*f*P

J OSEPH S OBRAN

THE FREE PRESS

New York   London   Toronto   Sydney   Singapore

A L I A S

SHAKESPEARE

Solving the Greatest

Literary Mystery of All Time

THE FREE PRESS
A Division of Simon & Schuster Inc.
1230 Avenue of the Americas
New York, NY 10020

THE FREE PRESS and colophon are trademarks
of Simon & Schuster Inc.

Designed by Carla Bolte

Manufactured in the United States of America

10   9   8   7   6   5   4   3   2

Library of Congress Cataloging-in-Publication Data

Sobran, Joseph.
    Alias Shakespeare : solving the greatest literary mystery of all
time / Joseph Sobran.
        p.   cm
    Includes bibliographical references and index.
    ISBN   0-684-82658-5
    1. Shakespeare, William, 1564–1616—Authorship—Oxford theory.
    2. Oxford, Edward De Vere, Earl of, 1550–1604—Authorship.
    3. Dramatists, English—Early modern, 1500–1700—Biography.
    4. Nobility—Great Britain—Biography.   I. Title.
    PR2947.O9S63   1997
    822.3'3—dc21   97-1504
                                                                  CIP

ISBN 0–684–82658–5

To my descendants

Kent, Vanessa, Mike, and Chris. And Joe, John, Willie, Jim, and Elizabeth

And I haven't forgotten you, Joe Paul.

Contents

APPENDIXES

The Authorship Debate

And this man is now become a god.

*A*fter four centuries, Shakespeare remains the most haunting of authors. He seems to know us better than we know him. He has put our deepest feelings into his own magnificent language, which, though now semiarchaic, still fills us with "wonder and astonishment," as Milton wrote. But he seems to escape all our attempts to know him: "[Shakespeare's] personality always evades us, even in the Sonnets," as Harold Bloom observes in *The Western Canon*. And for over a century now, the Shakespeare authorship question has appeared to be a strange circus at the edge of the town of literary studies. We are told not to waste too much time there, nor expect to find anything profound. Professional Shakespeare scholars question the good sense, the competence, and even the sanity of authorship heretics—the anti-Stratfordians, as they are usually called—and commonly charge them with a snobbish refusal to believe that a man of modest origins and education, who was born and died in a provincial town, could have been the greatest genius in English literature.

There is good reason for the scholars' dismissive attitude. Until I was nearly forty, I shared it myself. From my early teens through graduate school (I planned to make a career of Shakespeare studies), I never for a moment doubted the authorship of "the Stratford man," as the heretics call him—the phrase still makes me uneasy. And a great deal of the heretical literature is outlandish.

Still, I always found the standard Shakespeare biographies—those of Sidney Lee, Marchette Chute, Peter Quennell, F.E. Halliday, A.L. Rowse, and Samuel Schoenbaum—oddly frustrating. They never managed to connect. The author seemed unrelated to his work. How could this nondescript man have created Falstaff and Cleopatra? I assumed that if we knew more about him, we would have some sort of answer. We at least had his will, written shortly before his death in 1616. Why didn't that will contain a single bright turn of phrase? How could Shakespeare write even a thousand words without leaving his touch? I was puzzled, disappointed, but not yet skeptical. Like a good soldier, I suppressed my doubts, even after leaving graduate school for a career in journalism.

The difficulty of knowing Shakespeare the man has been summed up with unusual candor by an orthodox scholar, Irvin Leigh Matus:

> It was said of William Shakespeare that "In the shadowy throng of the Great he cuts an uninspiring figure." He certainly is an elusive one. During his lifetime we do hear something of the poet and playwright in contemporary sources, but of the man himself little more than business transactions and law suits. One letter exists that was written to him, but not one written by him. Tales of Shakespeare abound, but they did not begin to surface until 50 years or more after his death—there is only one contemporary anecdote. Of the numerous documents in which his name appears there are five legible signatures of "William Shakespeare," but it is not certain all are by his hand. Even when his play *Richard II,* long associated with the ambitions of the Earl of Essex, became a prelude to rebellion, Shakespeare is not once mentioned in the trial that sent the Earl to the block. Thus, although his genius was acknowledged in his lifetime, Shakespeare himself stubbornly insists upon remaining in the shadows . . .

A few years ago, when I began to be persuaded that there was more to this story than the conventional view, I entered a bizarre world of colorful people, totally unlike the academic world I'd known before.

The anti-Stratfordian tradition had begun with the champions of Francis Bacon, who in their heyday a century ago specialized in finding cryptograms and anagrams claiming Bacon's authorship buried in the plays. The first renowned Baconian, coincidentally named Delia Bacon, is renowned for her attempt to dig up Shakespeare's bones in the hope of proving her namesake's title to the works. From there it only got wilder. The cipher craze began with a fiery American congressman and utopian reformer named Ignatius Donnelly, who in 1888 published a thousand-page tome called *The Great Cryptogram: Francis Bacon's Cipher in the So-Called Shakespeare Plays*. Donnelly also credited Bacon with the so-called works of Marlowe, Montaigne, and many others—780 plays in all. Others followed suit, in the apparent conviction that *Hamlet* and *King Lear* were less interesting as tragedies than as brainteasers. One erudite Baconian, Sir Edward Durning-Lawrence, discovered that the playfully pedantic word *honorificabilitudinitatibus* in *Love's Labour's Lost* could be rearranged to read *Hi ludi F. Baconis nati tuiti orbi,* or "These plays, F. Bacon's offspring, are preserved for the world." Rarely has classical learning been put to such ingenious use.

Other candidates eventually included Christopher Marlowe and various earls—of Oxford, Derby, Rutland, Essex, and Southampton. Among the more unlikely candidates who have been advanced are Elizabeth I, James I, Anne Hathaway, and Daniel Defoe. Setting aside whatever case may exist for their majesties or Mrs. Shakespeare, Defoe was not even born until 1629, after nearly all the Shakespeare works had been published!

During the 1940s, Percy Allen, a leading Oxfordian, converted to a theory of group authorship after conducting interviews at séances with the shades of Oxford, Bacon, and Shakespeare. He published his conversations with these three worthies, over the anguished pleas of what I suppose we must call mainstream Oxfordians, in a little book titled *Talks with Elizabethans*. The three collaborators did agree that chief credit for their plays belonged to Oxford. Bacon told Allen, "I wrote none of the plays; but I was fortunate in being consulted frequently. A circle of interested parties was formed; I had the honour of being one of those. I also acted as critic and adviser. You understand. It was a case of joint authorship." Shakespeare, for his part, allowed: "I am responsible for parts of the plays, and for suggestions as to production of the plays. . . . I was quick at knowing what would be effective on the stage. I would find a plot, consult with Oxford, form a skeleton edifice which he would furnish and people, as befitted the subject." Oxford confirmed this: "My work was but the filling of a frame, in most cases. I would have you know that I never wrote a play from the beginning to the end. I filled in the framework." (He recalled Shakespeare himself as "a good friend of mine" and "an entertaining rogue.") Orthodox scholars received these revelations with reserve, and cackles.

One leading Oxfordian, renowned for his temper, accused me of implying that he and other Oxfordians were either fools or liars because I had spelled the Stratford man's name "Shakespeare" rather than "Shakspere"—the prescribed form among anti-Stratfordians, who attach great significance to the matter—in a short article on the authorship question. Fallings-out among different anti-Stratfordian sects, or divisions within them, are common. A Baconian of my acquaintance was refused admittance to an Oxfordian Internet group because of his schismatic views—Baconians and dogs need not apply! Oxfordian factions, after complaining that their ideas are denied a fair hearing by orthodox scholars, often conspire to squelch dissident opinions at their own gatherings. The suggestion that Oxford was bisexual is enough to make some of his partisans livid: apparently, he must not only be accorded the glory of authorship but must also be, as far as possible, idealized.

At one point I was approached by a rich old lady who, having learned that I was a professional writer with an interest in the authorship question, arranged for me to visit her at her Mississippi home. This woman shared with me her somewhat fantastic beliefs about various amorous intrigues at the court of Elizabeth I; she had even written, and published at her own expense, a book on these matters in doggerel verse. I found her charming but almost incomprehensible. At length she offered me a staggering amount of money—she mentioned a million dollars—to write a book, in prose if necessary, arguing not only that Edward de Vere, seventeenth Earl of Oxford, was the true author of the Shakespeare plays, but that Oxford had secretly begotten the Earl of Southampton on Elizabeth herself (a notion widely held by Oxfordians, who consider this supposed liaison romantic rather than dishonorable). She specified a number of other pet ideas that the proposed book must include: for example, that Southampton had been the rightful king of England, bastard though he was. I tried hard to see it her way, but I just couldn't follow her reasoning. To my occasional regret, I turned her down.

On the other hand, the heretics have included people of intellectual, literary, and artistic distinction: Walt Whitman, Henry James, Mark Twain, John Galsworthy, Sigmund Freud, Vladimir Nabokov, David Mc-Cullough. Several are notables of theater and cinema: Charlie Chaplin, Orson Welles, Sir John Gielgud, Michael York, and Kenneth Branagh. Yet these famous anti-Stratfordians have made no important contributions to the debate. Only Twain, in his pamphlet *Is Shakespeare Dead?*, wrote about the authorship question at any length. The bulk of the anti-Stratfordian literature has been produced by a few amateur scholars and a great many eccentrics.

In fact, the great comedy of the authorship question is that so many important discoveries have been made by dubious scholars, intellectual misfits, and outright cranks; mainstream scholars, meanwhile, ignoring their challengers, have insisted that there is no real authorship question at all. Under the circumstances, we do well to set aside credentials (which can carry their own whiff of snobbery) and sift all the evidence carefully. I have learned how often a priceless gem may be found in a pile of intellectual rubbish. More than once I have been reminded of St. Paul's dictum that God has chosen the foolish things of this world to confound the wise.

Samuel Schoenbaum, foremost among recent orthodox biographers, derides "the dark power of the anti-Stratfordian obsession." But we should not leap to the conclusion that the heretics have eaten of the insane root that takes the reason prisoner; many, in fact, appear quite normal. As a cruel fate would have it, one of the shrewdest of them was named Looney (rhymes, I hasten to add, with "bony")—John Thomas Looney, who first named the Earl of Oxford as the real author. Twain (more or less Baconian), Sir George Greenwood (agnostic), Calvin

Hoffman (Marlovian), and Charlton Ogburn Jr. (Oxfordian) exemplify the best of the anti-Stratfordian advocates. Suffice it to say that thousands of sane readers have found all of them to some extent compelling, and that any cause has to be judged by the case made by its ablest advocates.

The orthodox scholars' methods are cautious enough to make their conclusion plausible. And though I sympathize with the heretics in their challenge to the received view, their methods are often so haphazard as to make them sound hysterical. Skeptical of "the Stratford man," they can be astoundingly credulous about their pet candidates. Their faults are not the ravings of lunacy, but the almost unavoidable errors of isolation from a stabilizing mainstream. Professional scholars constantly criticize each other and harmonize their findings; amateurs, living in a more anarchic state, rely too much on self-criticism. The Shakespeare heretics have produced an abundance of wild fruits, but so far these have never been carefully sorted. The authorship question needs an overhaul.

The deeper trouble with most of the anti-Stratfordian theories, aside from illogicalities and deficiencies of evidence, is that they have very little *literary* relevance. They have nothing to do with our experience of reading Shakespeare or watching the plays in performance; they reduce the interest of a supreme poet to the level of a whodunit with a creaky plot. Shakespeare becomes a gigantic puzzle, to which the solution is "F. Baconis." Even if a theory of that kind were true, it would tell us nothing about the Shakespeare works except that the wrong name had been attached to them—leaving us to wonder why the prosaic rationalist Bacon would write a haunting sonnet like "No longer mourn for me when I am dead." Bacon must have written the great plays and poems only for the purpose of proving that Shakespeare didn't.

The excesses and fantasies of some heretics do not endear them to the professional scholars, and they make any alternative authorship theory seem hopelessly farfetched. The scholars believe, with every appearance of common sense, that Shakespeare was born in Stratford-upon-Avon, received a good education at the local school, married young, had three children, went to London, became a successful actor and playwright, wrote a few nondramatic poems along the way, bought property in Stratford, finally retired there, and died in 1616.

Yet this "official" account of Shakespeare's life also fails to offer any literary insights. Its apparently sensible premise never brings us close to the mind and heart of the author himself. Indeed, unbeknownst to many, the orthodox account teems with difficulties and has never successfully answered certain basic questions.

For example: How did Shakespeare know so much about court life, heraldry, law, Ovid, and Italy, as the plays suggest? The orthodox answer is that he did not. The scholars all agree that he got a sound education in his hometown, supplemented that knowledge sufficiently for his pur poses through his own reading, and still made gaffes no highly educated man would have made—giving Bohemia a seacoast, for example, and making his characters travel by water between the inland cities of Verona and Milan. The standard view is that Shakespeare acquired much of his wide knowledge casually, perhaps from the thousands of travelers, merchants, soldiers, and sailors who milled about in Elizabethan London and frequented its taverns. Gareth and Barbara Lloyd Evans offer a hypothetical anecdote: "The dusty traveller sitting in the Mermaid Tavern in London, just arrived from wars on the Continent, never realized what was to happen to his replies when the quiet stranger sipping his beer turned and asked him—'How is it with you, cos?'" The legendary Mermaid Tavern becomes Mermaid University, with Shakespeare its most distinguished alumnus. It seems a reasonable supposition—at least not impossible.

The late Louis D. Wright, in the introduction to the Folger Library series of Shakespeare plays, disposes of the authorship question in one patronizing remark:

> The anti-Shakespeareans base their arguments upon a few simple premises, all of them false. These false premises are that Shakespeare was an unlettered yokel without any schooling, that nothing is known about Shakespeare, and that only a noble lord or the equivalent in background could have written the plays. The facts are that more is known about Shakespeare than about most dramatists of his day, that he had a very good education, acquired in the Stratford Grammar School, that the plays show no evidence of profound book learning, and that the knowledge of kings and courts evident in the plays is no greater than any intelligent young man

could have picked up at second hand. Most anti-Shakespeareans are naive and betray an obvious snobbery. The author of their favorite plays, they imply, must have had a college diploma framed and hung on his study wall like the one in their dentist's office, and obviously so great a writer must have had a title or some equally significant evidence of exalted social background. They forget that genius has a way of cropping up in unexpected places and that none of the great creative writers of the world got his inspiration in a college or university course.

Schoenbaum writes sardonically of the growth of authorship heresy: "In the fullness of time, alternative candidates were offered, preferably candidates with university degrees and blue blood coursing through their veins." After recounting the story of Delia Bacon, one of the first to champion the cause of her namesake Francis Bacon as Shakespeare, he adds:

> Other dissidents have since championed Bacon, or argued for one earl or another: Oxford, or Derby, or Rutland—almost any earl will do. These anti-Stratfordian theories do not agitate the great majority of readers or playgoers, or those professionally concerned with Shakespeare and his times. As children of a democracy, we do not need to be persuaded of the potentialities for literary accomplishment in plebeian citizens—even the offspring of unlettered immigrants.

Other academic biographers agree. Gerald Eades Bentley accuses the heretics of "irresponsible fancy" and remarks "the great majority [of them] share the firm conviction that the author must have been a blue-blooded aristocrat." Russell Fraser charges the heretics with "snobbery": they believe that the real author must be endowed with "either noble lineage or academic honors." Stanley Wells indicts them for both "snobbery" and "the desire for self-publicity."

These chiding remarks show how deeply democratic ideology has become entwined with the cultural icon known as "William Shakespeare." The issue is not merely factual; it is moral, political, and even spiritual. For twentieth-century readers, Shakespeare without his plebeian identity wouldn't quite be Shakespeare. In his recent book *The Western Canon,* Harold Bloom celebrates Shakespeare in strikingly extraliterary terms: "There is an inverse ratio, a little beyond our analytical skills, between Shakespeare's virtual colorlessness and his preternatural dramatic powers. . . . The creator of Hamlet and Lear died a not very momentous death after an uneventful life. There are no great biographies of Shakespeare, not because we do not know enough but because there is not enough to know. . . . At once no one and everyone, Shakespeare *is* the Western Canon." Shakespeare the man is "ordinary-seeming" and "unassuming," even "someone with whom you could have a relaxed drink," in Bloom's view. That is precisely what makes his genius so astounding. The less flamboyant his outward show, the more miraculous his genius appears. Two other recent commentators, Germaine Greer and Garry O'Connor, agree in calling Shakespeare "invisible."

But to suspect that the real Shakespeare was a lord, or at least a courtier, may not necessarily be snobbery; it may be sociology. The ardent democrat Walt Whitman sensed the hand of one of the "wolfish earls" in Shakespeare's comedies, which he pronounced "non-acceptable to democracy." As Whitman shows, one needn't be a partisan of the feudal nobility to raise the authorship question. The real issue is not whether anti-Stratfordian views reveal the reactionary sympathies of the doubter, but whether the Shakespeare plays suggest an author of privileged background—one who not only received the best education available, but who also knew court life, traveled widely, and enjoyed other advantages beyond the reach of a man of rustic origins, however intelligent. In the end, calling the Shakespeare plays works of genius tells us very little about them. "Genius" is not an explanation. Nor is it a motive. We can't make up the deficit in our knowledge of Shakespeare with superlatives. *A Streetcar Named Desire* may not be as great a play as *Hamlet,* but the author of *Hamlet* couldn't have written it and Tennessee Williams could. This is a matter not of genius but of individuality.

The fact is that we know very little about Shakespeare—certainly not enough to warrant 300- to 600-page "biographies" that inflate a few dry documents, mostly business records, into the semblance of a full life. Most readers would be surprised to learn that the actual records of the first half of Shakespeare's life consist of five spare entries in parish registers: the date of his baptism, the date of his betrothal, the date and terms of his marriage, the dates of his three children's baptisms (two of whom were twins). Everything else from those years—1564 to 1590—must be deduced.

Furthermore, there is no match between the known facts about the man and the works assigned to his authorship. Shakespeare's life and personality have no discernible relation to the plays and poems bearing his name. As Emerson put it, "I cannot marry the life to the work." It is not only that we lack information. We don't know much about most of his contemporaries either, but nobody doubts that Marlowe, Spenser, and Jonson wrote the works ascribed to them. Even from the meager records and rumors that we have, Marlowe sounds like just the sort of man who would write Marlowe's works. The same may be said of Spenser and Jonson. Consider other great European poets. "Of Dante's life we know as little as we know of Shakespeare's," Pablo Milano writes. "Yet the harmony between Dante's character and his work is such that the meager facts are almost enough for us." The same could be said of Virgil. We do know a lot about Milton, and his identity has never been in question. But doubts about Shakespeare have actually increased as time has passed.

The name "Shakespeare" itself may be germane. The family name was usually spelled "Shakspere" in Stratford. This may or may not signify something important; Elizabethan spelling is notoriously irregular and it is hard to be sure. I would leave the matter there, but anti-Stratfordians of all denominations tend to treat it as definitive evidence that the man of Stratford wasn't "Shakespeare" the author; the debate over this point has been endless and inconclusive.

The distinction between "Shakspere" and "Shakespeare" does, however, have one convenience for this book. For clarity's sake, I will call the Stratford gentleman "Mr. Shakspere" and the author in dispute "Shakespeare." Whether they are the same man is, of course, the question.

By 1623, two dozen works, some of them spurious, had been published bearing the name William Shakespeare but not identifying the author further. It was in 1623 that the First Folio of the plays appeared, identifying Shakespeare with Mr. Shakspere of Stratford. If this testimony had not pegged Mr. Shakspere as the author, and the works had come down to us with no name attached, it would probably never have occurred to anyone to suggest that he had written them. Nothing in the records or impressions of his life would lead us to believe he was a writer at all, or anything but an actor and shareholder in a London theater company and a successful businessman in his hometown.

The Folio has given us the famous woodcut portrait of Shakespeare by Martin Droeshout—though this dull, pudgy face has been supplemented, in modern iconography, with a more seemly countenance, based on the Chandos portrait: lean, high-domed, goateed, with penetrating eyes and an earring. The experts admit that the authenticity of the Chandos portrait is doubtful, but it has certainly provided us with an arresting image of Shakespeare: intellectual but rather swashbuckling, rather like a psychoanalyst with a dash of pirate in him.

Unfortunately, the Folio is sparing with the kind of information we crave about Shakespeare. It omits such essential facts as the dates of his birth and death; it offers no anecdotes or reminiscences by friends. It praises him lavishly without actually describing him. It doesn't include the two narrative poems, *Venus and Adonis* and *The Rape of Lucrece,* for which he was most famous in his own time, or his self-revealing Sonnets or minor poems. The Folio tells us that Mr. Shakspere wrote the plays between its covers, nothing more. The scholars, taking his authorship largely on faith, have been forced to piece his life together as best they can from other sources. Later generations have emulated the Folio in lauding Shakespeare's universality—"his infinite variety"—at the expense of any *individuality.*

Whoever he was, he was not, in Professor Bloom's phrase, "at once no one and everyone"—or a man who never had to blot a line, as the Folio suggests. The superlatives used to describe Shakespeare tell us nothing useful about Mr. Shakspere.

As a result, dozens of questions about Mr. Shakspere have never been fully answered by the scholars, despite their best efforts. For instance: How did he zoom from being a young man in the provinces, with a wife and three children as of 1585, to being the most polished poet in England, writing amorous verses to a young nobleman, by the early

1590s? Nothing is known of this crucial period, known to scholars as "the lost years." Yet almost as little is known of Mr. Shakspere's years in London, when he should have been at the height of his success and fame. His death in 1616 apparently passed unnoticed in the city that adored the plays and poems bearing his name. And as we shall see, some of the most impenetrable mysteries have been posed by the one work that would seem to tell us most about the poet himself: the little book published in 1609 as *Shake-peares Sonnets*.

Some may still ask: What difference does it make who Shakespeare really was, as long as we have the plays? It is a perfectly sensible question. The Elizabethans felt the same way. They weren't curious about authors. Being interested in poetry rather than in the poet's psyche, they no more considered a play a self-revelation of the playwright than they considered a table a self-revelation of the carpenter. Drama, a popular art, was public and self-explanatory. Nobody sought hidden depths in it. For better or worse, we moderns are different. We *are* curious. We have made literary biography a genre. We can't always justify it theoretically, and we debate endlessly about the relation between art and the artist, but we want a peek at him anyway.

When it comes to the Sonnets, the poems don't make much sense unless we know something about the sonneteer himself. Most of the scholars try to shoo us away from taking a biographical interest in these intimate poems, even though the Sonnets, unlike the plays, are explicitly about real people—at least four of them, including the poet. That poet sounds so unlike Mr. Shakspere that the scholars are driven to classify the Sonnets as fictions, in spite of all evidence to the contrary.

It has become fashionable in recent literary criticism, notably in the extreme school of deconstruction, to deny the relevance of the author—an awkward postulate for would-be biographers. It is odd to find the biographers saying much the same thing. Whatever justification our personal interest in Shakespeare may have, I can only say that I feel no need to apologize for it. Our curiosity is too natural and too common to be blushed at. Like millions of others, I am interested in who Shakespeare was as a simple matter of historical fact; and if the doctors of literature condemn our inquiry, we can appeal to the historians.

Further, if we are accused of snobbery for doubting Mr. Shakspere's authorship, we can reply that a sort of inverted snobbery seems to be driving his partisans. And it does seem strange that an author whose biases are so obviously aristocratic should be made an icon and test of democratic faith. Whoever Shakespeare was, he seems to have taken little interest in the sort of self-made man his champions suppose him to have been.

Finally, we must face the charge of crankery, or even lunacy, for pursuing this inquiry at all. This charge has been given its fullest expression by Schoenbaum:

> In certain recurring features of anti-Stratfordian behavior we may discern a pattern of psychopathology. The heretic's revulsion against the provincial and lowly; his exaltation of his hero (and, through identification, himself) by furnishing him with an aristocratic, even royal, pedigree; his paranoid structures of thought, embracing the classic paraphernalia of persecution: secrets, curses, conspiracies; the compulsion to dig in churches, castles, river beds, and tombs; the auto-hypnosis, spirit visitations, and other hallucinatory phenomena; the descent, in a few cases, into actual madness— all these manifestations of the uneasy psyche suggest that the movement calls not so much for the expertise of the literary historian as for the insight of the psychiatrist. Dr. Freud beckons us.

Taken to its limit, this approach implies that rational discussion of Shakespeare's authorship is pointless, since anyone who rejects the orthodox view must be somewhat crankish; it also implies that cranks can be persuasive only to other cranks. If so, orthodox scholars who try to stop the susceptible from being seduced are wasting their breath, while there is no need to warn normal people against the anti-Stratfordians, since normality itself is sufficient to immunize them.

One can understand Schoenbaum's psychoanalytic conceit as a joke, or even as a burst of exasperation with the generally prolix, often fanciful, and sometimes occult anti-Stratfordian literature, in which 800-page tomes are the norm. A sober scholar who has read them all may be pardoned for a bit of spleen. Still, he shows little compassion for the putatively diseased wits of the heretics; he evidently judges them more to be censured than pitied.

Schoenbaum's is a common attitude among the orthodox scholars, who seem a shade too eager to stigmatize the doubters and to warn others away from them. They assume that there is no fate worse than being an isolated crank, and that the threat of being excommunicated by academia should suffice to keep others in line.

The most dispiriting trait of the professional scholars is not their consensus about Shakespeare's identify, but *their refusal to admit that there can be any room for doubt.* Realizing very well how little is known about Mr. Shakspere of Stratford, they should at least allow for an agnostic middle ground. It is one thing to say that the testimony in favor of Mr. Shakspere's authorship remains, on balance, more satisfying than all the arguments made against it. It's quite another matter to concede nothing to dissent, or even uncertainty. In the writings of orthodox scholars on the anti-Stratfordian heresies, it is rare to find a concessive note. Animadversions, often vituperative, are the rule. It is almost never admitted that any of the heretics has ever raised a point worth taking into account. The impulse to scold the dissenter; the inability to acknowledge even the possibility of reasonable doubt; suspicion even of the noncommittal; the denial of ambiguities in our imperfect records of the past; intense frustration with anything less than unanimity; the conviction that dissent reveals a moral or psychological defect—these are the marks of the brittle belief systems we call cults or ideologies, as opposed to the balanced judgment that tries to come to terms with all the available evidence.

Most of the anti-Stratfordian writings present a mirror image, and sometimes a parody, of these orthodox attitudes. The reader gathers that the Stratfordian position is less an opinion than a plot, stretching from the court of Elizabeth I to the curators of the Folger Shakespeare Library, to deny the true author credit for his immortal works. Presumably, if we could get the leading Stratfordian scholars in a cellar, we could beat the truth out of them with a rubber hose. On this side, too, disagreement is presumed dishonest; every professed Stratfordian is really an anti-Stratfordian who won't admit what he knows.

I don't mean these observations to sound evenhanded—heaven forbid! There are some differences that can't be split, and I think the evidence about Shakespeare's authorship is clear enough. I merely mean to acknowledge that I bear the same burden of proof as anyone else who takes up a point of long contention. If I turn out to be a crank with aristocratic sympathies and a paranoid mentality, so be it.

If it comes to that, what is so bad about cranks? The charge of crankery is apt to be thrown at people for no better reason than that they insist on making up their own minds at all costs, in spite of all social pressures and conventions. Personally, I would much rather be in the tradition of great American cranks like Thoreau, Ambrose Bierce, Lysander Spooner, and H.L. Mencken, or even obscure cranks like the aforementioned lady in Mississippi, than belong to the mass of scholars who, ever mindful of tenure, promotion, grants, and that last infirmity of ignoble minds, respectability, never deviate from scholarly consensus.

At least I have the advantage of having been on two sides of the authorship question, of knowing what can be said for each, and of bearing debts to astute people of clashing persuasions. Above all, perhaps, I have known what it is to be uncertain about a question so close to my heart as this one is. It's because I was torn between two utterly incompatible views that I am finally able to render my own verdict.

I have not tried to answer every disputed point about the authorship question; some very interesting problems have been left hanging because I believe they are, for the time being anyway, unanswerable. In many cases, I have not tried to refute orthodox criticisms of common anti-Stratfordian arguments, for the simple reason that those arguments are often weak, and in some cases I think the orthodox are quite right. A great deal of energy has been spent—and in my opinion, wasted—on such marginal questions as whether the Ashbourne portrait was originally a portrait of the Earl of Oxford; whether the original Stratford monument of Mr. Shakspere has been altered; whether the Droeshout portrait in the Folio contains hidden clues; whether Ben Jonson's "hadst" (in "And though thou hadst small Latin and less Greek") is to be construed subjunctively; and so on. Questions of this kind unnecessarily confuse and demoralize readers, giving the impression that the authorship debate pivots on hopelessly arcane, disconnected, and irresolvable mysteries. The key issues are sufficiently demanding and, happily, soluble.

In order to keep this book short and to avoid distractions, I have confined myself to the issues that in my judgment lie at the heart of the question. I think these essential points can be addressed fairly briefly. We have strong circumstantial evidence that Mr. Shakspere didn't write the plays and poems, and even stronger circumstantial evidence that someone else did. The reader may decide in the end that the testimony in Mr. Shakspere's favor deserves more weight than any other evidence. But I hope that even the reader who rejects my answer will at least agree that there *is* a question.

THE SHAKESPEARE MYTH

The Life of Mr. Shakspere

*W*hat is known about the man generally accepted as William Shakespeare, and how do we know it? The standard account of Shakespeare's life is given succinctly on a single page in the Bantam paperback editions of Shakespeare's plays, edited by David Bevington:

William Shakespeare was born in Stratford-upon-Avon in April 1564, and his birth is traditionally celebrated on April 23. The facts of his life, known from surviving documents, are sparse. He was one of eight children born to John Shakespeare, a merchant of some standing in his community. William probably went to the King's New School in Stratford, but he had no university education. In November 1582, at the age of eighteen, he married Anne Hathaway, eight years his senior, who was pregnant with their first child, Susanna. She was born on May 26, 1583. Twins, a boy, Hamnet (who would die at age eleven), and a girl, Judith, were born in 1585. By 1592 Shakespeare had gone to London, working as an actor and already known as a playwright. A rival dramatist, Robert Greene, referred to him as "an upstart crow, beautified with our feathers." Shakespeare became a principal shareholder and playwright of the successful acting troupe the Lord Chamberlain's men (later, under James I, called the King's men). In 1599 the Lord Chamberlain's men built and occupied the Globe Theater in Southwark near the Thames river. Here many of Shakespeare's plays were performed by the most famous actors of his time, including Richard Burbage, Will Kempe, and Robert Armin. In addition to his 37 plays, Shakespeare had a hand in others, including *Sir Thomas More* and *The Two Noble Kinsmen,* and he wrote poems, including *Venus and Adonis* and *The Rape of Lucrece.* His 154 sonnets were published, probably without his authorization, in 1609. In 1611 or 1612 he gave up his lodgings in London and devoted more and more of his time to retirement in Stratford, though he continued writing such plays as *The Tempest* and *Henry VIII* until about 1613. He died on April 23, 1616, and was buried in Holy Trinity Church, Stratford. No collected edition of his plays was published during his lifetime, but in 1623 two members of his acting company, John Heminge and Henry Condell, published the great collection now called the First Folio.

Apart from business records, mostly in Stratford, not a great deal more than this is known about Mr. Shakspere. A strictly factual biography of him would be no longer than this chapter.

The orthodox scholars agree with Louis Wright that "more is known about Shakespeare than about most dramatists of his day." That familiar claim is true in the sense that we know more about Mr. Shakspere than we know about Thomas Kyd or Christopher Marlowe, to name two of many Elizabethan playwrights. But what we know about Marlowe has more bearing on his literary career: we know that he was educated at Cambridge and we know something of his connections with at least one patron, Sir Thomas Walsingham, and with other writers of his day. (Kyd's testimony against Marlowe, obtained under torture, might have led to his death even if he hadn't been killed in a brawl.) We actually know far more about Ben Jonson, not only in quantity of data but in the sheer presence of his personality and in his interactions with other noted contemporaries. We know about relations among such writers as Sidney, Spenser, Lyly, Harvey, Greene, Nashe, and many others. Only

Mr. Shakspere seems strangely aloof from his literary peers. He remembers other actors in his will, but no writers.

It is instructive to see how, and from what sources, the scholars have had to piece together Mr. Shakspere's life.

- A single line from the Stratford parish register from April 1564 records Mr. Shakspere's baptism: "26 Gulielmus filius Johannes Shakspere xxx."
- Similarly terse entries record the christenings of his three brothers and two sisters. No other document mentions William Shakspere himself for eighteen years. Stratford had a grammar school, which he may or may not have attended. Because of his father's status as alderman and bailiff, he would have been entitled to attend the school, but the record, as we have it, tells us nothing.
- His name next appears in a diocesan register of betrothals for November 27, 1582, showing that "wm Shaxpere" and a woman identified as "Anna whately de Temple grafton" were licensed to marry. The next day, November 28, the same register records the marriage bond of "willm Shagspere" and "Anne hathwey of Stratford in the Dioces of worcester maiden," noting that they were permitted to marry with only one reading of the banns instead of the usual three. (Presumably the clerk had confused two local families, the Whatelys and the Hathaways, in the first entry).
- The Stratford register for May 26, 1583, notes the baptism of Mr. Shakspere's first daughter: "Susanna daughter to William Shakespeare"—one of the few Stratford documents that uses the now standard spelling of his name, incidentally. (The date of the baptism implies that Mrs. Shakspere was already pregnant at the time of the marriage, which explains the deletion of the banns.) And on February 2, 1585, we find the baptism of twins: "Hamnet & Judeth sonne and daughter to William Shakspere."

This is the entire documentary record of the first half of Mr. Shakspere's life of fifty-two years. None of these records was known, by the way, until the early eighteenth century, when Shakespeare scholarship actually began and had to pick up a cold trail. By then, no reliable tradition about him survived; everything had to be reconstructed like a dinosaur, from scattered bones. (The first biography, a short essay by the editor Nicholas Rowe, appeared in 1709. Most of its facts are now generally agreed to be wrong.)

As of February 2, 1585, Mr. Shakspere would seem to have had his hands full: at twenty, with a modest education at best and no important social connections, he was a provincial lad with a wife and three children. Few could have predicted, from such a start, that in less than a decade he would be the rage of literary London—not only a popular playwright, but also a supremely polished poet writing daringly amorous verses to one of England's leading young lords. If the standard account is right, he rose above his class and established himself as a literary genius with amazing rapidity.

What happened in between remains a puzzle. The years from 1585 to 1592 are known as "the lost years," since there is no trace of Mr. Shakspere, his attachment to the theater, his development as a poet, or his ascent to high society. No record of any kind helps us to explain how he achieved such mastery of English, as well as a knowledge of other languages; how he acquired apparent firsthand familiarity with Italy; how he came to know so much about law, court life, aristocratic pastimes, and the arcana of heraldry.

The trail resumes in 1592, when a pamphlet titled *Green's Groatsworth of Wit* violently attacked an unnamed actor, who is believed to be Mr. Shakspere. Soon afterward, Henry Chettle, the pamphlet's publisher, issued a soothing apology to an unnamed playwright whom the pamphleteer had also addressed. Most scholars believe that this playwright, too, was Mr. Shakspere. The *Groatsworth* episode will be dealt with at length in the next chapter. For now we may simply note that neither the pamphlet nor its publisher named Shakespeare. The inference that they were referring to him was drawn nearly two centuries later.

"William Shakespeare" actually made his debut in print the following year, 1593, as the author of *Venus and Adonis,* a long poem dedicated to Henry Wriothesley, the young Earl of Southampton. The poem was an immediate success. So was *The Rape of Lucrece,* another long poem, published in 1594 and also dedicated to Southampton. Both poems were extremely popular and went through many printings over the next three decades. In 1594 the lays of Shakespeare also began appearing in print, but without the author's name. None of his plays bore that name until 1598; it is clear that to the literate public of his day, "Shakespeare" was a poet, not a playwright. Most contemporary references speak of him as the author of *Venus* and *Lucrece,* and only secondarily, if at all, as the author of the plays, until the publication of the Folio in 1623.

It is widely believed that Shakespeare began writing his Sonnets in the early 1590s and that Southampton is the young man most of them address. Though these are arguable guesses, the interesting fact is that the Sonnets weren't published until 1609 and did not identify the young man. One of the many confusing facets of the Sonnets is that although they are evidently private poems not intended for publication, they speak in an aging man's voice, while at the apparent time of their composition Mr. Shakspere was only about thirty.

In 1594, the Lord Chamberlain's Men acting company was formed, and there is a record of payment for two performances to "William Kempe, William Shakespeare, & Richard Burbage." It seems likely that this refers to Mr. Shakspere, who appears from other records to have been in London by about this time; he was certainly associated with the company as a shareholder and probably as an actor, too. At some point, his younger brother Edmund also came to London, dying there in 1607; the funeral record identifies Edmund as a "player."

From 1593 on, *someone* is certainly using the name William Shakespeare both as the author of published poems and in connection with the theater. But the record is surprisingly thin. We do have abundant theater records from the 1590s and some of them mention plays of Shakespeare. But few mention Mr. Shakspere personally, and even those that do merely record property purchases and similar transactions, usually in entries as frustratingly terse and impersonal as his baptismal record. For example, in 1596 Mr. Shakspere and three others were accused of threatening one William Wayte, who sought an order restraining them. The court records give us only a single line in Latin to this effect, and we know little about the incident that occasioned Wayte's action. (Even the book-length biographies usually ignore it.) Mr. Shakspere is also listed in the tax records of that year as a resident of Southwark, London. He is given two or three other London addresses over the next few years, but we always feel we have gotten there after he left.

In 1599, he and others were listed as owners of the new Globe Theater. In 1597, he had bought a large house in Stratford called New Place for the considerable sum of 60 pounds. From this time on he appears as a rather substantial citizen of Stratford, acquiring more property and selling grain and other commodities over the years, and applying for the title of "gentleman," with a coat of arms for himself and his father. (His only son, Hamnet Shakspere, had died in 1597—a touching fact whose only record is the usual one-line entry in the parish register.) From 1602 to 1604, according to his later testimony in a lawsuit, Mr. Shakspere lodged in London with a family named Mountjoy. He apparently never owned a residence in London

From mid–1604 through 1611 Mr. Shakspere does not appear in any London records (except as a partner in a purchase that would not have required his presence). He seems to have been absent from the city for most of the decade, and four documents place him in Stratford during those years. The paucity of London references during this period is striking, since these were the years in which he is thought to have written most of his greatest plays. A few scholars actually believe that he retired to Stratford as early as 1604. In any case, he apparently left no mark in the city while writing such supreme works as *Othello, King Lear, Macbeth, Antony and Cleopatra,* and *The Tempest.* Indeed, the records are so brief that we can determine Mr. Shakspere's whereabouts on only a handful of dates in his entire life. We can only guess how much of his time he spent in London and how much in Stratford. Most scholars surmise that Mr. Shakspere retired to Stratford around 1611. Yet there is no record of his being in London between 1604 and 1611, while the records from 1611 to 1615 show him doing business in London as well as Stratford.

Mr. Shakspere reappears in London in 1612 to testify in a lawsuit over a dowry. The suit concerned a family named Mountjoy, with whom he apparently lodged from about 1602 to 1604. His memory of the details was too dim to be helpful. He is given neither a residence nor an occupation in London; he is identified only as a "gentleman" of Stratford-upon-Avon, where he seems to have been living for some time.

He reappears in London in March 1613 to purchase a "dwelling-house or tenement" in Blackfriars (the record again identifies him as a gentleman of Stratford) and once more in April 1615 on a related matter. One of his trustees is John Heminge, his fellow shareholder in the King's Men and the Globe Theater. During the 1613 visit, he and Richard Burbage also seem to have made an impresa (a painted paper shield bearing mottoes) for the Earl of Rutland. Both Heminge and Burbage would be remembered in the will that Mr. Shakspere wrote in early 1616 and revised in March, a month before he died on or about his fifty-second birthday.

Mr. Shakspere's will might be expected to provide some correlation with the literary life of a man of the theater. Instead, it tends to embarrass the orthodox biographers. Few of them quote it in its entirely. In all the years—whether five years or twelve or even more—during which Mr. Shakspere was spending most of his time in Stratford, he left only a single written artifact, one that furthermore looks very like the work of a virtual illiterate. Some scholars contend that he may not have written it, despite its opening statement that "in perfect health and memory" he did "make and ordain" it. Having read the document in full (see Appendix 1), could anyone think it was written or dictated by the author of *The Tempest?*

In his *William Shakespeare: A Compact Documentary Life,* Samuel Schoenbaum devotes eleven pages to the dry, three-page will, even though it has little or no bearing on the lays and poems. "Shakespeare's will," Schoenbaum tells us, "is not a poetic testament but [in G. E. Bentley's phrase] a characteristic will of a man of property in the reign of James I. In such a document it is futile to seek metaphor or dark conceit, or even intimate revelation."

Perhaps he did not care about how his will was composed, but why no mention of anything indicative of an interest in literature? He left no books or manuscripts; no sign of any intellectual interests; no mention of any literary patrons or friends. His half-dozen surviving signatures have themselves aroused skepticism, not so much because they are barely legible as because they are so irregular, lacking the consistency of a man who wrote habitually. And though Mr. Shakspere's will left small remembrances to three of his fellow actors, including Richard Burbage, there is no recorded notice in London of this celebrated author's death. In an age of effusive eulogies, nobody bothered to salute him.

In the age of the paperback, we must remember that books were far more expensive then than now; often they were chained to desks. We can be confident that the author of the Shakespeare plays would have owned at least a small library since the plays so consistently make references to published texts. Over the years, Shakespeare often used the Bible (especially the Geneva translation), Holinshed's *Chronicles,* Plutarch's *Lives* (in Sir Thomas North's translation), Ovid (both in Latin and in Arthur Golding's translation), and Chaucer. But there is no sign that Mr. Shakspere owned a single book. Schoenbaum suggests, "Books might have been separately itemized in the inventory post-mortem. . . ." But this is hard to accept, considering that Mr. Shakspere's own son-in-law, Dr. John Hall, left a will directing his son to dispose of his books and manuscripts as he saw fit. The author and translator John Florio, who dedicated books to the earls of Southampton and Pembroke, bequeathed many of his books and manuscripts to Pembroke. Mr. Shakspere supposedly enjoyed the patronage of both earls, yet his will mentions neither of them.

In her biography *Shakespeare of London,* Marchette Chute usefully contrasts Mr. Shakspere's will with those of others of his own circle:

> The tone of Shakespeare's will is impersonal throughout, although most of the wills of this period are personal and affectionate. Henry Condell's will speaks of his "well-beloved wife," and John Heminges asks to be buried "near unto my loving wife Rebecca." Augustine Phillips uses the same term, and Thomas Pope even includes in his affections "my loving friend John Jackson." But Shakespeare was one member of the company whose will does not show a flicker of personal feeling.

Compare the warm sentiment of the 1624 will of Edmund Heywood, uncle of the playwright and poet Thomas Heywood:

> And whereas my intent and meaning was to have given and left to Magdalen, my well-beloved wife, with whom I have by the goodness of God lived a long time, the greatest part of mine estate for her maintenance during her life, and to have been disposed of by her after her death; but considering how it hath pleased God to visit her long with lameness whereby and by reason of her other weakness and imperfections which commonly

doth attend old age, she is now unfit to take care of the things of this world, I thought it better to dispose of these temporal blessings with which God hath endowed me, according as it is declared in this my will; and to leave my said wife to the care of her natural and only child, than to expose her and my substance to strangers that may happen to regard it more than her.

Jane Cox of the Public Records Office in London, a specialist in old legal documents, unsentimentally calls the famous bequest to Anne Hathaway Shakspere of the poet's "second best bed" a "miserable souvenir." She comments:

> This was no "affectionate little bequest," neither was it usual for a seventeenth-century man, of any rank, to make no overt provision for his wife in his will. Of [a] sample of 150 wills proved in the same year, . . . about one third of the testators appointed their wives as executrixes and residuary legatees. None left his wife anything as paltry as a second-best bed. Bedsteads and bedding were without doubt valuable and prized items and they were normally carefully bequeathed, best beds going to wives and eldest sons.

Mr. Shakspere's will does leave a small bequest to three of his colleagues in the King's Men: Richard Burbage, John Heminge, and Henry Condell. But he mentions no *literary* colleagues—not a single fellow writer from all his years in a city teeming with notable authors. This is a strange omission, since Francis Meres refers to the circulation of Shakespeare's "sugared sonnets among his private friends." Presumably he would have had many lively literary conversations with those friends. Yet the only London acquaintances the will names are Mr. Shakspere's theatrical business partners. Even Jonson, his reputed drinking companion and friendly rival, does not rate a farewell gesture. It may not be surprising that we have no record of his Stratford boyhood, with its bright promise of what he would become. But it is extremely strange that the records of his life in Stratford after his London years should yield no sign of what he had *been*.

The will bears three of the six surviving signatures believed to be Mr. Shakspere's. Jane Cox thinks these signatures may have been written by another hand than his. In fact, she believes the six Shakspere signatures are the work of four different hands. Schoenbaum cites her opinion, but avoids acknowledging its clear implication: that Mr. Shakspere may have been *unable to write his own name*. Whether or not the six Shakspere signatures match each other, none of them looks like the penmanship of a writer. Joseph Quincy Adams assures us that when Mr. Shakspere signed his will, "he was in such a state of weakness and exhaustion that his hand shook." Schoenbaum surmises that he was "gravely ill." This, of course, directly contradicts the second sentence of the will itself.

Finally, we must consider his famous gravestone inscription, commonly but mistakenly referred to as his epitaph. No one could call it honey-tongued, mellifluous, or Ovidian:

> Good friend, for Jesus' sake forbear
> To dig the dust enclosed here:
> Blest be the man that spares these stones,
> And curst be he that moves my bones.

Most scholars think the author of *Hamlet* did not write this crude doggerel. However, some recent editors include among Shakespeare's poems a few similar verses ascribed to Mr. Shakspere during the seventeenth century. One concerns a Stratford usurer named John Combe:

> Ten in the hundred here lies engraved;
> A hundred to one his soul is not saved.
> If anyone asks who lies in this tomb,
> "O ho!" quoth the devil, "'tis my John-a-Combe."

These gauche couplets do sound like the work of the poet who composed the verse for Mr. Shakspere's bones. If Mr. Shakspere wrote both, he may have a fair claim to the title of Stratford's foremost poet.

Nothing else in the Stratford papers and relics gives the slightest intimation that Mr. Shakspere was a man of any cultivation; it is not even clear that he was literate. His biographers believe that Mr. Shakspere spent at least the last five years of his life in Stratford; yet in all those years he didn't manage to leave *any* clue that he was the author William Shakespeare. Since we have no firm evidence that he was in London at all between 1604 and 1612, while we have several records of his pres-

ence in Stratford during those years, it may be that he lived in his hometown for a dozen years without leaving any sign of a literary personality.

The 1623 Folio seems to atone abundantly for the silence of 1616—
which makes that silence all the more curious. Shakespeare the poet had
been generously praised since 1593. Shakespeare the playwright made
his formal debut in 1598: Francis Meres had praised him for his poems
and plays alike, and individual plays bearing the byline "William Shakespeare" began to appear as well. These plays were so popular that from
1605 onward, several bogus plays were also published under his name.
(Mr. Shakspere apparently didn't protest.) Shakespeare's printed works
were selling well and his plays were still being performed when Mr.
Shakspere died in 1616. Seven years later, his name was sufficiently
commanding to warrant the Folio itself—a very expensive production,
complete with copious tributes to the author, which must have sold for
the equivalent of $100 a copy.

The Folio does identify Shakespeare with Mr. Shakspere; it is the
chief evidence of Mr. Shakspere's authorship. Unfortunately, it reveals
nothing useful about the author, giving us neither basic biographical
facts nor any sense of what the man himself was like.

Given the poverty of the documentary record, it is no surprise that
Shakespeare's plays have come to be treated as documents of Mr.
Shakspere's life. Unfortunately, the dates of the plays are highly uncertain. We know when they were published; we know some of the dates
when they were performed (or referred to in print or writing); we think
we can tell from their style the general order in which they were written; but there are few clues as to *when* they were written, and no links
with the life of their presumed author. The biographers are therefore reduced to circular reasoning. They stipulate that the plays must have been
written between roughly 1590 and 1612, and spread them out evenly
over those years, making each play a minor event in Mr. Shakspere's life.
Two of the most venerable scholars, Edmond Malone and Sir Edmund
Chambers, explicitly base their dating schemes on the presumed dates of
Mr. Shakspere's career. Other scholars have followed suit, explaining
away evidence to the contrary. This method of dating the works produces its own problems. Thus, faced with references to *Hamlet* as early
as 1589, long before the standard date of about 1601, the scholars posit

the existence of an earlier version, the "Ur-*Hamlet*," by another, unknown playwright. This Ur-*Hamlet* had to be invented, because hardly anyone thinks Mr. Shakspere could have written the familiar *Hamlet* before 1600.

Most recent scholars have been wary of trying to connect the works with Mr. Shakspere's life, particularly his inner life. Some read the Sonnets as autobiography, but the general tendency has been agnostic. The Shakespeare of the scholars—and of our classrooms, monuments, and iconography—has no human authenticity. He is an uneasy composite of the nondescript man from Stratford and the man with the superb imagination, insight, and wit that give life to the plays and poems. Under the circumstances, it is hardly surprising that a number of authorship "heresies" have sprung up. Lacking coherent individuality, Shakespeare has been endowed with a vague aura of "universality." The scholarly establishment has stuck together an image of Shakespeare from a few loose pieces that fit together very awkwardly, ignoring a number of pieces that do not fit at all. As we consider the history of this scholarship, it becomes clear that it says more about ourselves than about Shakespeare.

Before considering the case for an alternative author of William Shakespeare's works, let us carefully consider the Shakespeare myth itself, what it grew from and what sustained it.

Chapter 2

The Origin of
the Shakespeare Myth

For modern readers, the chief mental obstacle to any doubt about who wrote Shakespeare's plays is the assumption that Shakespeare must have been a public personality, even a celebrity, in his own day. Many of his contemporaries must have known him, seen him in and around the theater, shared a pleasant drink with him at the Mermaid. Could they all have been fooled? The records about Mr. Shakspere make it clear how difficult it is to reconstruct his life, how few clues we have. No question, people knew him. And a certain number would certainly have known if Mr. Shakspere and Shakespeare were two different men. Ben Jonson, for one, surely would have known. But in general it is hard to say who knew what.

We must also bear in mind that Shakespeare, though popular and respected as a writer in his own time, was by no means the cultural icon he became nearly two centuries later. He was not even a public personality; many of his most popular plays weren't yet associated with him; the literary public had no sense of the complete body of his work. Many contemporaries praised Shakespeare *as a writer*. But we have only a handful of personal references that (as scholars believe) point to Shakespeare the man.

Two such supposed references to Shakespeare, essential to the standard account of his career, don't even mention his name: a passage in the pamphlet called *Greene's Groatsworth of Wit* and the publisher Henry Chettle's apologetic follow-up, both dated 1592. A gossipy poem called *Willobie his Avisa* tells a tantalizing story about an "old player" identified only as "W. S." in 1594; this may mean William Shakespeare, whose *Lucrece* the poem also cites, but the orthodox view cannot explain why Shakespeare would be described as "old" so early in his career. Two plays performed at Cambridge University around 1600 include jokes about "sweet Mr. Shakespeare." A bit of bawdy gossip about Shakespeare is repeated by one John Manningham in 1602. Yet another reference is an oblique one (again, not mentioning Shakespeare's name) by the poet Thomas Heywood in 1612. The 1623 Folio speaks of Shakespeare, but tells us remarkably little about him. Finally, there is Jonson's brief, affectionate, but slightly caustic reminiscence of Shakespeare in his posthumous *Timber, or Discoveries,* published in 1640.

Of these, the Greene and Jonson references are the most important to the orthodox account. It is notable that they occur nearly half a century apart—one at the beginning of Shakespeare's career and the other long afterward. In between, while he was an active and successful playwright, virtually nothing was written about him aside from tributes to his work. Both Greene and Jonson, along with the Folio, therefore deserve a close look.

According to Edmund Chambers, the most conservative of the orthodox scholars, "Greene's letter in itself is sufficient to show that by September 1592 Shakespeare was both a player and a maker of plays." The late Samuel Schoenbaum, who is generally as cautious as Chambers, asserts that "the *Groatsworth of Wit* contains—no question—a desperate shaft directed at Shakespeare." This is very nearly the scholarly consensus about the pamphlet. But as we shall see, many questions have been raised about the identity of the person it refers to.

Greene's Groatsworth of Wit is a long pamphlet, supposedly written by Robert Greene as he lay dying, recounting Greene's life in the form of an autobiographical fable whose wastrel hero is named Roberto. It ends with a bitter warning addressed to three fellow playwrights to beware of unscrupulous actors, who depend on playwrights for the very words they speak but later cheat and abandon them. How a dying man could have written with such vigor, at such length, we are left to wonder.

The pamphlet, for all its splendid invective, is probably a forgery. Warren Austin, of Stephen F. Austin State College, has reached this conclusion from a computer-aided analysis of its style, but Peter Moore has also reached the same conclusion on simpler grounds. The author of the pamphlet, purporting to be the dying Robert Greene, urges his wife to take good care of their son Fortunatus. The boy was actually Greene's son by another woman, a prostitute he lived with after leaving his wife. Evidently the forger didn't realize this.

Not that the pamphlet's authorship proves whether or not it is an attack on Shakespeare. But the rather late discovery that Greene could not have written it shows that, since a scholar named Thomas Tyrwhitt came across the pamphlet in 1766, few have subjected it to rigorous scrutiny.

The famous passage about the "upstart crow"—actually only a single sentence in the lengthy pamphlet—occurs in the warning to the playwrights, one of whom (probably the scandalous Marlowe) is particularly cautioned against atheism and other notorious sins. "Base-minded men all three of you," says the writer impersonating Greene, "if by my misery you be not warned." The actors are "those puppets (I mean) that spake from our mouths, those antics garnished in our colours," even "apes." The writer singles out one actor (I reproduce the original spelling and punctuation):

> Yes trust them not: for there is an upstart Crow, beautified with our feathers, that with his *Tygers hart wrapt in a Players hyde,* supposes he is as well able to bombast out a blank verse as the best of you: and being an absolute *Johannes fac totum,* is in his owne conceit the onely Shake-scene in a countrey.

This supposed swipe at Shakespeare is mentioned in every biography, and appears even in the shortest biographical sketches. It has been quoted so often that most readers, including most English professors, have formed the mistaken impression that not only this sentence but the whole pamphlet is directed against Shakespeare. "Tygers hart wrapt in a Players hyde" mockingly echoes the line "O tiger's heart, wrapp'd in a woman's hide!" in the play now known as *Henry VI, Part 3*. And for most scholars, the word "Shake-scene" confirms that the target is Shakespeare.

Yet there are problems with this interpretation, apart from its assumption of a rather poor and awkward pun. For one thing, *Henry VI, Part 3,* was not yet publicly known to be Shakespeare's in 1592. In fact, when it was first published three years later, it bore no author's name—a curious fact, if its author was already a subject of controversy. Only the Folio, many years later, definitely connected it with Shakespeare. So the writer could not have expected a single oblique reference to remind his readers of the play's author. But what else could the passage mean?

In his book *Tiger's Heart,* Jay Hoster argues that the real "upstart crow" was the actor-manager Edward Alleyn, the greatest star of the Elizabethan stage (at least before Burbage), whom the real Greene had earlier attacked for underpaying playwrights. Alleyn was known for his violent ranting; audiences loved it. He once literally broke the boards of the stage—a real "shake-scene," so to speak. A playwright who had dealt with Alleyn might well resent him. Hoster suggests that Alleyn had starred in *Henry VI, Part 3,* as the character who spoke (or roared), "O tiger's heart, wrapp'd in a woman's hide!" and that the line was associated with him, not with the anonymous playwright. We should also note that the line is spoken by a major character: Richard, Duke of York. When the play was printed in 1595, its title was not *Henry VI,* but *The True Tragedy of Richard, Duke of York.*

Years later, the real Shakespeare would base his play *The Winter's Tale* on Greene's novella *Pandosto.* If the standard story were correct, this would mean that Shakespeare was incurring a literary debt to the very man who, at the beginning of his career, had called him an ape and a parasite. A more plausible explanation is that Shakespeare didn't mind *Greene's Groatsworth,* because it had nothing to do with him. Neither he nor anyone else ever referred to it later in connection with him.

In 1592, however, *Greene's Groatsworth* excited alarm. Another of the brilliant pamphleteers of the age, Thomas Nashe, denounced it in print:

"[A] scald trivial lying pamphlet, called *Greene's Groatsworth of Wit,* is given out to be of my doing. God never have care of my soul, but utterly renounce me, if the least word or syllable of it proceeded from my pen, or if I were any way privy to the writing or printing of it." This protest shows that not only Nashe but others, too, believed it a forgery.

The publisher of the pamphlet, Henry Chettle, felt constrained to issue an apology for it two months later. He denied having forged the pamphlet, but acknowledged some responsibility and apologized to one of the two "play-makers" who had taken offense at "Greene's" remonstrations:

> With neither of them that take offense was I acquainted, and with one of them I care not if I never be. The other, whom at that time I did not so much spare, as since I wish I had, for that as I have moderated the heat of living writers, and might have used my own discretion (especially in such a case), the Author being dead, that I did not, I am as sorry as if the original fault had been my fault, because myself have seen his demeanor no less civil than he excellent in the quality he professes: besides, divers of worship have reported his uprightness of dealing, which argues his honesty, and his facetious grace in writing, that approves his art.

Most scholars have assumed that the subject of the "handsome apology" is Mr. Shakspere, thus rounding out the story of their hero's first professional contretemps on an inspiring Horatio Alger note: Mr. Shakspere, his budding genius provoking bitter envy in a dying rival, is fully vindicated by the sponsor of the attack. The virtuous hero, with his native gifts and natural good manners, has withstood everything a university wit could hurl at him. He has survived the gibe that he is an upstart with no talent of his own; and so he has arrived.

Yet Chettle is clearly apologizing to one of the *playwrights* the pamphlet addressed, not to the actor (the "upstart crow"). Indeed, the pamphleteer was warning those playwrights *against* such people. Edmund Chambers comments on Chettle's apology with this admission: "It is probable that the first play-maker here referred to is Marlowe and the second Shakespeare, although this implies some looseness in Chettle's language, *since Greene's letter was obviously not written to Shakespeare*" (my emphasis). Chettle is not even thinking of the crow in his apology. It would be silly to say that the crow "took offense" at a robust insult that would have totally misfired if it *had not* offended him. The point of saying that someone has *taken* offense is to imply that the offense was not *intended*. This one was. Shakespeare might be either the playwright or the crow, but not both. In all probability, he was neither.

Greene's Groatsworth caused an immediate stir and was still being mentioned more than a decade after it appeared—yet none of the references to it implies that it had anything to do with Shakespeare. That inference was never made until Tyrwhitt's time. Nevertheless, Samuel Schoenbaum calls this supposed reference to William Shakespeare "the first glimpse we get of him as a man." The scholars have leaned heavily on the Greene–Chettle episode, and most of the biographies devote more attention to it than to the definite references to Mr. Shakspere or even, in some cases, the intimate and confessional Sonnets, whose apparent disclosures about their author are hard to square with the recorded data of Mr. Shakspere's life.

By contrast, Edmund Spenser's *The Teares of the Muses,* published in 1591 (and probably written earlier), laments the recent absence from the theater of a playwright who sounds very much like Shakespeare. His name is "Willy," he is "gentle," "honey and sweet nectar" flow from his pen, he is "the man whom Nature self had made To mock herself, and Truth to imitate," and his retirement has grieved the Muse of Comedy. It all sounds like Shakespeare, whose later eulogists would praise him in these very terms; commentators from Dryden on assumed that it could be nobody else.

Modern scholars deny that Spenser's Willy could be Shakespeare as vehemently as they insist that the "upstart crow" *must* be. They argue that Mr. Shakspere couldn't have established such primacy as a playwright, and also taken temporary leave of the theater, before 1591; whereas he could have been resented as an upstart by 1592. Of course, their governing assumption in rejecting the one allusion while accepting the other is that Mr. Shakspere was Shakespeare, and that references to Shakespeare have to fit the dates within which Mr. Shakspere could have made his mark in London. Nevertheless, Shakespeare's contemporaries seemed to recognize him in the paean to Willy, but not in the attack on the crow.

Both passages are open to dispute. My present point is that the scholars prefer the *Groatsworth* passage to the Spenser verses not because it is more self-evidently about Shakespeare, and certainly not because the Elizabethans thought so, but simply because it is more in accord with their presumption that Mr. Shakspere and Shakespeare were the same man.

In any case, even if the standard account of it could be taken as fact, the *Groatsworth* incident would hardly have loomed large in the playwright's life. It would never have received such inordinate prominence in the biographies if information about Shakespeare were really sufficient to leave no room for doubt about his identity.

Far from being established as a playwright by 1592, "William Shakespeare" never appeared in print as the name of a playwright until 1598. Not that it remained unknown in the interval. The name soon achieved renown—not for plays, but for two great narrative poems.

In 1593, the first published work of Shakespeare appeared. This was *Venus and Adonis,* a long, witty, amorous poem dedicated to the young Henry Wriothesley, Earl of Southampton. The poem was an immediate and lasting success. Overnight, Shakespeare became a famous poet. Then, in 1594, *The Rape of Lucrece* was published—also dedicated, with a startling declaration of love, to Southampton. *Lucrece* was longer than *Venus,* and far more serious. Its tragic sexual theme had none of the arch naughtiness of the earlier poem. It proved nearly as popular, and also earned its author renown and respect among what the scholar Gabriel Harvey called "the wiser sort." From then on, Shakespeare's greatness was unquestioned.

Beginning in 1594, Elizabethan literature yields many references to the stories of Lucrece and of Venus and Adonis. In 1594, we find three references to Lucrece, one of which, in the cryptically gossipy poem *Willobie his Avisa,* mentions Shakespeare by name: "And Shakespeare paints poor Lucrece' rape." A 1595 note by William Covell, in his book *Polimanteia,* has the words, "All praise worthy Lucrecia Sweet Shakespeare," showing again the association between the poet and the Lucrece tale. Francis Meres' famous praise of Shakespeare in 1598 begins by praising not his plays, but "his *Venus and Adonis,* his *Lucrece,* his sugared sonnets among his private friends." A poetic tribute addressed to Shakespeare by Richard Barnfield the same year mentions none of the plays but declares that *Venus* and *Lucrece* his "name in fame's immortal book have plac'd."

After 1598, there are also scattered references to the plays, but most praise of Shakespeare continued to begin with the two long poems. A 1599 sonnet addressed *"Ad Gulielmum Shakespeare"* by John Weever speaks of Shakespeare's characters as his "issue" and "children":

Rose-cheek'd Adonis with his amber tresses,

Fair, fire-hot Venus charming him to love her,

Chaste Lucretia virgin-like her dresses,

Proud lust-stung Tarquin seeking still to prove her:

Romeo, Richard, more whose names I know not . . .

Two books of quotations published in 1600 also contained many passages from Shakespeare, the great majority of which—192 out of 310—were taken from the two long poems rather than the eight or so plays that had been printed by then. Beyond any doubt, then, Shakespeare was first defined for the reading public not by *Greene's Groatsworth* but by *Venus and Adonis* and *The Rape of Lucrece.* Nobody in that age ever mentioned him in connection with *Groatsworth.*

At least six of his plays were printed between 1594 and 1597—that is, after his poems had made his reputation. Yet none of those plays bore his name. Shakespeare was never publicly identified as a playwright before 1598. Why not? His name on the title pages would have increased sales considerably. The scholars have not attempted to explain this fact.

In 1598, Shakespeare's name began to appear on the individual, or quarto, editions of his plays. Coincidentally or by design, it was in that same year that Francis Meres, in his survey *Palladis Tamia,* saluted him as both poet and playwright, likening him to the great Latin authors. From then on, Shakespeare was officially a playwright, so to speak, and nearly all of his plays, as they appeared in print singly, carried his name on the title page. After 1605, even some plays he *didn't* write were passed off as his.

In 1596, as mentioned above, William Wayte obtained sureties of the peace against Mr. Shakspere and three others, evidently fearing violence at their hands. The incident remains obscure, but it appears to have been part of a feud connected with the Swan Theater. And unlike *Greene's Groatsworth* and Chettle's apology, the document refers to Mr. Shakspere by name. We don't know that he was really at fault or had actually made threats against Wayte. But here at least is a clear reference to him, discovered by the scholar Leslie Hotson in the 1920s. Yet the biographers hardly mention the Wayte incident, and some of them omit it altogether. Why the neglect of this explicit reference to Mr. Shakspere, in contrast to the heavy emphasis on the obscure Greene–Chettle episode? Perhaps because it clashes with the image of Shakespeare as a placid genius, and with Chettle's supposed description of him as a "civil" person.

No personal information about Shakespeare *or* Mr. Shakspere appeared in print before the 1623 Folio. And the Folio itself, in both its lack of information and some of its assertions and omissions, seems designed to mislead. Mr. Shakspere had acquired the title "gentleman," a significant social distinction, yet the Folio doesn't mention it. With Ben Jonson taking the lead, the Folio creates Shakespeare's lasting image as a sort of self-made rustic. This was probably necessary if he was to be identified with Mr. Shakspere. Jonson implies that he had "small Latin and less Greek," yet Shakespeare uses nearly four hundred classical names in his works and shows familiarity with many Latin authors. In fact, *Venus* and *Lucrece* (neither of which is included or even mentioned in the Folio) are taken directly from classical sources; neither has ever been accused of erring in the slightest in its treatment of ancient history and myth.

Before Jonson, Shakespeare was known as a supremely *urbane* poet. Virtually every contemporary tribute praises him as "honey-tongued" or "mellifluous." Meres himself avers that "the Muses would speak with Shakespeare's fine-filed phrase, if they would speak English." It is in the

Folio that we see a subtle attempt to wrench Shakespeare's image, to make him not a polished gentleman-poet but a popular actor-playwright, the "friend and fellow" of other common players, who hardly bothered to revise his work. The epistle to the readers, allegedly by Mr. Shakspere's colleagues John Heminge and Henry Condell (but probably by Jonson, whose phrases are sprinkled through it), calls him "a happy imitator of Nature": "His mind and hand went together: and what he thought, he uttered with that easiness, that we have scarce received from him a blot in his papers."

The Folio set the tone for such future praise of Shakespeare as Milton's picture of him "warbling his native woodnotes wild." For a century afterward, Shakespeare was said to personify "Nature" and Jonson "Art," and debate raged over which was superior. That became the conventional way to speak of Shakespeare, and to explain how Mr. Shakspere could have written so brilliantly without being highly educated. It helped that Shakespeare's two great poems were soon all but forgotten.

Jonson died in 1637. In 1640, his *Timber, or Discoveries,* a series of casual notes on literary matters, was published, with a famous paragraph of barbed affection for Shakespeare:

> I remember, the players have often mentioned it as an honour to Shakespeare, that in his writing (whatsoever he penned) he never blotted out [a] line. My answer hath been, would he had blotted a thousand. Which they thought a malevolent speech. I had not told posterity this, but for their ignorance, who choose that circumstance to commend their friend by, wherein he most faulted, and to justify mine own candour, for I loved the man, and do honour his memory (on this side idolatry) as much as any. He was indeed honest, and of an open, and free nature; had an excellent phantasy, brave notions, and gentle expressions, wherein he flowed with that facility, that sometime it was necessary he should be stopped: *Sufflaminandus erat* [He had to be braked], as Augustus said of Haterius. His wit was in his own power; would the rule of it had been so too. Many times he fell into those things [that] could not escape laughter, as when he said in the person of Caesar, one speaking to him, *Caesar thou dost me wrong.* He replied: *Caesar never did wrong, but with just cause,* and such like, which

were ridiculous. But he redeemed his vices with his virtues. There was ever more in him to be praised, than to be pardoned.

This is accepted as the nearest thing we have to an actual description of Shakespeare the man—the only evidence of its kind, in fact. For many, it has constituted proof that Mr. Shakspere was Shakespeare. But if Jonson were keeping his friend's secret, he might well continue to refer to him in print as "Shakespeare," even when reminiscing about him.

If we read his words closely, we notice that in charging Shakespeare with a thousand gaffes, Jonson cites only one. Yet that one—"Caesar never did wrong, but with just cause"—does not appear in Shakespeare. Shakespeare's Caesar actually says. "Know, Caesar doth not wrong, nor without cause/Will he be satisfied."

The scholars have generally explained this apparent contradiction by positing that Shakespeare wrote the line Jonson cites in an early version of the play, but changed it in response to Jonson's needling. But the point of Jonson's complaint is that Shakespeare *didn't* amend his faults. Shakespeare makes mistakes here and there, though nowhere near a thousand, and most people wouldn't notice them without the guidance of scholarly notes. The truth is that every reader's direct impression of Shakespeare is the same as that of Meres and everyone else in his time: he set the all-time standard for English eloquence. Passing Shakespeare off as a blunderer, an inspired rustic, was an audacious absurdity on Jonson's part; and yet it has had its effect.

It is remarkable that Shakespeare never speaks in his own person except in the very private Sonnets and in his two dedications to Southampton. He is otherwise totally aloof from the literary give-and-take of his time. He never comments on public events (with two or three exceptions in the plays), never acknowledges or returns the praise of his contemporaries, never enters into controversy or feud, never exchanges the normal courtesies of commendatory verse with which Elizabethan poets boosted each other, never joins his fellow poets in eulogizing a dead queen or prince. The only hints of his awareness of any other poet of his time are his touching allusions to Marlowe, the "dead shepherd" who is saluted briefly and discreetly in *As You Like It,* and perhaps a subtle glance at Spenser in *A Midsummer Night's Dream.*

And yet our overwhelming impression of his personality is that he was hypersensitive to everything around him, and to everything within himself. Therein lies the real mystery of Shakespeare.

Mr. Shakspere is inexpressive, but not mysterious. His Stratford records are devoid of emotion and eloquence. His will is banal and businesslike. His gravestone inscription is a crude rhyme. He apparently had no love of literature or music; at any rate, the will mentions neither books nor musical instruments. Nothing in his Stratford records would lead one to suspect him of taking any interest in poetry, let alone of writing it. Any inference to the contrary is based entirely on the assumption that he wrote the plays in London.

The iconography of Shakespeare is so powerful that it takes a feat of imagination to separate the orthodox assumption of his authorship from what is actually known about Mr. Shakspere. We are so used to picturing Shakespeare and Ben Jonson clinking flagons and swapping jests at the Mermaid Tavern, for example, that it comes as a mild shock to realize that there is no warrant for such a scene.

Once one accepts that some doubt is justified regarding the authorship question, that it is some sort of mystery, certain questions immediately present themselves. First, if Mr. Shakspere wasn't William Shakespeare, how could such a great secret have been kept? For one thing, it would not have been a sensational secret in its own time. Shakespeare was by no means the towering icon he is today. Elizabethan and Jacobean critical opinion would have ranked Sidney and Spenser far above him as a poet, and Jonson and Beaumont beside him as playwrights. Nobody before the late eighteenth century would have placed him in the celestial company of Homer, Virgil, and Dante. Further, if the real author was in fact of high rank, concealment would have been not only routine but almost mandatory. His class and position would have forbidden him to publicize his connection with the theater. In an age of primitive communications and heavy censorship, it was relatively easy to maintain at least a formal secrecy. Many people might have known the truth, but it would have been kept out of print.

Indeed, everything that was printed had to be licensed by the censor, in the same way that everyone who drives a car today has to have a driver's license. For people of any rank, suppression was easy. And if a respected author who was also a man of importance wanted his identity concealed, his friends would naturally respect his wishes. Only an enemy, and a powerful enemy at that, would have been able to expose him.

Under modern conditions the truth might have quickly leaked out. Then again, even the much freer press of this century has helped suppress the widely shared knowledge of Edward VIII's affair with Mrs. Simpson, Franklin Roosevelt's infirmity, and John Kennedy's amours. If all these things have been successfully hushed up, it has not been for lack of intrinsic interest. More people are curious about royal and presidential dalliances, we can safely assume, than would have cared who Shakespeare was in 1600.

Chapter 3

The Development of
the Biography

The Folio's initial deception about Shakespeare's identity led to a long comedy of further errors. Not only was Mr. Shakspere quickly accepted as Shakespeare; misinformation about Mr. Shakspere himself soon came into currency. Thus a legend was created that continues to shape our image of the playwright, even though scholars have by now identified much of it as myth. The mythic Shakespeare began his career as a nimble tavern wag, the poet of "nature" who competed with his learned friend Ben Jonson, the master of classically inspired literary rhetoric. Later, during the eighteenth century, Shakespeare became an icon of British nationalism. For Victorians in the nineteenth century, his work was bowdlerized "for family reading" and became a fixture of home and hearth. Adopted by Americans, he was turned into an exemplary quasidemocratic, self-made man, universal in his sympathies and insights, an enemy of snobbery and prejudice.

The author of *Venus and Adonis* and *The Rape of Lucrece* appeared to contemporaries like Francis Meres a poet of consummate polish. Nobody in his own time except Ben Jonson professed to find his works bristling with imperfections and gaffes. Jonson, the literary solon of the next generation, imperiously took charge of Shakespeare's reputation, claiming to have been the author's friend and affirming his great love for him (though falling well short of idolatry). Even so, he made his famous criticisms only after Mr. Shakspere was dead. Then Shakespeare turned out to have "wanted art," to have had "small Latin and less Greek," to have written a thousand lines he should have blotted. Jonson's disparagements were soon echoed by others such as John Aubrey and Thomas Rymer—though Shakespeare's admirers turned his supposed faults into the virtues of a "natural wit" that had no need of erudition. John Milton wrote of "sweetest Shakespeare, fancy's child,/Warbling his native woodnotes wild."

Echoing Milton's characterization of Shakespeare, criticism of the period typically paired Shakespeare with Jonson. Jonson had all the prestige of learning, classical models, and French neoclassical theory on his side; Shakespeare represented the home team, the trusty English man of war. Thomas Fuller, in his 1662 book *The History of the Worthies of England,* expanded the point and contrasted Shakespeare with Jonson in what proved to be a long debate over the relative merits of "nature" and "art." Note in the following account from Fuller that neither poet had yet established clear preeminence, and more important, that the Shakespeare myth was already becoming entwined with English national pride.

> He was an eminent instance of the truth of that Rule, *Poeta not* [sic] *fit, sed nascitur,* one is not *made,* but *born* a Poet. Indeed his Learning was very little, so that as *Cornish diamonds* not polished by an Lapidary, but are pointed and smoothed even as they are taken out of the Earth, so *nature* it self was all the *art* which was used upon him.
>
> Many were the *wit-combates* betwixt him and *Ben Johnson,* which two I behold [sic] like a *Spanish great Gallion* and an *English man of War;* Master *Johnson* (like the former) was built far higher in Learning; *Solid,* but *Slow* in his performances. *Shake-spear,* with the *English-man of War,* lesser in *bulk,* but lighter in *sailing,* could turn with all tides, tack about and take advantage of all winds, by the quickness of his Wit and Invention. He died *Anno*

Domini 16 . . , and was buried at *Stratford* upon *Avon,* the Town of his Nativity.

If Fuller witnessed these "wit-combats," he must have begun frequenting the Mermaid at a very tender age: he was born in 1608. Nevertheless, the coupling of Shakespeare with English patriotism has clearly already begun.

Others in the mid-1600s related apocryphal anecdotes of "Shakespeare" topping Jonson in duels of wit. John Ward, vicar of Stratford from 1662 to 1681, wrote in his diary: "I have heard yt Mr. Shakespeare was a natural wit, without any art at all." He also recorded a pair of legends few biographers accept: that "hee spent att ye Rate of 1000*l.* a year, as I have heard," and that "Shakespeare, Drayton, and Ben Jhonson, had a merry meeting, and itt seems drank too hard, for Shakespeare died of a feavour there contracted."

John Aubrey, writing around 1681, recounts colorful gossip that is in accord with the growing legend's unreliability; it has often been quoted by scholars as if it were authoritative:

> [H]is father was a Butcher, & I have been told heretofore by some of his neighbors, that when he was a boy he exercised his father's Trade, but when he kill'd a Calfe, he would doe it in a *high style,* & make a Speech. There was at that time another Butcher's son in this Towne, that was held not at all inferior to him for a naturall witt, his acquaintance & coetanean, but dyed young. This Wm. being inclined naturally to Poetry and acting, came to London I guesse about 18, and was an Actor at one of the Playhouses and did act exceedingly well: now B. Johnson was never a good Actor, but an excellent Instructor.

Like the others, Aubrey keeps pairing Shakespeare with Jonson. He has the two men on intimate terms, traveling through the countryside and visiting taverns together: "Ben Johnson and he did gather Humours of men dayly where ever they came." He offers a somewhat garbled version of the familiar legend: "He was wont to say, That he never blotted out a line in his life: sayd Ben: Johnson, I wish he had blotted out a thousand." Aubrey's brief life of Shakespeare (barely a page) concludes, "Though as Ben: Johnson sayes of him, that he had but little Latin and lesse Greek, He understood Latin pretty well: for he had been in his younger yeares a Schoolmaster in the Countrey." One modern biographer, A. L. Rowse, says flatly, "There is no reason at all to reject this."

On the contrary, there is reason to question nearly every statement Aubrey makes. He would have Mr. Shakspere teaching school before he went to London at age eighteen—after working as a butcher's boy. Moreover, we have no record that John Shakspere was ever a butcher. Aubrey's sketch wasn't published for over a century. It quickly became part of Shakespeare's virtual identity, even though the most careful scholars consider it dubious in nearly every detail.

In his 1709 edition of Shakespeare's works, Nicholas Rowe attempted the first substantial biography of Shakespeare. Running forty pages in large type, it contained errors large and small. Rowe was the first to put in print several persistent legends, such as that Mr. Shakspere fled to London and began his career as an actor after getting into trouble at home for poaching deer. He also repeated Jonson's comments about Shakespeare's lack of learning. Rowe did no real research, but his biography remained the standard for most of the eighteenth century; Samuel Johnson had little to add and merely reprinted Rowe's account in his own 1765 edition of the plays. Rowe's biography was only gradually picked apart by later scholarship; like Aubrey, he gave his readers a more colorful characterization of Shakespeare than more careful later scholars would allow. In that respect, critical scholarship leaves us knowing less about the poet than earlier readers thought they knew. The more we learn, the more remote he seems.

Critical biography of Shakespeare began nearly two centuries after Shakespeare wrote. It was a labor of reconstruction from scattered documents more akin to archaeology than to biography as we usually think of it. It follows that if Ben Jonson and the 1623 Folio were unreliable, everything built on them is unreliable too.

Immediately following the Restoration, Shakespeare's plays became something of an embarrassment to neoclassical taste. They sprawled extravagantly, defying the prescribed unities of time, place, and action.

The tragedies were too violent, the comedies too buffoonish. But Shakespeare's undeniable greatness eventually forced critical theory to accommodate him. As Dryden put it, "genius must be born, and never can be taught." The very idea of genius, in this modern sense, grew up with Shakespeare's reputation. English literary theory, culminating in Coleridge and Hazlitt, continued to be shaped by the need to justify Shakespeare, who was bound to fall short by the standards of Neoclassicism. To judge Shakespeare by the rules of Aristotle, Pope wrote, "is like trying a man by the Laws of one Country, who acted under those of another." Still, the English remained self-conscious about their somewhat coarse native-born genius. For a long time he did not travel well; no translation of Shakespeare into a European language was made until the 1740s. Voltaire and others sniffed at his "barbarism." Even his defenders at home acknowledged his frequent "obscurity," his tendency to "quibbling" and "bombast."

From the Restoration on, Shakespeare held the stage, but usually in revisions that made him both palatable and "correct" in the eyes of audiences and critics. Such poets as Dryden and Sir William Davenant tried to "refine" Shakespeare's diction; coarse scenes were omitted altogether; elaborate music and spectacular stage business were added. Nahum Tate even gave *King Lear* a happy ending, with the edifying moral that "truth and virtue shall at last succeed." Such editors as Rowe, Pope, and Lewis Theobald freely "improved" Shakespeare's text, seeking to cure his supposed faults with their own words. We must not judge these improvers too harshly. If they strike us as presumptuous, we should bear in mind that they were merely trying to broaden Shakespeare's appeal to readers and audiences. They took for granted that Shakespeare, though great and popular, was only human.

All this changed dramatically in the second half of the eighteenth century. When David Garrick staged his huge Jubilee at Stratford in 1769, Shakespeare seemed to ascend at last to the status of England's cultural god, never to be toppled. Garrick's wildly popular productions of the plays in London did their part too; though Garrick retained some of the adapted versions of Tate and others, his own powerful acting did for Shakespeare in the eighteenth century what Laurence Olivier's film versions would do in the twentieth.*

Shakespeare's glory grew along with the British empire. Gary Taylor, coeditor of the recent New Oxford edition of Shakespeare's works, notes that the one was enlisted to serve the other as Britain and France competed for global power. If the French had their effete neoclassical tragedians Racine and Corneille, England could boast its honest, earthy Shakespeare. "During the 1760s," Taylor observes,

> [British] writers fell over one another in proclaiming Shakespeare the world's greatest dramatist and poet. Such praises were almost nationalistic in tone and often specifically anti-French. . . . The opposition between Shakespeare's practice and French aesthetic theory, the focus of critical argument for a century, became the foundation of Shakespeare's expanding international reputation. Shakespeare became the exemplar of literary liberty, the titular champion of anyone who wanted to overthrow an exhausted critical system.

The Shakespeare craze reached such a pitch that after 1769 Stratford became a mecca, with hawkers selling old furniture and bric-a-brac as "relics" of the great poet. The trade soon led to one of the great hoaxes of literary history: the brief but amazing career of William Henry Ireland, a young man who managed to fool nearly all of literate England with his absurd forgeries.

Ireland was the legal son of Samuel Ireland, an avid Shakespeare lover, who had married the lad's mother after she was cast off by the no-

---

*We should note that Olivier and other modern actors and directors have also "adapted" the plays, not so much by altering the text as by superimposing fashionable interpretations on them. Olivier's heavily Freudian film version of *Hamlet* illustrates that the more up-to-date such things appear in their own time, the more dated they seem afterward. Ian McKellen has recently played Richard III as a protofascist, a reading that overlooks the obvious difference between an old-fashioned usurper, who merely wants a crown on his own head, and a modern totalitarian who wants to remake all social institutions. In other productions, Shylock, Othello, and even Caliban become victims of prejudice, imperialism, and other evils. The urge to improve on Shakespeare—usually in an earnest effort to enlist him in democratic and other progressive causes—is perennial. But it interferes with the understanding of Shakespeare on his own terms.

bleman who had been her lover. His lordship may have paid Samuel to take the woman and the children she had borne him. The boy found his putative father cold to him but very warm to Shakespeare. The result was a droll story tinged with pathos.

On a pilgrimage to Stratford, Samuel Ireland bought a love seat in which, he was assured by a local merchant, Will Shakespeare had wooed Anne Hathaway. Even eighteen-year-old William could see how gullible Samuel was. But he may also have thought, correctly, that he had found the way to his father's heart. Whatever the motive, he began forging his own Shakespeare relics. First he wrote a love letter from Will to Anne. Clever and modestly literate, William Henry simulated archaic spelling and poetic language, as he conceived them, then held the paper over a fire until it yellowed like an old manuscript.

> O Anna doe I love doe I cheryshe thee inne mye hearte forre thou arte ass a talle Cedarre strehtchynge forthe its branches and succourynge the small-ere Plants fromme nyppynge Winneterre orr the boysterous Wyndes . . .

Samuel Ireland was ecstatic with the find. And as William continued to "discover" love letters, poems, business records of Shakespeare—even letters to Shakespeare from the Earl of Southampton and Queen Eliza-beth—Samuel showed them to others. The forgeries swiftly created a national sensation. Among the multitudes of duped Shakespeare lovers was the aging James Boswell, who knelt tearfully before these purported tokens of the great genius and cried, "I now kiss the invaluable relics of our bard, and thanks to God I have lived to see them!"

Supply met demand as William Henry kept producing Shakespearean documents with a rapidity that should have aroused suspicion. But few, even among scholars of the day, perceived the laughable coarseness of his forgeries. People obviously *wanted* to believe, and perhaps it seemed cynical to doubt such welcome discoveries. William himself, in his later memoirs, marvelled at the credulity of the public. Fearing that his dis-coveries might be claimed and taken from him by some descendant of Shakespeare, Ireland forged a deed of gift from Shakespeare, granting the title to all his papers to one William Henry Ireland—a fictitious an-cestor of his own! Laying it on thick, Ireland had the poet describe how he had fallen into the Thames one night, whereupon his friend Ireland "pulledd off hys Jerrekynne and jumpedd inn afterre mee withe muche paynes he draggedd mee forthe I beynge then nearelye deade and soe he dydd save mye life."

The English public gobbled up even this. Emboldened by unbroken success, William Henry produced a magnum opus: his own Shakespearean tragedy. *Vortigern* was based, with fitting audacity, on a painting in Samuel's own study. The play, produced with much fanfare at Drury Lane, was to star the Prince of Wales' mistress, Dorothea Jordan. But on the eve of what should have been his supreme triumph, Ireland's imposture was exploded. The great Shakespeare scholar Edmond Malone wrote a pamphlet debunking his frauds. Ireland was finished overnight. He had to shelve his plans to favor the world with Shakespeare's authentic versions of *Hamlet* and *Lear*. Only one man believed to the last that Ireland's forgeries were real—Samuel Ireland, who could not believe his stupid William capable of writing such sublime letters and verses.

The Ireland frauds have one lasting value: they remind us how primitive the state of Shakespeare studies remained as late as the end of the eighteenth century. It would take a long time to sift documented fact from legend and fraud. During the eighteenth century, even reputable scholars created bogus Shakespeare documents. Lewis Theobald, who edited the works of Shakespeare, claimed to have a manuscript of a lost Shakespeare play called *Cardenio,* but he never showed it to anyone; today his claim is almost universally rejected. Later, George Steevens, a more reliable editor who had also assisted on Johnson's edition, fashioned an authentic-sounding letter from the Elizabethan poet-playwright George Peele, purporting to recall a conversation with Shakespeare about *Hamlet;* Steevens may have meant the letter as a harmless prank, but it fooled readers for more than a century.

In the nineteenth century came the most serious fraud of all. John Payne Collier was the foremost Shakespeare scholar of his time, and he made lasting contributions to Shakespeare studies. But he also made expert forgeries of documents about the dramatist, and even now it is hard to tell some of his false creations from true records of the time. Unlike Ireland, whose crude efforts he immeasurably surpassed, Collier never confessed to his misdeeds. He avoided simulating any work by Shakespeare himself, instead mixing his real discoveries with almost perfectly executed forged papers by the actor Edward Alleyn and the Earl of Southampton. Lesser scholars hesitated at first to voice their suspicions of Collier's finds, but by 1860 they had been exposed and he was plunged into disgrace.

In time, honest scholars learned to start from scratch. But their project began late, and has been dogged by false starts and errors as well as outright deceits. During the late nineteenth century, it was fashionable to round out the sparse facts of Mr. Shakspere's outer life with freestyle inferences about his inner life drawn from the plays, based on their supposed dates. Thus, Edward Dowden, in his 1872 book *Shakspere: A Critical Study of His Mind and Art,* divided the poet's career into four phases. First came his apprenticeship, "during which Shakspere [sic] was learning his trade as a dramatic craftsman." Second came the period of early mastery, "strong and robust," during which "he was making rapid advance in worldly prosperity, and accumulating the fortune on which he meant to retire as a country gentleman." Third, and most interesting, was the tragic period, resulting from the fact that "Shakspere had known sorrow: his son was dead; his father died probably soon after Shakspere had written his *Twelfth Night;* his friend of the Sonnets had done him wrong." During this period, "Shakspere's genius left the bright surface of the world, and was at work in the very heart and centre of things." Finally, in his late romances, the poet achieved a sense of reconcilation: "The tragic gloom and suffering were not, however, to last for ever. The dark cloud lightens and rolls away, and the sky appears purer and tenderer than ever." The poet had come "out of the darkness and tragic mystery" to "a pure and serene elevation."

Dowden's naive way of blending criticism with biography appears in such comments as these:

> In Shakspere's [sic] late play, *The Tempest,* written when he was about to retire for good to his Stratford home, he indulges in a sly laugh at the principles of communism. He who had earned the New Place, and become a landed gentleman by years of irksome toil, did not see that he was bound to share his tenements and lands with his less industrious neighbours. On the contrary he meant to hold them himself by every legal title, and at his decease to hand them down to his daughter and her sons, and sons' sons.

Dowden's biographical scheme had great influence for half a century. But a reaction against it was inevitable, and in 1934 C. J. Sisson delivered a powerful, sardonic rejoinder on "the mythical sorrows of Shakespeare." Without raising the authorship question in any way, Sisson pointed out that the few known facts of Mr. Shakspere's life simply didn't support what were essentially no more than guesses about his moods. There was no evidence that his "tragic period" in any way reflected his personal fortunes or misfortunes. Sisson helped set the tone for all subsequent Shakespeare studies. Since his time, Shakespeare criticism and Shakespeare biography have gone their separate ways. What Sisson showed, albeit inadvertently, was that orthodox biography has nothing to say about the Shakespeare works. It did not occur to Sisson that the chief reason for this odd disjuncture might be that the biographies were about the wrong subject.

Edmond Malone, who left his work unfinished when he died in 1812, is considered the dramatist's first true biographer. After him came Collier and James Halliwell-Phillips. At the beginning of the twentieth century, Sir Sidney Lee completed the definitive life of Shakespeare, purging old legends and severely pruning unsupported surmise, leaving only the arid outline of a life. Lee's Shakespeare is even more of a nonentity than Rowe's. Orthodox Shakespeare scholarship culminated in the work of Sir Edmund Chambers in the 1930s. His two-volume critical study of the Shakespeare documents remains nearly the last word on the Shakespeare we have come to know. A heroic labor, it nevertheless disappoints anyone who hopes for a living glimpse of the great author. The leading Shakespeare biographer of our time is Samuel Schoenbaum, whose *William Shakespeare: A Documentary Life* pares the life to the bone. So severe is Schoenbaum in rejecting all the unproven legends about the playwright that he leaves Shakespeare a mere specter. And of course he adds nothing to what was known before—the records of baptisms, marriages, business dealings, taxes, will, and burial, filled out with speculative dates of his poems and plays. Schoenbaum rejects even the Sonnets as a source of biographical knowledge. His biography leaves the dramatist himself, creator of hundreds of vivid characters, with no personality at all. From Schoenbaum it would seem a short step to doubting the whole standard account of Shakespeare. Yet Schoenbaum snorts at such suggestions. He insists that Mr. Shakspere of Stratford, or what is left of him, is beyond question the real author.

As this orthodox tradition progressed, heresy began to appear, though only furtively at first. In the 1780s, a retired clergyman named James Wilmot, a friend of Samuel Johnson, moved to Stratford to attempt a full-scale biography of Shakespeare. But after searching everywhere within fifty miles of the town, he had found nothing useful—no letters, papers, books, or other records of Mr. Shakspere beyond what was already known. Finally he concluded that Mr. Shakspere was not Shakespeare the writer. He suspected that Francis Bacon had written the works. But he prudently kept his doubts to himself, confiding his suspicion to only one close friend.

By the 1850s, many readers, examining the scholars' lean findings, concluded that the whole hunt was following a false scent. Delia Bacon, an American, was the first anti-Stratfordian to achieve a kind of celebrity. She championed her namesake Sir Francis as the real author; she even went to Stratford, hoping to resolve the mystery of authorship by opening the sacred grave. Unsurprisingly, this was not permitted.

Others agreed with Miss Bacon in rejecting Shakspere, but not everyone accepted Sir Francis. Dozens of rival candidates, plausible (Christopher Marlowe) and absurd (Daniel Defoe), were proposed; a minority of the doubters remained agnostic. Baconians leveled some trenchant criticisms at the orthodox view, but made themselves ridiculous with their absurd efforts to find Bacon's claim enciphered in the Shakespeare works themselves.

Walt Whitman wrote of Shakespeare's history plays that "only one of the 'wolfish earls' so plenteous in the plays themselves, or some born descendant and knower, might seem to be the true author of those amazing works." He judged the comedies "made for the divertissement only of the elite of the castle, and from its point of view." Whitman dropped a provocative hint: "Beneath a few foundations of proved facts are certainly engulf'd far more dim and elusive ones of deeper importance—tantalizing and half suspected—suggesting explanations that one dare not put into plain statement." Why not? Was Whitman, outspoken on most matters except his own discreet homosexuality, thinking of the adoring sonnets addressed to the beautiful young man?

Henry James privately admitted his "conviction that the divine William is the biggest and most successful fraud ever practised on a patient world." But much as he scorned the Stratfordian version of Shakespeare, he found it nearly as hard to believe that Bacon had written the plays.

Mark Twain's last published work, *Is Shakespeare Dead?* (1909), was a long, bumptious pamphlet in all-out assault on Shakespeare's claim. Twain based much of his argument on the brilliant writings of an English lawyer, Sir George Greenwood, who had no candidate of his own to offer but certainly wasn't buying Shakespeare (or Shakspere, as most anti-Stratfordians called him by then). Greenwood argued that the Shakespeare plays implied an author of a totally different background and education from the Stratford man's—in all likelihood, a learned aristocrat trained in the law. Twain reinforced the argument in his tart style:

> When Shakespeare died in Stratford *it was not an event*. It made no more stir in England than the death of any other forgotten theatre-actor would have made. Nobody came down from London; there were no lamenting poems, no eulogies, no national tears—there was merely silence, and nothing more. A striking contrast with what happened when Ben Jonson, and Francis Bacon, and Spenser, and Raleigh and the other distinguished literary folk of Shakespeare's time passed from life! No praiseful voice was lifted for the lost Bard of Avon; even Ben Jonson waited seven years before he lifted his.

In time dozens of rival candidates would be proposed, and popular doubts persisted. But none ever succeeded in displacing Mr. Shakspere. As we have seen, most scholars hold that the dissenters are driven by "snobbery." Among recent scholars, only Gary Taylor has grasped that the anti-Stratfordian movement that erupted in the mid-nineteenth century was not an elitist phenomenon, but a populist one: "the revolt of the layman" against academic authority.

Easily dismissing the doubters, orthodox biographers have carried on their quest for a plausible picture of Shakespeare. But many of them have shown a gift for invention worthy of William Henry Ireland. The

Shakespeare of the orthodox biographers, Mark Twain observed, "is a Brontosaur: nine bones and six hundred barrels of plaster of paris." But the meager facts are heavily reinforced by iconography. Every literate person learns to imagine Shakespeare exchanging witticisms with Ben Jonson at the Mermaid; rehearsing new plays at the Globe Theater; performing with his acting company at the court of Elizabeth I; pondering his next profundity as he sits at his writing table with quill poised. Chess books even record the moves of a game he supposedly played against Jonson.

So familiar is Shakespeare as a cultural icon, his face appearing even in advertisements, that we almost feel we have seen him ourselves. It is easy to forget how scanty the biographical materials really are. They can be printed in a pamphlet of thirty pages or so, even if the entire texts of the 1616 will and the long prefatory tributes of the 1623 Folio are included, and many of the records are legal documents with no bearing on Mr. Shakspere's presumptive career as a playwright. So the orthodox biographers tell us that Shakespeare *may have* done this, *must have* known that; *probably* read this, *almost certainly* was aware of that. By such means, they have achieved impressive length. Sidney Lee, for example, produced a Shakespeare biography of 476 pages. Joseph Quincy Adams, not long afterward, achieved 561 pages. More recently, A. L. Rowse made 484 pages out of the same meager materials, and Peter Levi reached 392 pages. Russell Fraser recently published a two-volume Shakespeare biography: *Young Shakespeare* (217 pages) takes its hero to the age of thirty; Fraser completes the story in *Shakespeare: The Later Years* (380 pages).

Samuel Schoenbaum, until his recent death the dean of contemporary scholars, is far more scrupulous than most in sifting documents and questioning old legends (most of which date from the late seventeenth and early eighteenth centuries), and much of the bulk of his 384-page (in the 1987 revised edition) *William Shakespeare: A Compact Documentary Life* is due to his careful discussion of critical problems. Yet even Schoenbaum occasionally lapses into romantic guesswork.

By now the methods of Shakespeare biography have become almost comically formulaic. The biographer begins, of course, with the town of Stratford-upon-Avon, where Mr. Shakspere was born and died, giving a lengthy, nostalgic description of Stratford in Shakespeare's time, refulgent with the glow of small-town boyhood. This includes a reconstruction of the circumstances of Mr. Shakspere's father—a small tradesman, sometimes an alderman and bailiff, in and out of debt, in minor trouble with the law—and some information about the Ardens, the family of Mr. Shakspere's mother. Siblings can also be listed, and even an uncle or two.

Next, one must say something of the young genius's school days. The first small hurdle is that we have no certainty that he ever went to school: again, the only record of his first eighteen years is the single line recording his baptism. But there indubitably was a Stratford Grammar School, and one can follow the example of Louis B. Wright: "Though the records are lost, there can be no reason to doubt that this is where young William received his education." With such reasonable-sounding stipulations, Wright lulls skepticism to sleep while maintaining a tone of certitude and authority.

In his introduction to each volume of the old Folger Library paperback editions of Shakespeare, Wright provides a nine-page biography. This short account tells about all there is to tell, according to scholarly consensus. Even at that, it is heavily padded. Two pages are devoted to attacking authorship heresies. Another page is given to repeating, then rejecting, such apocryphal stories as Shakespeare's apprenticeship to a butcher, his purported deer poaching, and the legend that he started his career in the theater with the entry-level job of holding horses outside the playhouse. Much of the rest is the usual article: Shakespeare perhaps, Shakespeare probably, Shakespeare may have, Shakespeare seems to have.

Wright goes on: "His learning in books was anything but profound, but he clearly had the probing curiosity that sent him in search of information, and he had a keenness in the observation of nature and of humankind that finds reflection in his poetry." Well, he *probably* had that probing curiosity—if he was Shakespeare. That assumption generates any number of inferences about the sort of pupil young Mr. Shakspere must have been. Note Wright's exemplary assertiveness: "There is little documentation for Shakespeare's boyhood. There is little reason why there should be." As Wright knows, there is no documentation *at all* for Mr. Shakspere's boyhood. His baptism in 1564; his betrothal in 1582 at eighteen; and nothing in between. "Nobody knew that he was going to be a dramatist about whom any scrap of information would be prized in the centuries to come. He was merely an active and vigorous youth of Stratford [how do we know he wasn't passive and sickly?], perhaps assisting his father in his business [but perhaps not], and no Boswell bothered to write down facts about him." One must admire Wright's tone of magisterial impatience with anyone who would deny the virtually tautological. "The most important record that we have is a marriage license issued by the Bishop of Worcester on November 27, 1582, to permit William Shakespeare to marry Anne Hathaway, seven or eight years his senior." Being virtually the only document we have, it is no doubt the most important. Of course, as we have seen, it spells the couple's names "Shagspere" and "whately." This may mean nothing, but it shows that the sources are less unequivocal than Wright's tone suggests.

As we come to Mr. Shakspere's courtship, let Wright yield to Charles Norman, author of *So Worthy a Friend: William Shakespeare:*

> Now comes the personable son of the former high bailiff of Stratford, to entertain the two Hathaway girls with talk of poetry and the theatrical companies, which were performing in the borough with greater frequency of late. Perhaps he read to them, which would have been more than mere entertainment, for with such a responsive audience, William Shakespeare would see ever more clearly where his ambitions tended; his enthusiasm would be contagious, and be reflected back.
>
> Catherine is a shadowy figure in all this. Anne is not, particularly in view of what happened. Her heart must have been lighter in her side every time she saw the youth from Stratford coming over the fields—he was young, to be sure, younger than herself, younger even than Catherine; but old for his years. He brought tidings of the busy borough and of the world outside, of books, and great and glamorous events.
>
> She marked him for her own.

Even the austere Schoenbaum can't resist indulging in some romantic fancy here:

> If his apprentice days were cluttered with the merchandise of his father's shop, pungent with the aroma of leather, he nevertheless found time—and

occasion—for other pursuits. During the long summer twilights of 1582, he must more than once have found his way along the narrow footpath that led west from his home, through green fields, to a clump of farm-houses called Shottery, a mile distant, where the large Hathaway family dwelt.

All this springs from a well-placed "if," but it's no nicely evocative that the reader forgets that everything that follows is guesswork. (Elsewhere, Schoenbaum himself has well described the biographer's temptation: "In the absence of verifiable data, speculation flourishes, biography (like nature) abhorring a vacuum.") He proceeds: "Shakespeare wooed and bedded the farmer's daughter—or did she seduce her boy lover?"

For the answer to that provocative question, we turn from Schoenbaum back to Norman:

> By the summer of 1582 her father was dead. She had no fear of her step-mother. It could have been love at first sight; but it could have been some-thing else. Given a woman of twenty-six, and a youth of eighteen, plus a seduction, and it is not difficult to determine who was the seducer.
>
> In the heat and very midsummer of that year, in the sweet-smelling meadows of Shottery, Anne Hathaway clung gratefully to William Shake-speare with all the pent-up ardor of her spinsterhood.

F.E. Halliday's *The Life of Shakespeare* runs a modest 248 pages. But Halliday (an especially genial writer, I feel bound to say) is unrivaled at getting mileage out of his material. His treatment of Mr. Shakspere's entirely supposititious school days is at least inventive:

> As there are no records of the period, we do not know that Shakespeare went to the grammar school, but the only early mention of his education, that of Rowe, presumably on the authority of Betterton, states that he went to "a free school." But there is no need of such authority; of course he must have gone there. It is inconceivable that one of Stratford's leading townsmen should not send his son to the local grammar school, a particu-larly good one, which for the children of burgesses was free.
>
> We can therefore imagine John Shakespeare, early one morning in 1571, reassuring his reluctant though excited son as they walked along

Henley Street to the High Cross, and then down High Street, past the Quiney house on the right, past New Place on the left, to the Gild Chapel, on the south side of which was the school . . .

And so on. If, perhaps, probably, may well have, must have, we can imagine, there is no reason to doubt—such phrases make possible a paragraph or even a few pages of appealing fantasy. "It may well have been in the next year that the little boy caught his first glimpse of the Queen." "Then we can imagine the gathering excitement of the little boy as he began the study of his first play, a comedy of Terence." "It must have been a happy time for the boy." "Then there were relations to be visited. Perhaps William did not make a point of going to see his uncle Henry Shakespeare, who was not farming at Ingon, two miles north of Stratford." "What exactly happened we do not know, but it seems clear that . . ." "It seems probable, therefore, that . . ."

Halliday carries us through Mr. Shakspere's career in London, and finally back to retirement in Stratford: "But there was work to be done as well as leisure to be filled with reading, music, and the conversation of friends." This is consoling; but apart from the assumption that Mr. Shakspere was Shakespeare the author, we don't even know that he could read, let alone that he listened to music. That he probably talked to his friends may be conceded.

Less tentative and more confident than other biographers is A.L. Rowse. In his 1963 best-seller *William Shakespeare: A Biography*, he supplies the local color of Stratfordian school days:

> In the upper school he went on to Ovid, and this was the love of his life among Latin poets. . . . It is nice to think, however, that the boy sometimes played truant from all this and went off into the fields blackberrying.

> He picked up everything. It was noticed in his own day that everything came easily to him—though on the basis of that natural gift, how he worked to make the most of it! There can be no doubt that the methodical training of the memory at Elizabethan grammar school and church entered largely into it.

> That Shakespeare heard [Queen Elizabeth] speak we need not doubt.

He was an orthodox, conforming member of the Church into which he had been baptised, was brought up and married, in which his children were reared and in whose arms he at length was buried.

By nature he was a poet, and one fine day in the later 1580s . . . he took the road to London.

He lived in lodgings in London, but went home to Stratford for the summers.

We must always remember that, among other things, he was a good, if good-tempered, man of business.

Rowse's habitual assurance does not desert him when he confronts the puzzles of the Sonnets. He announces that

historical investigation, by proper historical method, . . . has enabled me to solve, for the first time, and definitively, the problem of the Sonnets, which has teased so many generations and led so many people into a morass of conjecture. The key to the resolution of their problems, all of which are now cleared up—except for the identity of Shakespeare's mistress, which we are never likely to know—has been to follow strict historical method and establish a firm dating and chronology.

He launches his solution by sweeping away one silly notion: "We can be quite sure that it was no aristocrat who wrote the Sonnets." He has no doubt who the Rival Poet was: "[T]here is no reason now for doubting that Marlowe was the rival poet of the Sonnets. . . . I am not proposing yet another thesis: the problem is solved, as is clear for all to see." And the poet's mistress? "All kinds of wild-cat notions have been proposed as to the identity of the Dark Lady. In fact we do not know, and are never likely to know, who she was; nor is this a matter of much importance—of more sentimental interest, than scholarly."*

Rowse maintains this confident tone over 484 pages. But even Rowse can't rival Garry O'Connor in the assurance of his conjectures.

---

*Only a few years after he wrote these words, Rowse positively identified the dark lady as one Emilia Lanier, roundly abusing those who resisted this solution, until it transpired that he had misread a key word in the document on which he had based it.

In *William Shakespeare: A Life,* O'Connor enters the thoughts not only of his subject but of his subject's wife. He begins his book with a certainty that never flags:

> In the early summer of 1585, a short time after celebrating his twenty-first birthday, William Shakespeare left home. Forsaking his wife and young family—or so his wife Anne felt—Shakespeare was quitting the crowded provincial home in Henley Street where they had been living with his parents and brothers.

The record supports not a syllable of this. Of Anne we know only the dates of her birth, her marriage, her children's births (and one child's death), and her death and the fact that she incurred a small debt in Stratford. What she "felt" when William left in the early summer of 1585 we can only guess. But then it is only a guess that he did leave in the early summer of 1585, or that they had been living on Henley Street with his family.

O'Connor manages to give his wildest guesses the tone of well-informed gossip and discriminating judgment: "Anne's relationship with William's mother was sound. . . . It may have been in many ways a failed marriage, but it was never a dead marriage."

> She was competent, practical, literal, and sensual. It is not too fanciful to see her as dark-haired and dark-eyed, features common enough with yeomen's daughters.... Anne was wilful, individual, guarded her middle-class "heiress" status, later refused to become an actor's wife, or a camp follower in any way, fought ferociously to preserve this dual nature, her first allegiance being to that truth of feeling and to family values, not to art. She became, as a mother of twins, outwardly a primal force of nature, and however much the often variable emotional nature of Shakespeare wanted to run away, he knew always that he must remain rooted in that dark and eternal female nature.

O'Connor even offers a physical description of Anne later in life:

> Anne Shakespeare, sixty now, fed on beef and ale, but with a more refined moral diet, had broad shoulders and a well-developed bust, with a boldness and rotundity of speech which well suited her round and ruddy cheeks.

This of a woman whose documented life makes her husband's look like a Russian novel! Even the year of her birth has to be deduced from her gravestone inscription. All these excesses, ludicrous as some of them may be, arise from the necessity of filling in the long silences in Mr. Shakspere's life—the "vacuum," as Schoenbaum calls it. But those same silences, insofar as they excuse the biographers for speculating, amply justify the skeptics.

The attempt to forge a single coherent "Shakespeare" out of Shakespeare's plays and Mr. Shakspere's life produces only confusion. The poet-playwright sounds like a polished courtier; Mr. Shakspere sounds like a shrewd, tough businessman with some rough edges. Each is a distinctive character, but together they don't add up to a human being, no matter how many biographers apply their intuition and eloquence to the problem.

Shakespeare biography has been a fruitless quest. It has thrown no light at all on the Shakespeare plays and poems, and the greatest of the critics and commentators have simply disregarded it. Shakespeare's personal inaccessibility has helped give rise to the various schools of modern literary criticism that deny the relevance of the author's life and personality to his work, from the New Criticism of the 1930s to deconstruction. In some respects, this may be a defensible postulate; an author's work should not be reduced to disguised autobiography, since a literary work by definition is a distinct object of interest. But because authors and their language are rooted in real history, literary biography remains a legitimate and illuminating enterprise. Its popularity as a genre is likely to ensure its survival despite all philosophical attacks. Thus, given the rickety if towering edifice that Shakespeare biography has become, sooner or later we may expect a thorough and widespread reconsideration of Shakespeare's identity—one that effectively marries the historical and literary evidence.

Chapter 4

Disconnections Between the Poetry and the Life

Nothing we know of Mr. Shakspere fits the sense of Shakespeare the man we get from the plays and Sonnets. Kenneth Muir has confessed to doubts about the possibility of "relating Shakespeare's works to his private life," but the real problem is relating Shakespeare's works to Mr. Shakspere's private life. The biographers' frustration, far from giving rise to second thoughts about their subject, has been transmuted into further evidence of Shakespeare's transcendent genius. "The elusiveness of Shakespeare's personality," writes Stanley Wells, "is a function of his supremacy as a dramatist." Shakespeare becomes everyone and no one by a logical fallacy that derives its premise from its conclusion.

Actually, Mr. Shakspere's life makes good sense on its own terms, once we quit trying to make him into something he was not. He grew up in a provincial town, had perhaps a modest education, married an older woman while in his teens, went to London where he became an actor and shareholder in the Lord Chamberlain's Men, and bought some choice real estate in his hometown, where he spent the last decade or so of his life. He was a tough, canny businessman who dealt in various commodities—grain, stone, land, tithes on church properties. His marriage appears to have begun with a shotgun wedding and to have continued unhappily. After the birth of twins in 1585, when he was only nineteen, he and his wife had no more children. He spent some years away from her in London. At one point, she contracted a substantial debt in his absence, which he did not pay, despite his ample means. When he wrote his will, he wasted no endearments on her; he left her only their second-best bed, perhaps the one in which he had slept alone most of the time he was at home.

Shakespeare the playwright, whoever he was, had widely varied interests; the question of Shakespeare's education has been endlessly debated. Modern scholars have written whole books about Shakespeare's knowledge of literature and history (classical and modern), horticulture, law, music, heraldry, court life, foreign lands, and such aristocratic sports as tennis, bowling, and falconry, but nothing in Mr. Shakspere's Stratford records suggest that he knew or cared about any of these things.

Shakespeare uses hundreds of legal, musical, medical, and horticultural terms, as well as hundreds of names from classical history and mythology. Did he pick them up casually from books and tavern talk, as most orthodox scholars contend, or did he enjoy a privileged schooling? Mr. Shakspere was so obviously a man of limited formal education that his partisans are forced to assume that the plays pretty much "use up" his learning, such as it was. I believe that Shakespeare was in fact very well educated, and that the knowledge he displays in the plays is only the tip of a large iceberg rather than a random collection of scraps.

In many areas this would be hard to prove, because we have no way of determining the ratio between the knowledge that he actually displays and what else he may have known. Certainly Shakespeare never gives the impression of concentrated erudition that we get from Marlowe, Jonson, and Milton (Marlowe and Milton took degrees at Cambridge; Jonson never attended university, but he had studied with the scholar William Camden at the Westminster School). On the other hand, Shakespeare always has as much learning as he needs, and he seems to draw on it so effortlessly, without flaunting, that we have the sense of an inexhaustible fund. He never sounds as if he is overreaching, running dry, or straining his resources.

Consider Shakespeare's detailed knowledge of Italy, which supplies the background for a dozen of the plays. The documents of Mr. Shakspere's life record his presence only in Stratford and London. As far as we know, he never left England, and it is generally agreed that he never went anywhere near Italy. For a long time it was assumed that Shakespeare knew Italy from books and from that great class-mixing institution of miscellaneous learning, the Mermaid Tavern. Three of the famous "gaffes" in his plays which support this view involved apparent errors in Italian lore, which strengthened the assumption that his knowledge was secondhand. In *The Two Gentlemen of Verona,* for example, he has characters traveling by water between Verona and Milan, two inland cities; in *The Taming of the Shrew* he refers to sail-making in Bergamo, also an inland city; and in *The Winter's Tale* he refers to the painter Giulio Romano as a sculptor.

But all of these gaffes have turned out not to be mistakes at all. Far from proving Shakespeare's ignorance of Italy, they actually prove a high degree of intimacy. In Shakespeare's time and long afterward it was possible to go by boat between Milan, Verona, Venice, Bologna, and other northern Italian cities, which were connected by rivers and canals. A French scholar, Georges Lambin, observes that the travels Shakespeare depicts are "not an ignorant invention of the playwright. It exactly corresponds with what was taking place in his time. A boat was the only comfortable conveyance from Verona to Milan. *But one must have made use of it oneself to be so well informed*" (my emphasis). In Verona, Shakespeare rightly speaks of "the river," the Adige, not the sea or seacoast. An Italian scholar, Ernesto Grillo, notes that the city of Bergamo "has been famous for that industry [i.e., sail-making] until recent times." As for Giulio Romano, he was a sculptor and architect as well as a painter. His many talents are fully appreciated in Vasari's *Lives of the Artists* (published in Italy between 1550 and 1568, but not available in England for many years thereafter). But again, a man who had never visited Italy would be unlikely to know this—or to have heard of Romano at all.

In *The Merchant of Venice,* Shakespeare demonstrates familiarity with obscure features of Venetian law and local topography. The name Launcelot

Gobbo refers to the statue of a kneeling hunchback known as the Gobbo di Rialto, where the laws of the Republic were officially promulgated. Shakespeare refers to the "tranect" (possibly a misprint, sometimes emended as "traject"), the *traghetto* or ferry running between the city and the mainland; he also knowingly refers to "the liberty of strangers" as prescribed in the Venetian constitution. He even knows the exact distance—twenty miles—between Padua and Belmont. The name of Gratiano comes from one of the stock characters of the *commedia dell'arte*. And in *Othello* we find a reference to Venice's *signori di notte,* "the special officers of night."

Shakespeare certainly knew something of the Italian language. Several of his sources—for *Merchant, Othello, Much Ado about Nothing,* and probably *The Tempest*—existed only in Italian, which was not taught in English grammar schools (and would not have been understood at the Mermaid). Possibly a linguistic genius who knew some Latin could piece out as much Italian as was necessary for his purposes, but we have a strong hint that Shakespeare's acquaintance was more than bookish: the clown in *Othello* makes a joke to the musicians about the Neopolitan accent—"Why masters, have your instruments been in Naples, that they speak i'th' nose thus?" This suggests the sort of familiarity with regional Italian accents that only a traveler would be likely to have.

In his invaluable book *Shakespeare and Italy,* published in 1949, Ernesto Grillo dispels any doubt that Shakespeare was not only familiar with Italy and its culture, but profoundly saturated in them. A puzzling sentence in *Twelfth Night*—"The Lady of the Strachy married the yeoman of the wardrobe"—remained obscure until Professor Grillo explained:

> In view of the dramatist's love for everything Italian, and of the Italian source and flavour of *Twelfth Night,* is it not possible to derive "Strachy" from the Italian *stracci*—i.e., rags? "The Lady of the Strachy" is, in fact, the English rendering of the Italian, *La Signora degli Stracci,* a sarcasm still common in many parts of Italy in allusion to a lady poor but haughty. "Strachy" may reasonably be a corruption or a phonetic adaptation of *stracci,* for in Shakespeare we meet with a large number of Italian names and words anglicized.

Grillo is worth quoting at length:

Shakespeare evinces a varied and profound knowledge of the country in general and of our cities in particular. . . . Innumerable are the passages where he speaks of the special characteristics of our peninsula, of her history, and of her customs. He knew that Padua possessed a great university and was the majestic Alma Mater of the arts.

> for the great desire I had
> To see fair Padua, nursery of arts,
> I am arrived for fruitful Lombardy,
> The pleasant garden of great Italy . . .

He knew that Padua with all its learning was under the protection of Venice and that Mantua was not. Besides he assigns special and precise attributes to various cities, e.g., Pisa, renowned for her wealth but still more for her "grave citizens," an expression used by Dante; Milan is "the fair" and possesses a "royal court" and the famous St. Gregory Well. Elsewhere he speaks of the Florentines and Neapolitans, and accuses the inhabitants of Pisa of being avaricious. He knew that the Florentines were notable merchants and mathematicians, making frequent use in their commerce of letters of credit and counting their money by ducats; and he was also aware that they were constantly in conflict with the Sienese. And here the poet uses a phrase which is pure Italian—The Florentines and the Sienese are by the ear (*si pigliano per gli orecchi*).

Grillo also notes Shakespeare's fondness for Italian proverbial phrases like "sound as a fish" in *Two Gentlemen*—from *sano come un pesce,* "an expression still in common use in certain parts of Italy." Moreover, he observes, "Shakespeare has a perfect knowledge of the correct use of names belonging to the Italian aristocracy of his own time."

The various scenes of *Othello* are no mere Venetian reminiscences, but pictures exhaling the very spirit of Venice, which Shakespeare has transferred to his drama. The darkness of morning, the narrow and mysterious "*calli,*" Brabantio's house with its heavy iron-barred doors, the Sagittary, the official residence of the commanders of the galleys, the hired gondolier witness of gallant intrigues, the gondola where the lovers had been seen, the galleys sent on a multitude of errands, the armaments, the attendants with torches, the special night guards, the council chamber, the senators, the Doge—the beloved Signor Magnifico—the discussions about the war, Brabantio's accusation that his daughter had been stolen and seduced by means of drugs and witchcraft, the history of Othello with all the sacrifices made in defence of the republic . . .

The local colour of *The Taming of the Shrew* displays such an intimate acquaintance not only with the manners and customs of Italy but also with the minutest details of domestic life that it cannot have been gleaned from books or acquired in the course of conversations with travelers returned from Padua. The form of marriage between Petruchio and Katharine, which was later recommended by Manzoni's loquacious Agnese to Renzo and Lucia, was Italian and not English. . . . The description of Gremio's house and furnishings is striking because it represents an Italian villa of the sixteenth century with all its comforts and noble luxury.

> My hangings all of Tyrian tapestry;
> In ivory coffers I have stuff'd my crowns;
> In cypress chests my arras, counterpoints,
> Costly apparel, tents, and canopies,
> Fine linen, Turkey cushions boss'd with pearl,
> Valance of Venice gold in needlework,
> Pewter and brass, and all things that belong
> To house or housekeeping: (*Shrew,* 2.1.345–52)

These magnificent *objets d'art* were only to be found in Italy, in the palaces of the aristocracy of Milan, Genoa, Turin, Pavia, etc., since living conditions in England were very primitive, and not even Elizabeth's courtiers could boast of possessing such refinements.

Grillo is absolutely convinced that Shakespeare—whom he assumes to be Mr. Shakspere—must have visited Italy at some time in his youth. But of course he does not explain how young provincial Mr. Shakspere could have gained entree to the country's great aristocratic households. And nothing in Mr. Shakspere's effects, as we know them, suggests any knowledge of Italy or affinity with Italian culture.

Here is striking evidence that Mr. Shakspere was not Shakespeare, a writer who so plainly knew and loved Italy. The real Shakespeare is distinguished not only by his general education, but by his direct personal experience of that enchanting country, which did so much to enrich his imagination.

Again and again we find a lack of congruence between the apparently humdrum Mr. Shakspere and the exuberantly cultivated author he is supposed to be. We know enough about him to expect that some link would appear between the records of his life and those of the author, if they are the same man; but none ever does.

Nothing exposes the futility of the biographers so well as their total failure to accommodate Shakespeare's only traces of autobiography. Only in the Sonnets does Shakespeare speak directly from his heart and in his own person, rather than through his dramatic characters, and it is one of the gravest flaws of the Stratfordian tradition that no one has been able to integrate these poems with the life of Mr. Shakspere, or even to suggest plausible points of connection with that life. Most of the recent biographies give up the attempt. Shakespeare's single extensive self-revelation, which ought to endow the biographies with their deepest insights, instead produces their most awkward chapter.

The Sonnets are mysterious, deliberately so. Some of their secrets are no doubt locked away from us forever. Yet part of their mystery may be solved by solving the mystery of their authorship. This is precisely the reef on which the mainstream scholars founder: they refuse to admit any doubt about who Shakespeare himself was. This is the only certitude they bring to the Sonnets, and it makes them go wrong at nearly every point.

Before we turn to the Sonnets, we should bear firmly in mind that the most neglected pieces of the Shakespeare puzzle have long been his first two published works, *Venus and Adonis* (1593) and *The Rape of Lucrece* (1594), the two long narrative poems dedicated to the Earl of Southampton. The Sonnets also seem to have been addressed to Southampton, though this remains a matter of dispute; another point of contention is whether Southampton is the "Mr. W. H." of the publisher's dedication.

The standard assumption is that Mr. Shakspere wrote the long poems while the theaters were closed from 1592 to 1594 during an outbreak of the plague. Since it was pointless to write plays for the time being, the

story goes, he turned to writing verse as a bid for "literary respectability." (Muriel Bradbrook and others have even suggested that one of his
motives was to rebut the attack of *Greene's Groatsworth!*) At about the
same time, most (but not all) of the scholars agree, he fell in step with
the vogue for sonnet cycles that began with the posthumous publication
of Sir Philip Sidney's *Astrophil and Stella* in 1591. All the confusion over
Greene's Groatsworth has obscured the fact that every early comment referring to Shakespeare by name refers to him *solely* as the author of the
two long poems. Nearly every contemporary tribute to him mentions
these two poems first, whether or not it mentions his plays.

Today the Sonnets are held in high esteem, but not the long poems
that so impressed Shakespeare's contemporaries. Those poems are regarded as tedious, undramatic, artificial. This judgment is understandable when we compare them with the great plays; but we should
remember that for readers who had never heard of Shakespeare, the
long poems would have seemed a dazzling debut, displaying a fluent
command of every rhetorical figure known to the literate public of the
day. The very "artificiality" that repels modern readers would have impressed Elizabethans with its sheer virtuosity. Consider the passage describing Tarquin as he arises from his bed, tormented by lust for
Lucrece:

> Now stole upon the time the dead of night
> When heavy sleep had clos'd up mortal eyes.
> No comfortable star did lend his light,
> No noise but owls' and wolves' death-boding cries
> Now serves the season, that they may surprise
> > The silly lambs. Pure thoughts are dead and still
> > While lust and murder wakes to stain and kill.

> And now this lustful lord leapt from his bed,
> Throwing his mantle rudely o'er his arm,
> Is madly toss'd between desire and dread.
> Th' one sweetly flatters, th' other feareth harm,
> But honest fear, bewitch'd with lust's foul charm,
> > Doth too-too oft betake him to retire,
> > Beaten away by brainsick rude desire.

His falchion on a flint he softly smiteth,
That from the cold stone sparks of fire do fly,
Whereat a waxen torch forthwith he lighteth,
Which must be lodestar to his lustful eye,
And to the flame thus speaks advisedly:
  "As from this cold flint I enforc'd this fire,
  So Lucrece must I force to my desire." (*Lucrece,* 162–82)

The artifice may repel us, but for the poet it serves as a kind of slow motion, suspending the moment of Tarquin's supreme temptation and allowing his readers to contemplate it. To us, rhetoric means "empty" rhetoric. We forget that the Elizabethans loved rhetoric the way the Japanese love baseball.

The neglect of the long poems began early. Both, especially *Venus,* were reprinted often, even for a while after the 1623 Folio (which neither included nor mentioned them). But after that they were forgotten. They were never reprinted again until the next century; most editions of Shakespeare's works comprised only the plays—no long poems, no Sonnets, no other nondramatic verse. Some editions of the plays included works we no longer accept as authentic. The long poems have never recovered their original prestige or popular appeal, in part because they do not fit our image of Shakespeare. The Sonnets have fared better but, as we shall see, they have remained a literary enigma and a problem for the biographers.

Here is a summary, detailed but far from complete, of the story line of those 126 sonnets.

In the first seventeen sonnets, the poet urges the young man to marry, arguing that it is his duty to propagate his beauty. Then he abruptly leaves this theme behind and concentrates on exalting that beauty for its own sake, promising that it will be "eternal" in his verse (Sonnets 18 and 19). He declares his own love for the youth, "the master-mistress of my passion" (20), while denying that his love is sexual. He reflects on his own signs of aging (21) and continues to praise the youth. He remarks that he is denied "public honour" but takes consolation in the youth's love for him (25). He affirms his "duty" to the youth (26).

He confesses that he thinks of the youth day and night during his travels (27 and 28). He says that the youth's love consoles him for his "disgrace" (29), for other "sorrows" (30), and for the loss of other "lovers" (31). He urges the youth to remember his love after his death (32). Then, in three consecutive sonnets (33 to 35), he accuses the youth of hurting him but, seeing his contrition, forgives him. He proposes that they stay apart, lest his own "bewailed guilt" should bring "shame" on the youth (36). Again he says the youth consoles him for his own defects and disgrace (37). In another triad (40 to 42), he complains that the youth has stolen his mistress, but forgives him again. A longer series of sonnets (43 to 52) seems to tell of his obsessive thoughts of the youth while he takes another journey. Once more the poet lyrically praises the youth's beauty and faithful heart (53 and 54), and promises to immortalize him in verse (55). Three other sonnets (57, 58, 61), while declaring that the poet is the youth's "slave," hint at some jealous worry concerning his whereabouts. The poet contrasts his own aging face, "beated and chopp'd with tann'd antiquity," with the younger man's beauty (62), but reflects sadly that the youth himself must age, and that only the poet's verse will assure him a measure of immortality (63). Several subsequent sonnets offer more reflections on aging, death, and the power of poetry to survive the grave. The poet then warns the youth against becoming "common" and exposing himself to "slander" (69 and 70). He urges the youth not to mourn him after his death, lest the world "mock" the youth along with the poet; he hopes his own name will be "buried where my body is," lest it "shame" both of them (71 and 72). He thinks further on his aging and prospective death, telling the youth that "the better part" of him will remain, distilled, in his verse (73 and 74). He speaks of the alternating joy and yearning the youth creates in him (75). He says that he always writes in the same old style, so that "every word doth almost tell my name," because his only theme is "you and love" (76).

At this point (78 to 86), an important new development occurs. A rival for the youth's love enters the picture, "a better spirit" who also writes poetry (the poet speaks of "the proud full sail of his great verse"). The poet, though in anguish, seems resigned to coming out the loser in this rivalry. He expects to be "forgotten" after his death. Sonnet 81 deserves full quotation:

> Or I shall live your epitaph to make,
> Or you survive when I in earth am rotten;
> From hence your memory death cannot take,
> Although in me each part will be forgotten.
> Your name from hence immortal life shall have,
> Though I, once gone, to all the world must die.
> The earth can yield me but a common grave,
> When you entombed in men's eyes shall lie.
> Your monument shall be my gentle verse,
> Which eyes not yet created shall o'erread;
> And tongues to be your being shall rehearse
> When all the breathers of this world are dead.
> You shall live (such virtue hath my pen)
> Where breath most breathes, even in the mouths of men.

The poet accepts his bitter loss without anger: "Farewell! Thou art too dear for my possessing" (87). Three successive sonnets emphasize his unworthiness.

By Sonnet 91, a reconciliation seems to have occurred. The poet says he treasures the youth's love above all other things, and fears only its loss. He adds that he need not fear even that, since the loss of the youth's love would end his life at once (92). There is a hint here that the youth is fickle after all, in spite of the poet's earlier praise of his constancy. The poet likens himself to "a deceived husband" because he could never quite admit that the beautiful youth may be betraying him (93). He adds that if the youth is as innocent as his face appears, he is "the summer's flower," worthy of the admiration he receives; if not, he is worse than "the basest weed" (this seems the approximate sense of the enigmatic Sonnet 94, when set beside the others in the sequence). The poet becomes more explicit in suggesting that the youth is in danger of becoming corrupt (95 and 96).

At this point there is a sense of estrangement between the poet and the youth. They seem to have been apart for some time, possibly for years, when the sequence resumes in Sonnet 97. But now the poet is ecstatic again: he praises the youth as warmly as ever and scolds his muse for having so long neglected his favorite theme (97 to 108). Sonnet 107 may refer to the death of Queen Elizabeth in 1603 ("The mortal moon hath her eclipse endur'd"); some think its immediate subject is Southampton's release from prison, where he had been "confin'd" for his part in the Earl of Essex's attempt to overthrow her.

But now, in the final cluster of sonnets addressed to the youth, another cloud comes over the two men. The poet himself has in some way been unfaithful. He pleads that he has always loved the youth alone, however he may have wandered ("rang'd," 109; "gone here and there," 110). Others may have tested his love, but only to confirm it in the end. His "name" has "receive[d] a brand" (111) and he has suffered "vulgar scandal" (112); but still, he insists, "you are my all the world." He declares that he loves the youth more than ever; he even implies that his straying was a test of the youth's love for *him* (116 and 117). He should have remembered, he admits, how much he himself had suffered at the youth's earlier "crime" (120).

All these pleas leave the impression that the youth has not forgiven him. In these later sonnets, the poet avoids his earlier endearments: "my love," "sweet boy," "fair friend," and so forth. The sense that the poet has reached a limit is underlined by the startling new tone of Sonnet 121: he challenges charges or rumors against himself that seem to involve sexual scandal ("my sportive blood," "my frailties"). The next four sonnets almost defiantly reaffirm the poet's constancy: "No, Time, thou shalt not boast that I do change."

Sonnet 126, the last in the series, is really six rhymed heroic couplets, a farewell to "my lovely boy" reminding him one last time of his mortality. This poem all but proves that the 126 poems belong to one series, about the same youth, in chronological order; its echoes of Sonnet 4 ("Nature," "audit," "thy sweet self") are only a few of the many links between the early and late numbers.

However obscure their relation to real events, the voice of the Sonnets is intimate, even confessional. They have too much continuity to be read as unconnected verses, but they are also far too fragmentary to be read as a conventional narrative sonnet cycle. Instead, they seem to be the poet's private comments on some of his most intimate relations. The trouble is that they bear no discernible relation to anything we know of Mr. Shakspere; more important, they are hard to reconcile with the little that *is* known of him.

The Sonnets were published in 1609, apparently without their author's cooperation—but also without his objection, as far as we know. Either he was being reticent again or he inexplicably didn't care (or, like Philip Sidney, he was dead). If he was alive, he must have felt their publication as a mortifying invasion of his privacy. But there was only one edition, and no contemporary mention of *Shake-speares Sonnets* has survived. Robert Giroux and others suggest, plausibly enough, that the book was quickly and quietly suppressed, perhaps because it caused some scandal or offended some of the persons it concerned.

Of the 154 poems, the first 126 are addressed to a handsome young man, apparently of high rank, who is reluctant to marry. Most of the later numbers, 127 to 152, concern a dark woman about whom the poet has mixed feelings. The identities of the youth and the mistress—who at one point seem to have an affair of their own—have been the subject of endless controversy. Some commentators think there may be more than one young man; the poet's shifts of tone and range of emotion add to the confusion. One thing the Sonnets have not bred among Shakespeare scholars is consensus. In fact, they have created one of the deepest divisions within mainstream scholarship.

Until the twentieth century, most scholars assumed that the Sonnets contained a more or less literal account of Shakespeare's personal experience—in the words of David Masson, writing in 1852, "nothing else than a poetical record of his own feelings and experience . . . distinctly, intensely, painfully autobiographic." The poems seem to invite us to guess who the young man, the rival poet, and the dark mistress were in real life. And the scholars have devoted a great deal of effort to identifying these figures: the earls of Southampton and Pembroke, George Chapman, Christopher Marlowe, Mary Fitton, and many others were among the candidates proposed.

But the attempt to solve the multifaceted "riddle of Shakespeare's Sonnets," as Edward Hubler called it, has proved so frustrating that many commentators have abandoned it. Some have held that the Sonnets are essentially fictional. "I have long felt convinced, after repeated perusals of the Sonnets," Alexander Dyce wrote in 1832, "that the greater number of them was [sic] composed in an assumed character, on different subjects, and at different times, for the amusement, and probably at the suggestion, of the author's intimate associates." In 1862, Bolton Corney concluded that the Sonnets were, "with very slight exceptions, mere *poetical exercises.*"

The pure fictional view is hard to sustain, since nobody can prove that the Sonnets have no autobiographical basis. So a third position has arisen: the agnostic view that the biographical question should be set aside as insoluble and even irrelevant, and the Sonnets read purely as poetry. In the 1898 edition of his biography, Sir Sidney Lee argued that "the autobiographic element in the Sonnets, although it may not be dismissed altogether, is seen to shrink to slender proportions." On this view, the youth, the rival, the mistress, and the poet himself become virtually fictional characters like Romeo and Juliet. Or perhaps Antony and Cleopatra offer a better analogy, since they were remotely inspired by real persons who are, however, of little or no relevance to our interest in the play bearing their names. Just as some people dismiss the authorship question with the rhetorical question, What does it matter who Shakespeare was, as long as we have the plays?, the agnostic school of commentators asks, in effect, What does it matter who Shakespeare and his friends were, as long as we have the Sonnets?

This view certainly has its appeal, and at first glance it appears judicious and sophisticated. While avoiding dogmatic denial of the Sonnets' possible origins in the poet's experience, it dispatches a bundle of nagging problems at a stroke. It invites us to enjoy the Sonnets "for their own sake," or for their "poetic" and "universal" values, freeing us from the quest for information that may well be lost forever. After all, the idea that an appreciation of poetry should require any factual knowledge about the poet and his milieu jars with modern critical ideas, which tend to disparage curiosity about the sonneteer, his friend, his mistress, and his rival as somewhat vulgar, even prurient. The poems instead should "stand alone" on their "intrinsic merits."

The very opacity of the Sonnets has become part of the Shakespeare myth of the modest but inscrutable genius. Recall Harold Bloom's awed remark that "[Shakespeare's] personality always evades us, even in the Sonnets." Are the mysteries of these poems really so insoluble?

The "story" of the first 126 sonnets is self-contained; at least a sort of rambling narrative can be constructed from them. They don't constitute a "cycle" in the usual sense, because they follow no plan or design; they reflect what happened to the poet in the course of writing them, including unforeseen and unpleasant things. The twenty-six sonnets about the dark mistress record a series of situations, but not exactly a story we can follow, and I set them aside (along with the two Cupid sonnets, 153 and 154, which are indeed pure literary artifice).

Some of the individual Sonnets make excellent sense by themselves— for example Sonnets 2 ("When forty winters shall besiege thy brow"), 30 ("When to the sessions of sweet silent thought"), 65 ("Since brass, nor earth, nor stone, nor boundless sea"), 129 ("Th' expense of spirit in a waste of shame"), and 130 ("My mistress' eyes are nothing like the sun"). But many others make little sense in isolation: Sonnet 121 ("'Tis better to be vile than vile esteem'd") is a bitter but baffling poem, embedded in the poet's personal situation in a way that defies our understanding. And taken as a whole, the Sonnets make only partial sense unless we know what real people or events they refer to. They assume that their intended audience (which may amount to only one) knows something we do not. A complex case in point is the famous Sonnet 18 ("Shall I compare thee to a summer's day?") Millions know it from anthologies, and consider it a beautiful love poem. Many would feel differently if they realized that it is addressed to a young man, but the poem itself does not tell us this; the surrounding sonnets do. And such poems as Sonnets 33 ("Full many a glorious morning have I seen"), 34 ("Why didst thou promise such a beauteous day?"), and 35 ("No more be griev'd at that which thou hast done") not only refer to each other, but seem designed to be understood only by the young man they address.

In that sense the Sonnets aren't "universal" at all, and we may be doomed to final ignorance of their full meaning, as with topical satires whose targets have been forgotten. Francis Meres, writing in 1598, mentions Shakespeare's "sugared sonnets among his private friends." We do not know whether he means none, some, or all of the poems of *Shake-speares Sonnets*. But it is clear to readers that they are *private* poems, partly written in a private language.

Nothing in the life of Mr. Shakspere, as recorded in either London or Stratford, touches on or overlaps with anything in the Sonnets. Who were his "private friends"? His will mentions only a few Stratford neighbors and, as an interlinear afterthought, three members of the King's Men—Burbage, Heminge, and Condell—to whom he left a small remembrance. If he had been a man of letters, like the "Shakespeare" Meres had in mind, he would likely have remembered others outside this small circle. Those friends would surely have included some writers, certainly Jonson, plus any noblemen who had been his patrons and benefactors. Are we to assume that Mr. Shakspere, a renowned author, passed his "sugared sonnets" around only among his fellow actors? Put that way, it sounds ridiculous. Many of the Sonnets are anything but "sugared": they are sour, anguished, tortured, mournful. They express such acutely personal emotions about situations so peculiar and private that it is grotesque to call them "literary," let alone "universal." What is universal about Sonnet 20 ("A woman's face, with nature's own hand painted"), or the painful series about the Rival Poet?

The Sonnets are, or ought to be, a priceless revelation of the poet— the only writings (in a sparsely documented fifty-two years) in which we are apparently made privy to his inner life and loves. Scholars would be overjoyed if a sheaf of love letters by Chaucer or Milton were to turn up, no matter what perplexities they contained; they would hardly disparage such letters as superfluous or merely aesthetic additions to what we already know of these writers! Yet many scholars nervously dismiss the Sonnets as nearly useless for biographical purposes.

Samuel Schoenbaum counsels a general agnosticism about the Sonnets, and adds that he "takes satisfaction" in having no theory about them.

"With this key," Wordsworth said of the cycle, "Shakespeare unlocked his heart." But the doubt haunts us that the speaker may be, at least in part, another dramatic characterization. If the persona of the Sonnets addresses us with the resonance of authenticity, so do Shylock and Hamlet. Here, as elsewhere, the biographer, in his eagerness for answers to the unanswerable, runs the risk of confusing the dancer with the dance.

But the Sonnets are manifestly *not* a narrative cycle written according to a dramatic plan. They were evidently written not in one sustained effort, but irregularly, over several years, in response to events outside themselves and beyond the poet's control. And though we know all there is to know about Shylock and Hamlet (because they don't exist outside the plays), the same cannot be said of the poet who speaks in the Sonnets. Schoenbaum is closer to the mark when he allows that the Sonnets may be "sporadic entries, as it were, in a poet's rhyming diary." A diary is often written guardedly, against the chance that it may fall into the wrong hands. Shakespeare's most intimate poems are full of self-disclosure, but their disclosures are gradual, partial, sometimes ambiguous.

On the other hand, the inner life of Shakespeare, as limned in the Sonnets, is hard to square with the external life of Mr. Shakspere. One biographer, Peter Quennell, admits the odd fact that "where [Shakespeare] comes closest to deliberate self-portrayal, the effect that he produces should nowadays seem most mysterious." Stanley Wells acknowledges that "as an autobiographical document, the sonnets are most unsatisfactory." James Winny, in his study *The Master-Mistress,* allows: "What we learn of Shakespeare from the Sonnets throws no light upon his domestic affairs, any more than do the plays."

The stance has been adopted by many twentieth-century commentators. Edward Hubler, Gerald Eades Bentley, Stephen Booth, and John Kerrigan evade the question of the Sonnets' factuality. Booth, scornful of attempts to glean biography from the Sonnets, writes that "they reveal nothing and suggest nothing about Shakespeare's love life." F.E. Halliday surmises, "Probably the story [behind the Sonnets] is almost as mythical as that of Venus and Adonis, and little more than a framework to support the poet's meditations on love and friendship." He adds: "We have lost the key to the puzzle, and perhaps it is not very important, for the sonnets themselves remain, and the young man, whoever he may have been, was little more than a pretext for the poetry, without which our literature would be so immeasurably the poorer."

So much for the love and passion that make these poems real to us, across four centuries. Still, few scholars flatly and absolutely deny that the Sonnets may be rooted in fact; most straddle the issue with agnosticism, while belittling the importance or necessity of the missing information. And some commentators have continued to believe that the implied story does matter—both to the poet's life and to a full understanding of the poems themselves. Among these are Peter Quennell, Stanley Wells, E.K. Chambers, Dover Wilson, George Lyman Kittredge, Kenneth Muir, A.L. Rowse, Leslie Hotson, J.B. Leishman, Ivor Brown, Robert Giroux, G.P.V. Akrigg, Peter Levi, Paul Ramsey, Joseph Pequigney, Louis Auchincloss, Anthony Burgess, Philip Edwards, and S. C. Campbell. They have reached various conclusions (and in some cases no conclusion) as to just what that story may be, but they have no doubt a true story exists.

Most of these lean to the view that Southampton was the youth; others favor William Herbert, later Earl of Pembroke; still others think the youth was someone else. Nearly all agree that each of these possibilities raises difficulties for the traditional view. For if Shakespeare does reveal his true self in the Sonnets, he creates a self-portrait that defies integration with the image that the scholarly biographers have carefully built up.

The Sonnets form a huge riddle that demands a solution. But our natural curiosity about it meets with the sophisticated scorn of commentators who regard such an interest as somewhat improper. Douglas Bush deplores "misguided guesswork" about the story behind the Sonnets. He assures us that "the one fact is that we know nothing, and the wise reader will ignore the whole business [of biographical background]. . . . We do not know if the several characters (the poet included) and their relations with each other had some basis in fact or were entirely imaginary." Confusing the issue, Bush adds that "for poets and their readers alike, the difference between actual and imaginative experience is indefinable and meaningless"—a specious remark that equates the imaginative with the imaginary. After dismissing the vexed question of homosexuality in the Sonnets in a dogmatic parenthesis ("a notion sufficiently refuted by the sonnets themselves"), he declares sweepingly: "Indeed the 'story' has value only in the poet's distillation of *universal* emotions and values" (my emphasis).

This is a large claim, plausible only because it invokes the overworked notion of Shakespeare's universality. Some of the Sonnets may well be called universal, in the sense that they can speak for most of us when removed from their sequence, just as many speeches in the plays still have meaning when removed from their dramatic contexts. But the majority of the Sonnets puzzle precisely because they belong to a situation they assume but never explain. Far from being universal, these poems are— quite explicitly—private and particular. Bush is thus guilty of circular reasoning. He tells us that we should ignore what is *not* universal in the Sonnets because the Sonnets *are* universal. Shakespeare's own purpose in writing them—the purpose that makes them a sequence rather than a random collection—is presumed irrelevant.

In the same vein, C.L. Barber writes, "It is better to read the sonnets for [their] *universal values* than to lose their poetry by turning them into riddles about Shakespeare's biography" (my emphasis). Louis B. Wright intones: "The greatest enjoyment of Shakespeare's sonnets will come from reading them as individual poems rather than from treating them as riddles to be solved." The popular biographer Hesketh Pearson remarks that "for anyone who is not interested in crossword puzzles, the Sonnets are extremely irritating."

W.H. Auden deprecates the "illusion" that "if the identity of the Friend, the Dark Lady, the Rival Poet, etc., could be established, this would in any way illuminate our understanding of the sonnets themselves. [The] illusion seems to me to betray either a complete misunderstanding of the nature of the relation between art and life or an attempt to rationalize and justify plain vulgar idle curiosity." He adds, somewhat gratuitously, "Idle curiosity is an ineradicable vice of the human mind."

Northrop Frye, in his essay, "How True a Twain," ridicules the idea that the Sonnets should be read as "transcripts of experience" rather than as pure poetry. Frye comments that the Sonnets "still have power to release the frustrated Baconian who is inside so many Shakespeare scholars." The ultimate deadly epithet: Baconian! Shakespeare, says Frye, "was an expert in keeping his personal life out of our reach." We should therefore respect the great poet's hard-earned anonymity and abandon vain and prurient inquiries into his personal life. Of the poet's treatment of the youth Frye observes, "The world's greatest master of characterization will not give him the individualizing touch that he so seldom refuses to the humblest of his dramatic creations." But with this acute remark Frye undermines his own argument, for if the youth were the poet's creation, his maker surely *would* have given him the same illusion of autonomy with which he endows Richard III, Romeo, and Cleopatra. And if Shakespeare is telling a story, he is telling it badly. It lacks exposition, plot, pacing, suspense, and resolution as well as characterization. As Paul Ramsey writes in his study *The Fickle Glass,* "The sonnets have too much jagged specificity to ignore, too little development and completing of the events to be an invention." In *Shakespeare: A Writer's Progress,* Philip Edwards writes: "[T]hat there is a solid core of autobiography in the sonnets, in the events referred to, the relationships described, the emotions expressed, seems to me beyond dispute. It may not be their most important or interesting feature, but it can hardly be argued away." Esthetic interest in poetry need not preclude other kinds of interest, including the biographical.

Try as we may, we can't banish the sense that something real lies behind the Sonnets, if only we could find it. C.S. Lewis says they tell "so odd a story that we find a difficulty in regarding it as fiction." The most sensible word on the question of the Sonnets' factuality was spoken by the great critic A.C. Bradley:

> No capable poet, much less a Shakespeare, intending to produce a merely "dramatic" series of poems, would dream of inventing a story like that of these sonnets, or, even if he did, of treating it as they treat it. The story is very odd and unattractive. Such capacities as it has are but slightly developed. It is left obscure, and some of the poems are unintelligible to us because they contain allusions of which we can make nothing. Now all this is very natural if the story is substantially a real story of Shakespeare himself and of certain other persons; if the sonnets were written from time to time as the relations of the persons changed, and sometimes in reference to particular incidents; and if they were written *for* one or more of these persons (far the greater number for only one), and perhaps in a few cases

for other friends,—written, that is to say, for people who knew the details and incidents of which we are ignorant. But it is all unnatural, well-nigh incredibly unnatural, if, with the most sceptical critics, we regard the sonnets as a free product of mere imagination.

Put this way, it seems obvious that the Sonnets are about real people and events in the poet's life. Otherwise his artistry would have formed them all more perfectly. T.S. Eliot remarks that the Sonnets, like *Hamlet,* are "full of some stuff that the writer could not drag to light, contemplate or manipulate into art." That is why we find them so hard to understand at the simplest narrative level.

Those who resist this conclusion are driven to tortuous formulations. John Kerrigan, in the New Penguin edition of the Sonnets, argues that

> biographical reading, as we understand it now, has so little purchase on these poems that criticism directed along such lines soon finds itself spinning off into vacuous literary chitchat. . . . Shakespeare stands behind the first person of his sequence as Sidney had stood behind Astrophil—sometimes near the poetic "I," sometimes farther off, but never without some degree of rhetorical projection. The Sonnets are not autobiographical in a psychological mode.

What commentators like Schoenbaum and Kerrigan are saying, or perhaps trying *not* to say, is this: *The poet who speaks in the first person in the Sonnets simply doesn't match Mr. Shakspere of Stratford.* Thus, *the only way to salvage Mr. Shakspere's claim to their authorship is to posit that they have no factual basis.* This implicit concession is enormous. No wonder so many of the scholars don't want to spell it out. Northrop Frye speaks the truth with unconscious irony: the poet is indeed "an expert in keeping his personal life out of our reach."

The Sonnets refer to each other as well as to things outside themselves which the reader is expected to understand. And the only reader we can be sure was meant to read them is the youth himself. The poet keeps promising to make his name immortal, yet the poems never mention the youth's name. It would be extremely odd to invent a fictional character and make such a promise, then fail to keep it. (In the sonnet sequence *Astrophil and Stella,* Sidney disguised his love, Penelope Rich, under the name "Stella"; many contemporaries knew who Stella was, but posterity forgot until modern researchers rediscovered her.)

Those scholars who agree that the youth is a real person have usually agreed that the "lovely boy" is Southampton, who meets the description at every point. He was young, blue-blooded, handsome, popular, desirable. Born in 1573, he became the third earl of his line at his father's death in 1528, whereupon he also became a ward of Lord Burghley. In 1590, Burghley tried to marry Henry off to his fourteen-year-old granddaughter, Lady Elizabeth Vere. But Southampton resisted for years, despite great pressure. He also defied the queen by having an affair with one of her maids of honor, Elizabeth Vernon, whom he later impregnated and married. In 1601, he narrowly escaped death for his part in Essex's rebellion. It is fairly clear that the youth of the Sonnets is a nobleman; he is urged to beget an "heir" and to continue his "house." The Sonnets speak of his father in the past tense and his mother in the present; Southampton's father was dead, and his mother survived.

The Sonnets assume the youth's wealth and rank. They speak continually of the appurtenances of feudal life: titles, high birth, charters, privilege, portraits, gold, jewels, treasure, banquets, hawks, hounds, robes, rich garments, poms, canopies, vassals, servants, tombs, sepulchres, monuments. The youth has "fame," and is the subject of "all eyes" and "all tongues"—as well as gossip, "envy," "slander." In his weak moments he is in danger of growing "common." Great poets vie for his favor.

Sonnet 8 seems to play on Southampton's family motto, *Ung pour tout, tout pour ung*—Old French for "One for all, all for one."

> Resembling sire and child and happy mother,
> Who, all in one, one pleasing note do sing,
> Whose speechless song, being many, seeming one,
> Sings this to thee: "Thou single wilt prove none."

Sonnet 76 asks: "Why write I still all one, ever the same?" (possibly playing, too, on Elizabeth's motto, *Semper eadem*).

In Sonnet 53, the poet likens the youth to Adonis. This by itself nearly confirms the youth's identity. In Shakespeare's *Venus and Adonis,* dedicated to Southampton, Adonis is a beautiful youth who resists his duty to propagate, a duty urged on him in the very terms of the first seventeen Sonnets: "Thou was begot," Venus says, "to get [beget] it is thy duty." She pleads not only for love, but for "increase":

"Upon the earth's increase why shouldst thou feed,

Unless the earth with thy increase be fed?

By law of nature thou art bound to breed,

That thine may live when thou thyself art dead;

   And so in spite of death thou dost survive,

   In that thy likeness still is left alive."

Adonis is "more lovely than a man" and "thrice fairer" than Venus; the youth of the Sonnets resembles Helen of Troy (53) and has "a woman's face, with Nature's own hand painted" (20).

Queen Elizabeth's Lord Treasurer, Lord Burghley, was also Master of the Wards and Southampton's legal guardian. It was Burghley's prerogative to arrange marriages for his wards, and for Southampton he had chosen his own granddaughter. Eventually he fined Southampton 5,000 pounds for refusing to marry her. All this was happening at about the time the early Sonnets were probably composed. While Burghley was applying muscle, the poet was using charm. And Southampton is the only man the same poet did, in fact, immortalize through his verse. Sonnet 26 is a close paraphrase of the poet's dedication to *The Rape of Lucrece*.

Southampton had been the subject, or target, of an earlier poem, though a less admiring one: Burghley's secretary John Clapham had joined in the campaign to get him married with a Latin poem titled "Narcissus," whose dedication had wished the young man an increase in virility as well as honor (*"virtutis atque honoris incrementum"*). *Venus and Adonis* also makes a pointed reference to Narcissus.

It should be noted, too, that the poet assumes social equality with the youth. He doesn't have to ask or assert it; he takes it for granted. It is hard to imagine Mr. Shakspere saying to Southampton that "we must not be foes" (Sonnet 40); that would be up to Southampton, who would have little to fear from Mr. Shakspere's enmity. The poet tells the youth in Sonnet 88 that "thou, in losing me, shall win much glory." Surely Mr. Shakspere would be guilty of enormous self-importance if he thought

Southampton, one of the greatest and most admired young lords in England, could add a cubit to his stature by ending their friendship.

Even at his most adoring, he doesn't hesitate to criticize the youth. And he chides him with a moral authority that is almost parental. When he is abject, it is as a lover who knows he is in the wrong, with no hint of servility. When he pardons him, he does so with the confidence of a man who has the prerogative of withholding such generosity. It is hard to imagine Southampton weeping as he awaits the forgiveness of Mr. Shakspere. The poet tells the youth: "I may not ever more acknowledge thee" (Sonnet 36); if the poet were Mr. Shakspere, it would be up to his lord to acknowledge *him*.

The poet takes bold liberties with the youth, praising him in terms that would be incredibly presumptuous if he were a common poet addressing a man of Southampton's rank. He calls him "lovely," "beauteous," and so forth, with "a woman's face." He even jokes about the young man's genitalia, in the amazing Sonnet 20.

> A woman's face with nature's own hand painted
> Hast thou, the master-mistress of my passion;
> A woman's gentle heart, but not acquainted
> With shifting change as is false women's fashion;
> An eye more bright than theirs, less false in rolling,
> Gilding the object whereupon it gazeth;
> A man in hue, all hues in his controlling,
> Which steals men's eyes and women's souls amazeth.
> And for a woman wert thou first created,
> Till nature as she wrought thee fell a-doting,
> And by addition me of thee defeated
> By adding one thing to my purpose nothing.
> But since she pricked thee out for women's pleasure,
> Mine be thy love and thy love's use their treasure.

Such familiarities, addressed to an earl from a man of Mr. Shakspere's social status, would have been highly imprudent, if not suicidal—especially if the youth was, like Southampton, a ward of the mighty Burghley, who enforced a strict morality and kept spies and informers in every great house.

Bernard Shaw, who assumed the Stratfordian view, defended the poet against the charge of sycophancy in the Sonnets:

> A sycophant does not tell his patron that his fame will survive, not in the renown of his own actions, but in the sonnets of his sycophant. A sycophant, when his patron cuts him out in a love affair, does not tell his patron exactly what he thinks of him. Above all, a sycophant does not write to his patron precisely as he feels on all occasions; and this rare kind of sincerity is all over the Sonnets. (Shaw, preface to *The Dark Lady of the Sonnets*)

This is perceptive, given Shaw's Stratfordian assumption. If Mr. Shakspere had written these poems to Southampton, he would indeed deserve credit for moral courage.

The poet speaks continually of his "age," of being "old," "beated and chopp'd with tann'd antiquity," and laments the loss of "precious friends hid in death's dateless night." His "days are past the best." He looks forward to his grave and obscurity. In Sonnet 138, the poet smiles that he lies about his age to his mistress. But why would Mr. Shakspere, writing in the early 1590s, feel that he was old, looking death in the face, incurably disgraced, doomed to oblivion, and so forth? These are not the normal feelings of a man of thirty who is doing quite well for himself. Nor does a young man call another young man a "youth"; the word itself implies a considerable difference in age. If the youth was Southampton, the poet could hardly have been Mr. Shakspere.

Not all the commentators agree that the youth is Southampton. But those who reject him do so, for the most part, not because he doesn't match the description of the youth, but because it is so hard to imagine Mr. Shakspere as the poet who addresses a young nobleman in such familiar terms.*

---

*The case for Southampton is so strong that it is hardly necessary to weigh the case of the other chief candidate for the Lovely Boy, William Herbert, later Earl of Pembroke. But Pembroke would have been too young in any case. He was born in 1580. This pits him against Sonnet 144, published in *The Passionate Pilgrim* in 1599 and probably written some years earlier. It refers to the incident described in Sonnets 40 to 42, when the youth had had his own affair with the poet's mistress. This would require us to believe that Herbert had stolen an older friend's mistress while in his teens, possibly his early teens. It seems far-fetched.

Nothing is more obvious than that the poet is *in love* with the youth. He adores his beauty, lies awake thinking about him, idealizes him, is jealous of him, wants to "possess" him, speaks of his "desire" and "pleasure," worries about how his looks will affect his own attractiveness, and accuses first the youth and then himself of infidelity. He even praises the odor of the youth's breath!

What of the suspicion that the first 126 Sonnets are homosexual? At one time the question was derided as improbable, verging on blasphemy; today it has become fashionable. However we regard it now, to the England of Elizabeth I (and long afterward), sodomy was a monstrous sin and a capital crime. This ensured that any expression of what we call homosexuality would have been extremely guarded. Shakespeare can be startlingly explicit about his adulterous lust for his mistress (see Sonnet 151), but if he felt a similar passion for his young friend we should expect it to be more oblique.

The poet himself anticipates the suspicion in Sonnet 20, quoted earlier, and, at that point, tries to deflect it. In Sonnet 93 he compares himself to a "deceived husband" whom the youth may be betraying. Still later (Sonnet 121), he replies to reports about his "sportive blood." He speaks of some unnamed "shame," "disgrace," and "scandal"—"blots" that taint not only him but by association the youth as well; in Sonnet 71 he urges the youth not even to mourn him: "Lest the wise world should look into your moan,/And mock you with me after I am gone."

What can all this mean? An ordinary amour, even an adultery, would not have been a crippling shame in those days, any more than it is today. Not every disgrace rubs off on those who associate with the disgraced person. And the world doesn't usually "mock" a man for mourning a dead friend. What does the poet mean by the phrase "look into your moan"—unless to suggest that there is something about it that does not bear close scrutiny?

Read this way, the Sonnets appear very different from the sententious "universal" poems they are conventionally taken for. Rather, they would appear to be the private record of a long homosexual love affair.

If the Earl of Southampton was one of the lovers, could the poet have been Mr. Shakspere? Perhaps, but it seems improbable. When we left Mr. Shakspere in Stratford as of 1585, he was at eighteen enmeshed in a marriage which had quickly produced a child, then a set of twins. Though it is possible, we wouldn't expect him to be writing amorous verses to another man, especially a nobleman, only a few years later. Moreover, the poet clearly takes the initiative in wooing the youth. He wastes little time before addressing him (in Sonnet 13) as "my love." Those who say Elizabethan men spoke to each other this way should produce an example, preferably from Shakespeare's plays, where commoners speak with considerably less intimacy to their betters. (Apart from Lear's impudent Fool, they don't even say "thou" to them. Part of Falstaff's fatal effrontery, knight though he is, is that he presumes to address King Henry V as "thee" in public.)

In Sonnet 10, the poet urges the youth to "Make thee another self, for love of me." Whatever favors a poet might ask of his patron, they would probably *not* include begetting a son "for love of me." Nor would such a poet be presumptuous enough to think that some personal disgrace would be likely to ruin his patron. He would not, in the normal course of things, have to urge his patron to desist from mourning for him. Nor for that matter would he be apt to devote many poems addressed to his patron to his shifting moods and feelings.

The flirtatious tone of Sonnet 20 is almost enough to rule out Mr. Shakspere as the author. Yet here again, only one scholar, to my knowledge, has grasped the social implication. Tucker Brooke remarks in some puzzlement: "This sonnet has hardly the tone in which Shakespeare, the actor, could address a nobleman of high rank." That is putting it mildly.

There are indications that the Sonnets were suspected from the first of expressing a forbidden love. The first edition seems to have vanished; some scholars suspect that it was suppressed. No second edition appeared until 1640; even then, titles were added and pronouns changed to make it appear that the poems addressed to the youth were all addressed to the poet's mistress.

At least one man would have had a strong motive to suppress the Sonnets: Southampton himself—Henry Wriothesley, the famous "Mr. W. H." of the dedication. Reversing his initials and adding "Mr." was a thin disguise; sophisticated readers would recognize him. He was the only man whose name had ever been linked in print with that of Shakespeare—in the dedications of both the long poems. And there may well have been gossip about him and the real author, as the Sonnets themselves suggest.

The publisher's dedication suggests that he, Thomas Thorpe, knew the true story:

TO · THE · ONLIE · BEGETTER · OF

THESE · INSVING · SONNETS ·

MR. W. H. · ALL · HAPPINESSE ·

AND · THAT · ETERNITIE ·

PROMISED ·

BY ·

OVR · EVER-LIVING · POET ·

WISHETH ·

THE · WELL-WISHING ·

ADVENTVRER · IN ·

SETTING ·

FORTH .

T.T.

Note that the publisher, Thorpe, not Shakespeare, wrote the dedication—though the poet had written his own dedications to both *Venus and Adonis* and *The Rape of Lucrece*. Moreover, the Sonnets, unlike *Venus* and *Lucrece,* are sloppily printed and full of misprints. These facts have led most of the biographers to infer that the poet had no hand in this edition, and that in fact the Sonnets were pirated, no doubt to his extreme dismay.

The title page announces: "SHAKE-SPEARES SONNETS. Neuer before Imprinted." We may gather from this that Shakespeare was known to have written sonnets for private circulation well before 1609. Meres had said as much in 1598. Even if these were not the same sonnets Meres referred to, they had evidently existed for some years by the time Thorpe published them and, judging by this terse announcement, Thorpe himself expected their appearance to cause some excitement.

Scholars who deprecate biographical interest in the Sonnets recoil at the curiosity Thorpe's dedication has aroused, Hyder Rollins, the chief midcentury authority on the Sonnets, wrote in 1944: "No doubt the

Sonnets would be read more often *for their poetry* today if Thorpe had discarded his own thirty words!" His sentiment was echoed in 1964 by W.G. Ingram and Theodore Redpath in their own edition of the Sonnets: "There is no evidence that the Dedication stimulated attention until very late in the eighteenth century, but since then it has been the playground of theorists who have allowed it to distract their interest from *the poems as poems*." (My emphasis in both citations.)

If curiosity about the "facts" behind the Sonnets is irrelevant and crass, then Thorpe has played at the least a regrettable role in leaving the impression that there are any facts to be known. Rollins, in an introduction to a 1951 edition of the Sonnets, defined what has become the dominant view:

> Are the Sonnets autobiographical? Do they present real people, real events? Nobody knows for sure; but it is axiomatic that, as the greatest dramatist of all times, Shakespeare could hardly have penned a sonnet without making it sound sincere and revelatory. The male friend or friends, the dark woman or women, the rival poet or poets seem sketches from life, whereas actually they may be creatures of the imagination like Claudio or Mercutio, Rosalind or Beatrice, Orlando or Malvolio.
>
> The question of autobiography has been needlessly complicated by Thorpe's altogether cryptic dedication, from which Shakespeare is wholly disassociated. Thorpe, not he, dedicated the book to the only begetter, Mr. W.H., wishing him that eternity promised, in the Sonnets or elsewhere, by the ever-living or immortal Shakespeare. There is not the slightest evidence that Thorpe knew either Shakespeare personally or anything about his intentions, much less about his life and loves.

As we shall see, this is an injustice to Thorpe. Rollins then proceeds to denigrate his scholarly predecessors for believing that the Sonnets contained (or presupposed) extrapoetic information:

> Accordingly, those who are lucky enough to be approaching the Sonnets for the first time would be well-advised to ignore editors, commentators, critics, and to read the Sonnets simply as poems . . . If they have any literary taste, they cannot fail to notice and marvel at the depth of thought, the powerful imagination, the exquisite imagery, the surpassingly

beautiful phrasing, the altogether astonishing way in which individual sonnets or single lines are descriptive of almost every important occurrence in
human life.

Thus the publisher who gave us the Sonnets becomes the villain, and
those who wonder at his hints expose themselves as philistines for concerning themselves with anything but the universal genius of Shakespeare. But like most mainstream scholars, Rollins overlooks an obvious
problem: Why would a pirate publisher, involving the poems against the
author's will, have felt it necessary to supply a dedication at all? Thorpe
sounds far too respectful toward "our ever-living poet" for a publisher
who was supposedly disregarding his rights and invading his privacy.
Writing a dedication for another man under these circumstances would
be a cheeky gesture. But Thorpe does not sound at all presumptuous. In
this he is quite unlike all the other publishers of Shakespeare quartos,
real and bogus, before him. *Shake-speares Sonnets* is in fact a milestone: it
marks the first time any publisher of Shakespeare's work felt compelled
to speak for the poet, instead of letting him speak for himself.

Thorpe's proprietary "our" subtly supports the view that the poet
had already died and could not object to his poems' appearing in print;
otherwise, the publisher would hardly have presumed to use a pronoun
which implies that, by 1609, the poet was a common possession. And as
many have noted, the figurative compliment "ever-living" was used exclusively of persons who were literally dead. Donald Foster has been unable to find a single example of its being applied to a living person.

The dedication in fact displays considerable tact and shows Thorpe's
sensitive awareness of the Sonnets' theme. Over and over the poet
promises that his poems will give the youth immortality. The theme first
appears in Sonnet 17, where the poet tells the youth that he may "live
twice," both in a son and "in my rhyme." In Sonnet 18 he even more
boldly boasts of his "eternal lines": "So long as men can breathe, or eyes
can see,/So long lives this, and this gives life to thee." Sonnet 19 proph-
esies: "My love shall in my verse ever live young." Sonnet 38 promises
the youth "eternal numbers [verses] to outlive long date" in which
"thine shall be the praise." Sonnet 55 repeats the pledge most reso-
nantly—"Not marble, nor the gilded monuments/Of princes, shall out-

live this powerful rhyme."—And it is reiterated in a half-dozen later Sonnets.

But though the poet promises to immortalize the youth's name, he never actually mentions it. Meanwhile he predicts, and even begs, oblivion for his own "poor name." In Sonnet 36 he makes the mysterious complaint: "I may not evermore acknowledge thee,/Lest my bewailed guilt should do thee shame." And in the next three sonnets he says he will take his comfort both in praising the youth and in hearing others praise him

Later this theme becomes even more pronounced: he urges the youth not to mourn him longer than the tolling of the "surly sullen bell" (71), and asks that his name be "buried" with his body, lest it "shame" the youth (72). The poet describes his earthly remains as "too base of thee to be remembered," in contrast to "the better part of me," his "spirit," which is "consecrate to thee" and survives in "this," his poetry (74).

The contrast between the poet's exaltation of his friend and his own self-abasement is most explicit in Sonnet 81: he expects to be "forgotten" in a "common grave," while "Your name from hence immortal life shall have."

The poet's theme is mortality—or rather, the twin mortalities of his young lover and himself. He feels doomed to disgrace and oblivion, but he can bestow "eternity" on the youth through his verse (as Thorpe's dedication reminds us).

As the Sonnets harp on the poet's mortality, the standard authorship assumption again creates problems. The standard supposition that this is a poet of modest rank praising his lordly patron is simply absurd. A poet of Mr. Shakspere's age and rank, writing in praise of his noble patron, would hardly bring himself and his mortal prospects into the foreground so insistently; he would merely praise his patron, and leave himself and his own passions out of it. He wouldn't have to beg his employer to forget him and not mourn for him too much. His self-pity and emotional writhings would be totally out of place. The whole tone of the poetry would be different.

A nobleman who hired a painter to do his portrait would not thank the artist for including himself in the picture—particularly if the artist was shown in an illicit embrace with his subject. These Sonnets were all too likely to compromise the man they sought to glorify. We can safely rule out any notion that Southampton paid Mr. Shakspere for writing poems that might have led the public to infer, rightly or wrongly, that they were homosexual lovers.

The poet clearly was not hired, but is writing on his own initiative, one might even say his own authority, driven by his own self-declared "passion." The idea of glorifying the youth in verse is *his,* and his subject is as much himself as the youth—a fact underlined, not refuted, by his frequent self-disparagement. This is an aging man, evidently of some rank, writing to a much younger one with whom he has been furtively intimate. Their relationship is much more problematic than that of patron and poet.

Some commentators, thinking to sever the dedication from the poet's intention, argue that the "begetter" of the Sonnets is not the man who inspired them, but the man who procured the manuscript of them for Thorpe. But this is a strenuous reading. The word "begetter" links "Mr. W. H." to the theme not only of the first seventeen sonnets, but also of *Venus,* a work pointedly addressed to Southampton.

Two further clues in the dedication reinforce the view that Mr. W. H. is Southampton, though, surprisingly, all the scholars seem to have missed them. The strange construction "wisheth the well-wishing adventurer" echoes the last clause of the dedication to *Venus:* "which I wish may always answer your own wish." And in wishing Mr. W. H. "all happiness," Thorpe echoes the final phrase of the dedication to *Lucrece:* "long life, still lengthened with all happiness." I doubt that these are accidental echoes. Since both the earlier dedications are addressed to Southampton, Thorpe is making it as clear to his knowing readers as he dares that this one is too.

This tactic evidently didn't work as Thorpe had hoped, and the Sonnets were suppressed after all. The first edition quickly disappeared, and no contemporary mention of it survives, even though most of Shakespeare's published works were extremely popular and went through many printings. Southampton would have been enraged at the exposure in print of his affair with the poet; others, as we shall see, would also have been angry.

The "mistress" sonnets (written at around the time of Sonnets 40 through 42) have excited as much speculation as the sonnets to the youth. Who the mistress was we will probably never know. What is clear is that she was only a passing interest of the poet, who speaks of her with more contempt than love. He never idealizes her; on the contrary, he regards her as a whore and despises himself for his attraction to her. His revulsion against his own lust echoes the sexual disgust of the tragic heroes—Lear, Hamlet, Othello, Antony, Timon, and Troilus. It never occurs to the poet to promise her eternal fame in his verse; that he did immortalize her, after a fashion, is an accident. Apparently Thorpe managed to acquire the poems about her as well as the poems about the youth, and published them together (along with the two Cupid sonnets and *A Lover's Complaint*).

Thorpe's publishing gambit apparently resulted not only in the suppression of *Shake-speares Sonnets,* but in their virtual disappearance from the scene. The 1623 Folio makes no mention of them or, indeed, of Shakespeare's nondramatic poetry. The Folio creates the impression that "Mr. William Shakespeare" was solely a dramatist—though his first published works had been the two long poems dedicated to Southampton, both of which were still being reprinted in the 1620s. Nevertheless, we owe thanks to Thomas Thorpe that we have the Sonnets at all. But for his venture they would in all probability have perished.*

Thorpe's dedication tells us that he understood the situation better than modern commentators have. He understood it because he knew who the poet and the youth really were. By 1609, the "ever-living poet" was dead; the "only begetter" of these sonnets was still alive; and

---

*In his 1904 biography of Shakespeare, William J. Rolfe notes that certain textual imperfections in the 1609 quarto (the duplication of a final couplet in Sonnets 36 and 96, the parentheses that signify a missing couplet at the end of Sonnet 126) prove that Thorpe must have published the Sonnets without the author's cooperation; otherwise he might easily have consulted the poet and corrected these apparent flaws. This is a sensible and subtle observation. But Rolfe infers from it that Thorpe, in publishing the Sonnets, must have been acting in defiance of the wishes of the poet, whom he assumes to be Mr. Shakspere. He never considers the possibility that the author was somebody else, who could not have corrected the defective passages; in other words, that in 1609 the "ever-living poet" was no longer living.

Thorpe felt it appropriate to address the one in the name of the other. Yet he doesn't give either man's name. This makes it as clear as it can possibly be that a true story lies behind the Sonnets. Far from affronting Shakespeare, his dedication shows that Thorpe was trying to do what he thought the poet would have wanted. This was his justification for publishing the Sonnets, even if those to whom he offered it rejected it and moved to quash the most extraordinary volume of love poetry in the English language.

No further edition of the Sonnets appeared until 1711, and the 1640 arrangement was retained throughout most of the eighteenth century. When George Steevens finally restored the original version, he disparaged the Sonnets in general and wrote with special revulsion of Sonnet 20: "It is impossible to read this fulsome panegyrick, addressed to a male object, without an equal mixture of disgust and indignation." Another editor, George Chalmers, exclaimed, "Shakespeare, a husband, a father, a moral man, addressed a hundred and twenty, nay a hundred and twenty six *Amorous* sonnets to a *male* object!"; but he tried to rescue Shakespeare by concluding that the poems were actually meant for Queen Elizabeth, who was often "considered a man."

Rescuing Shakespeare from his own obvious meaning became a kind of duty in the age of Bardolatry. The great editor and scholar Edmond Malone came to the poet's defense against Steevens: "[S]uch addresses to men, however indelicate, were customary in our author's time, and neither imported criminality nor were esteemed indecorous." Coleridge, the most adoring of Shakespeare's commentators, likewise insisted that Shakespeare had nowhere made "even an allusion to that very worst of all possible vices," and that though the Sonnets expressed "something deserving the name of love towards a male object," it was "an affection beyond friendship, and wholly aloof from appetite" (though the poet himself uses the word "appetite" in Sonnets 56 and 110). At the same time, the infamous Bowdlers were purging Shakespeare of all indelicacies, making him fit for Victorian family reading.

Three eminent nineteenth-century men of letters, all homosexuals, may have sensed the truth. Walt Whitman spoke of certain facts about Shakespeare which remained "dim and elusive . . . tantalizing and half suspected—suggesting explanations that one dare not put into plain statement." Oscar Wilde and Samuel Butler were also fascinated by the Sonnets and wrote extensively about them, but neither dared to approach the forbidden subject publicly except in the most roundabout hints. Nearer to our own time, C.S. Lewis called the language of the 126 sonnets to the youth "too lover-like for that of ordinary male friendship," adding, "I have found no real parallel to such language between friends in sixteenth-century literature." But he stopped short of deeming the poems homosexual: "[O]n the other hand, this does not seem to be the poetry of full-blown pederasty. Shakespeare, and indeed Shakespeare's age, did nothing by halves. If he had intended in these sonnets to be the poet of pederasty, I think he would have left us in no doubt: the lovely *paidika,* attended by a whole train of mythological perversities, would have blazed across the pages."

Others are simply dismissive. Douglas Bush brusquely rejects, without explanation, the idea that the poems in question are homosexual. (He calls it "a notion sufficiently refuted by the Sonnets themselves"— referring to the Dark Mistress—but then why do the Sonnets themselves keep giving rise to that very notion?) W.H. Auden likewise ridicules any attempt to claim the poet for "the Homintern," on grounds that the poems to the dark mistress are "unequivocally sexual," while Mr. Shakspere himself was "a married man and a father."* Yet the suspicion has been so persistent that nearly every modern commentator has felt compelled to cope with it—a good indication that the "naive" interpretation has merit. As Samuel Johnson said, "I always suspect that reading to be true which requires many words to prove it false."

In recent years, liberal opinion has not so much abolished as reversed the old taboos, and a growing number of scholars and critics have held that the first 126 sonnets are indeed homosexual love poems. This view has been adopted (without reference to the authorship question) by G.P.V. Akrigg, S.C. Campbell, Leslie Fiedler, and most forcefully by Joseph Pequigney. In his book *Such Is My Love,* Pequigney assumes the traditional view of Shakespeare's identity, which leads him to conclude

---

*Auden, himself homosexual, privately took a different line: according to Robert Craft, he confided that "it won't do just yet to admit that the top Bard was in the Homintern."

that the youth could not have been Southampton since no commoner would have dared to address a nobleman in such erotic language. Pequigney's error illustrates how every time a commentator gets part of the truth, the assumption of Mr. Shakspere's identity throws the Sonnets out of focus again. It is true that if Mr. Shakspere is the poet, the youth can't be Southampton. But conversely, if the youth *is* Southampton, the poet can't be Mr. Shakspere.

The homosexual overtones of these Sonnets will be discussed in more detail later. For now we may pass on to the last of the series, Sonnet 126 (which is actually six rhymed couplets). Here, after many painful vicissitudes and a terminal estrangement, the poet permits himself a final burst of affection: "O thou, my lovely boy!" He returns to the theme of the earliest sonnets, warning Southampton that he is mortal. Nature will keep him as long as she can, but not forever:

> Yet fear her, O thou minion of her pleasure;
> She may detain, but not still keep her treasure.
> Her audit, though delay'd, answer'd must be,
> And her quietus is to render thee.

These lines somberly echo Sonnet 20, which describes Nature as "doting" on the youth and ends with a rhyme between "pleasure" and "treasure." But this time we also hear the solemn note of *Hamlet,* even to the legal language of "audit" and "quietus." The lovely boy no longer has his whole life ahead of him; the heartbroken poet bids him remember his end. He returns to the hortatory vein in which he began because the youth, no longer a boy, has ceased to welcome his love and praise.

It appears that the greatest passion of our greatest poet was a furtive homosexual love. Did this forbidden passion lead the poet to adopt the pen name by which we have confusedly known him, hoping to glorify Southampton forever while his own real name lay "buried"? Might this be a key to the identity of Shakespeare?

THE CASE FOR OXFORD

The Life of Oxford

W hen, by the midnineteenth century, a large number of readers began to realize that there was something radically amiss in the conventional portrait of Shakespeare as Mr. Shakspere, the respectable burgher, they began looking for other candidates. More than fifty have been advanced; most of them are Elizabethan authors, knights, and noblemen.

Some of the rival contenders are so farfetched—including Mary Queen of Scots, Elizabeth I, James I, Anne Hathaway Shakspere, and Daniel Defoe—that it is tempting to dismiss the whole authorship question as simply absurd. But considering the grounds for doubting the prevalent view, it is by no means absurd to weigh the claims of such candidates as Barnabe Barnes, Richard Barnfield, Richard Burbage, Samuel Daniel, Thomas Dekker, John Florio, Thomas Kyd, John Lyly, Thomas Nashe, George Peele, and other notable Elizabethan writers, though it would be exhausting to consider each of them singly. Only three alternative candidates for the authorship of Shakespeare's works have persuaded large numbers of people.

Francis Bacon, philosopher and statesman, is the most intellectually imposing of the rivals. Christopher Marlowe, the most brilliant Elizabethan poet-playwright aside from Shakespeare himself, is the most immediately plausible, apart from the detail that he seems to have died in 1593. Edward de Vere, better known as the (seventeenth) Earl of Oxford, has much to recommend him, even though the date of his death—1604—also contradicts the scholarly consensus about the probable dates of the plays.

Calvin Hoffman has made a fascinating case for Marlowe in *The Murder of the Man Who Was Shakespeare,* a book so enjoyable that I am reluctant to disparage it; but his thesis depends entirely on the argument that Marlowe's death was staged and that he went into hiding and began a second career, as William Shakespeare. This notion seems so improbable that it demands stronger proof than we are ever likely to find; further, Marlowe is so distinctive as a poet and dramatist that I find it hard to believe he could have been Shakespeare, too. One can almost imagine the fiery Marlowe writing Shakespeare's great tragedies, but not his serene and often silly comedies. Marlowe would probably have felt that creating such buffoons as Dogberry and Launcelot Gobbo was beneath his dignity. Falstaff, on the other hand, was far outside the range of his imagination; so were great comic heroines such as Rosalind and Beatrice. In any case, he has few partisans today.

Bacon delivers the sort of wise maxims many naive readers think of as typical of Shakespeare, but which really more resemble Polonius. (I omit discussion of the supposed ciphers implanted in the plays to assert Bacon's authorship; I can offer no better excuse for this dereliction than that life is short, and it seems to me farfetched to imagine *King Lear* doubling as a brainteaser.) However, Bacon can be ruled out on many grounds. Like Marlowe, he had none of Shakespeare's whimsy; more generally, the plays reflect little more of his life and experience than they do of Mr. Shakspere's. Nothing about the somber and inflexible Bacon suggests the Shakespearean capacity for a wide variety of moods, let alone the creation of a great diversity of characters; what Bacon has in gravity he lacks in quicksilver. He was, moreover, a busy man of affairs who could hardly have worked in a second career as the author of the Shakespeare plays. The most personal of Shakespeare's works, the Sonnets, seem utterly incongruous with Bacon's personality. The poet of the Sonnets complains of his public disgrace—a complaint Bacon could not have made until 1621, when he was convicted of taking bribes, over a decade after the Sonnets were published.

This is not to denigrate Bacon, but merely to say that his literary virtues are very different from Shakespeare's. So are his defects. He writes with an unvarying dignity and sonority, in a style that is now underrated. But though it is admirable, we can hardly imagine him writing any other way.

The best refutation of the Baconian case was made by a prominent Stratfordian scholar, J.M. Robertson. In his 1913 polemic, *The Baconian Heresy*, Robertson made a perceptive and definitive argument against identifying Bacon and Shakespeare. Both writers, he observed, have impressively large vocabularies—yet these diverge in important respects. For example, they consistently use different inflections of certain words. Bacon (like Jonson and others) uses "politique," whereas Shakespeare uses "politician." Bacon uses the plural forms "knowledges" and "harmonies"; Shakespeare never does. Bacon always uses the adjective "militar" (and sometimes "militare"); Shakespeare always uses "military." There are also differences of frequency. Bacon often uses the word "splendid," which occurs only once in all of Shakespeare's works. Robertson compiled a list of words in common use that Bacon employs often but that Shakespeare never does.*

Few of the distinctive words in Bacon's vocabulary are particularly rare even today. Shakespeare would have recognized and understood all of them. But they were not in his own distinctive vocabulary. The *Harvard Concordance to Shakespeare* gives 29,000 entries, counting separately the singular and plural forms of nouns and the different inflections of verbs. Although that is an awesome number for a single writer, it is still

---

*These include: *abstruse, accurate, allegory, alloy, amplitude, analogy, animosity, architecture, astrology, atheist, benign, collectively, commonplace, comparable, compatible, compendious, compression, concurrence, condense, conflagration, contexture, contrariwise, deduce, deficiency, delicacy, dialectic, disbanding, elementary, elevation, elocution, extraction, generate, geometrical, illumination, immerse, imposture, latitude, liturgy, luxuriant, magnify, magnitude, martyrdom, mediocrity, medium, multiplicity, mystical, overpower, proficiency, prolix, recede, relatively, renovation, repress, resplendent, retribution, righteousness, sanguinary, signature, similitude, subdivide, tabernacle, tacit, theology, transitory, transmit, veneration, version, vicissitude, voluptuous.*

only a slice of the full range of Elizabethan English. In spite of his amazing versatility, Shakespeare, like all writers, repeats himself a good deal. Repeated patterns are, after all, what we mean by "style."

The sort of Bardolatry that wants to credit Shakespeare with every excellence can blind us to his individuality and even his limitations. Robertson wisely pointed out that Bacon's prose is not only different from Shakespeare's, but in important ways much better. Bacon offers "a multitude of sonorous and long-breathed sentences in a style never to be found in Shakespeare's prose." Bacon's "prose is written with a new perception of the possibilities of cadence, of gracious movement without metre, of long breathing and restful fall." In Shakespeare's prose passages, Robertson writes, "we shall find infinite verve and vivacity, fluency and fire; and endless fecundity of phrase, image, and epithet; but we shall not find a great architectonic prose." These are the comments of a critic who appreciated both writers too intelligently to confuse them. Bacon could not have written Shakespeare, but equally, Shakespeare could not have written Bacon.

In our time, the most popular candidate to unseat Mr. Shakspere is Edward de Vere, seventeenth Earl of Oxford (1550–1604). Here too we are lucky enough to have abundant stylistic evidence by which to judge the question of his authorship. Oxford's letters, though they total only a few thousand words, display a rich vocabulary. Yet he uses only a handful that never appear in Shakespeare's works. In these letters, we find a recognizable ensemble of general or abstract nouns, nearly all of which not only appear in Shakespeare but are very typical of Shakespeare.*

---

*These include: *absence, abuse, accomplishment, account, achievement, acquaintance, admittance, admonition, advantage, adversary, advice, affairs, affection, alliance, alteration, amendment, amity, appointment, apprehension, arbitrement, argument, assistance, assurance, attendance, bargain, beauty, beginning, behavior, behoof, benefit, bestowing, breach, burden, business, care, cause, ceremony, change, charge, circumstance, comfort, command, commendation, commodity, commonwealth, compass, complaint, composition, comprehension, concealment, conceit, conception, concern, conclusion, condition, conference, confession, confidence, confirmation, confusion, consanguinity, conscience, consideration, constancy, continuance, contraries, convenience, correspondence, corruption, counsel, courses, courtesy, cozening, craving, credit, cumber, custody, custom, danger, dealings, death, deceit, deeds, defect, delay, delight, departure, desert, desire, despair, desperation, determination, detriment, device, devotion, difficulty, diligence, discontent, discouragement, disgrace, discovery, discretion, dispatch, disposition, dissembling, doubt, duty, effect, employment, enjoyment, error, estate, evil, excellence, exception, exclamation, excuse, expedition, experience, extenuation, extremity, familiarity,**

Oxford's vocabulary falls well within the Shakespearean (rather than, say, the Baconian) subset of Elizabethan English. This would be unremarkable if his vocabulary were small; but it is extensive, even in this chance selection of his nonliterary letters, some of which are as casual as phone calls.

Shakespeare often uses a given word only once, and he coins words freely. So did Oxford. Consider Oxford's apparent coinage "discommodities": Shakespeare uses the word "commodity" often, and he also has the habit of using the prefix "dis" to invert the meanings of otherwise ordinary words, such as "disfurnish," "disburdened," and even "dispark" (to convert park land to other uses); Oxford uses all three of these words. Shakespeare's fondness for the construction is evident not only in such common forms as *discharge, disallow, dispraise, disproportion, disjoin,* and so forth, but also in oddities (many of his own invention) like *disbenched, dismasked, disquantity, disjoin, discase, disseat, dispurse, disvalued, dishabited, disedged, disbranch, disannul, disanimate, discandy, disstained, disvouched, disgest,* and *disroot.* Oxford uses the verb "brandel," meaning shake or unsettle (as a sediment); Shakespeare never uses the word. But Oxford uses it in an image that would be perfectly at home in Shakespeare: "brandel the clearness of your guiltless conscience."

Most of Oxford's letters are essentially business correspondence, not works of literature. (The one important exception is Oxford's eloquent prefatory epistle to Bedingfield's translation of *Cardanus Comfort,* which

---

fault, favor, felicity, forbearance, forfeit, fortune, forwardness, foundation, frailty, friendship, fruit, furtherance, good, government, grace, gratitude, greediness, grief, happiness, harm, havoc, health, honor, hope, imperfections, impudence, ignorance, industry, infirmity, inheritance, injury, instant, interest, instrument, intention, invasion, judgment, justice, kindness, kindred, kinship, knowledge, law, leisure, liberality, likelihood, liking, love, loyalty, manner, marvel, matter, means, mercy, merit, mind, mischief, misfortune, mislikes, molestation, monument, motion, munition, nature, necessity, negligence, oblivion, occasion, offense, office, operation, opinion, oppression, opportunity, ornament, overthrows, pardon, patent, patience, perfection, performance, persuasion, pestilence, pity, pleasure, portion, possession, practice, precedent, prejudice, premises, prescription, presumption, pretense, proceeding, process, proffer, profit, proportion, promise, protection, providence, provision, punishment, purpose, readiness, reason, receipt, recompense, recreation, redress, remedy, remembrance, report, repose, request, resolution, respect, restoration, revenue, right, satisfaction, science, service, shadow, sovereign, state, strangeness, studies, substance, success, sufficiency, suit, supply, suspicion, tedium, thought, time, title, travail, treason, treacheries, trifle, trouble, trust, truth, tyranny, understanding, undertaking, violence, virtue, warrant, waste, weariness, will, wisdom, witness, words, wrong, youth, zeal.

is the only English prose composition that we know Oxford wrote with great care and deliberation *and meant to be published*. This preface is reserved for special attention in Appendix 3.) Most were written in haste, some in heat, reflecting Oxford's financial and marital problems and his often strained relations with his father-in-law, Lord Burghley. Most are emotionally guarded and rather formally respectful, though anger sometimes bristles, and now and then—especially at Queen Elizabeth's death—warmth, affection, and grief break forth. For all that, these letters have great interest as specimens of Oxford's everyday manner of expression.

It may still be objected that Oxford's letters, however congruent with Shakespeare's vocabulary, show nothing that we can call genius. But this is to misconceive genius as a source of unremitting inspiration, like a powerful electric current that can never be turned off. The author we are looking for may give himself away even when he isn't being a genius. Oxford provides us with particularly interesting evidence—even, at times, when he is making a fool of himself.

Edward de Vere, seventeenth Earl of Oxford, is startlingly different from the sage and placid Shakespeare of official iconography. His life sounds more like the subject of a Shakespeare play—comic or tragic, depending on which period we study. Roger Beckingsale, a biographer of his father-in-law Lord Burghley, describes Oxford as "the most brilliant of the young nobility" of Elizabeth's court, but adds that "all his life he attracted scandal and was involved in scrapes."

Oxford's life is far better documented than that of William Shakspere of Stratford. This is only natural. As a nobleman, Oxford, unlike most men of his time, was destined to be a subject of documentary attention. He was also a prominent courtier whose flamboyant doings made news and produced "embarrassing rumors," as Beckingsale puts it. His life was, at least for his first forty years, an eventful one, bearing the stamp of his strong and sometimes violent personality. Even so, there are gaps in the record, especially around the crucial period between 1590 and 1595. And though Oxford's life is more amply recorded than Mr. Shakspere's, the totality of known records about him isn't much longer than B.M. Ward's 1928 biography, *The Seventeenth Earl of Oxford,* which ran to 400 pages. A good deal of that is gossip, refracted through the eyes of interested parties. Some is hyperbolic praise, some malicious detraction; Oxford provoked plenty of both.

The earls of Oxford were an old and very distinguished line. In contrast to so many of the upstart nobility created by Henry VIII, the de Veres could trace their origins centuries back; they had come from France even before the Norman Conquest. Macaulay called them "the longest and most illustrious line of nobles England has seen." Edward de Vere took great pride in his ancestors, whose motto, a pun on the family name, was *Vero nihil verius*—"Nothing is truer than truth." The ninth earl, Robert de Vere, hated by the other nobles of his day, was the favorite of Richard II, and their homosexual amour helped ruin Richard. This episode was perhaps the most disgraceful in the family's history; it is notable that Shakespeare's *Richard II* neither includes Robert as a character nor makes any mention of him. He was killed by a boar during his exile in the Netherlands (the boar, coincidentally, was the de Vere family crest). The thirteenth earl, John de Vere, had helped restore the Lancasters during the Wars of the Roses, earning Tudor gratitude; he led Henry Tudor's troops at the battle of Bosworth Field. The earldom carried with it the office of Lord Great Chamberlain, a position of ceremonial importance on state occasions. A 1539 statute made the Lord Great Chamberlain fifth in formal precedence among the officers of state, though no real power attached to the position.

Oxford's uncle by marriage, Henry Howard, Earl of Surrey, was one of the leading court poets of his age. He created both the sonnet form we now call Shakespearean and English blank verse; he introduced blank verse with his translation of the second and fourth books of the *Aeneid*; Shakespeare refers to the second book often, as does one of Oxford's letters. Surrey ran afoul of Henry VIII and was beheaded at the age of thirty, three years before Oxford's birth.

Edward de Vere was born on April 12, 1550, at Castle Hedingham in Essex, forty miles east of London, to John de Vere, sixteenth Earl of Oxford, and the former Margaret Golding. John's first wife had died, leaving one daughter.

Curiously, during a hunt in France in 1544, John had had his own vivid encounter with a boar, a happier one than Robert's had been: to the amazement of his terrified companions, he fearlessly confronted the "enraged beast, with his mouth all foamy, his teeth whetted, his bristles up, and all other signs of fury and anger," and killed it with his rapier. When the French expressed astonishment at his valor, he lightly replied that "every boy in my nation would have performed it." The legend taught young Edward that he owed it to his family name to show courage.

John de Vere also loved the theater and kept a troupe of actors. In *The Children of Henry VIII,* Alison Weir notes that in October 1550, the Earl of Oxford's players performed a masque for the entertainment of a company of nobles, including Mary Tudor, the future monarch.

Edward entered Cambridge University at about the age of nine. In those days this betokened precocity, but not necessarily the prodigy it would signify today. It is unclear how often or to what extent Oxford actually attended the university, since he evidently lived elsewhere much of the time before taking his degree at fourteen. In 1562, his father died, and Edward became the seventeenth Earl of Oxford at the age of twelve. He rode from his father's funeral to London "with seven score horse all in black," a fair indication of his family's wealth at the time he inherited it.

At his father's death, young Oxford was sent to London to live as a royal ward under the supervision of Sir William Cecil, who was later made Lord Burghley (a figure many scholars accept as the prototype for Shakespeare's Polonius—see chapter 8). This proved to be a fateful moment in his life; the strong-willed Oxford's relations with the mighty Burghley were complex, and often strained, almost until Burghley's death in 1598.

As Elizabeth's Lord Treasurer, Burghley would be largely responsible for the emergence of Elizabethan England as a great European power. His large household included a number of sons of the nobility. We know that Oxford was tutored there in several subjects; a typical day's schedule included dancing, French, Latin, writing and drawing, cosmography, exercise with his pen, and common prayers. His regular pastimes included riding, shooting, and falconry. An elegant letter Oxford wrote in French at the age of thirteen to Burghley, then still Sir William Cecil, shows his linguistic aptitude and love of the courtly manner. It begins: *"Monsieur, j'ai receu votre lettres, plaines d'humanite et courtoysie, et fort resemblantes a vostre grand'amour et singuliere affection envers moy, comme vrais enfans deuement procreez d'une telle mere, pour la quelle je me trouve de jour en jour plus tenu a v[ostre] h[onneur]. Voz bons admonestements pour l'observation du bon ordre selon voz appointemens, je me delibere (Dieu aidant) de garder en toute diligence."*

One of his tutors was his mother's brother Arthur Golding, the great Protestant scholar and translator of Ovid, Calvin's version of the Psalms, Caesar's *Commentaries,* and the *Histories of Trogus Pompeius*; Ezra Pound called Golding's version of Ovid's *Metamorphoses* "the most beautiful book in the language." Shakespeare echoes Ovid so often that Francis Meres suggested the Roman's soul had transmigrated into the English poet (who sometimes borrows Golding's wording). Golding and his nephew shared a close literary friendship: he dedicated his *Histories of Trogus Pompeius* to Oxford in 1564, and his Psalms in 1573. Shakespeare quotes or borrows from both of these.

Oxford's mother remarried shortly after his father's death. In 1563, meanwhile, his half-sister's husband, the third Baron Windsor, challenged the validity of his parents' marriage, hoping thereby to invalidate Oxford's title and obtain his lands. The attempt failed; but had it succeeded, young Oxford would have become, in law, an impoverished bastard. This must have been, to say the least, an unsettling period in the boy's life.

Oxford took a bachelor's degree from Cambridge in 1564 and a master's from Oxford University in 1566. In 1567, he was admitted to Gray's Inn in London, where he studied law. Shakespeare adverts so readily to legal language for figures of speech that many scholars have surmised that Mr. Shakspere spent his "lost years" as a legal clerk; his name, however, has never turned up on any legal papers as clerk, notary, or witness. Oxford's legal training, on the other hand, is reflected in his dozens of surviving letters, several of which touch on legal questions.

In 1567, at age seventeen, Oxford gave what many read as the first recorded display of his famous temper. He stabbed Cecil's undercook, Thomas Brinknell, who died of the wound to his leg the following day. Cecil later wrote in his diary: "I did my best to have the jury find the death of a poor man whom he killed in my house to be found *se defendendo* [self-defense]"—though at the time he had written that the jury ruled it "*felo-de-se* [death as a result of one's own crime] with running upon a point of a fence-sword of the said Earl's." Some Oxfordians suspect that Oxford had caught Brinknell spying for Burghley. This is plausible enough—Cecil kept a huge espionage network, at home and abroad—but there is no evidence for it. The record indicates that Brinknell was drunk, and the verdict implies that he was the aggressor; if Oxford had meant to kill him, he presumably would not have settled for wounding his leg.

However it happened, the incident didn't prevent Cecil from arranging for his favorite child, Anne, to marry Oxford four years later. Oxford was the most eligible of all the young bachelors at Elizabeth's court—brilliant, gallant, witty, artistic, athletic, pedigreed, rich, the observed of all observers. He seemed to have a great future, if only he could add self-control to his other qualities.

Even in his youth, Oxford drew lavishly on his huge fortune. His tastes ranged widely. First among them was literature: surviving receipts record his purchases of books by Chaucer, Plutarch (in French), Cicero, and Plato, along with some Italian volumes and a copy of the Geneva Bible—all these by the time he was sixteen. He also bought plenty of velvet, satin, plumes, and other finery, including ten pairs of Spanish leather shoes in the space of three months, along with rapiers, daggers, and other appurtenances of a gentleman. When he was nineteen, it is recorded that he kept four geldings. It seems that his only sense of money was that it existed to be spent and given away without limit.

Oxford lived as if his fortune were infinite, when it was merely enormous—a distinction that was to prove his undoing. Later, he did try to augment his dwindling wealth with investments, but they were speculations that did more credit to his adventurous spirit than to his judgment: he lost large sums on them.

In 1569, Thomas Underdowne dedicated his translation of Heliodorus' *Aethiopian History* to Oxford. Oxford's love of literature and music, his wealth, and his utter profligacy combined to make him the most generous of patrons. Thirty-three books and works of music are known to have been dedicated to him, and he received the highest praise for his own talents. He is said to have been skilful at playing the virginal. The organist John Farmer, who dedicated two books to him, said that in musical talent Oxford surpassed most professional musicians: "For without flattery be it spoke, those that know your Lordship know this, that using this science [music] as a recreation, your Lordship have overgrown most of them that make it a profession." Of course, Oxford's favor was well worth cultivating; but he was praised just as highly by men who had no reason to flatter him, some long after his death.

During the Northern Rebellion of 1569, Oxford, after much pleading with Cecil, was given permission to join his mentor the Earl of Sussex in the campaign. He served during April and May as Sussex, an ally of Cecil's in the Protestant faction at court, routed the Catholic forces. What role Oxford played is not recorded, but the experience seems to have whetted his desire for military action. (Love of warfare ran in the family: his cousins Horace and Francis Vere were distinguished soldiers, so noted for valor that they became known as "the fighting Veres.")

One contemporary account shows again that Oxford spared no expense in self-display: on one occasion, he rode into London "with four score gentlemen in a livery of Reading tawny and chains of gold about their necks, before him; and one hundred tall yeomen in the like livery to follow him, without chains, but all having his cognizance of the Blue Boar embroidered on their left shoulder."

In 1571, he came of age and assumed his seat in the House of Lords, becoming a star at court when he took the prize in the tournament at Westminster, in the queen's presence, where it was noted: "The earl's livery was crimson velvet, very costly." He excelled in his first appearance in the tilt against older and more experienced competitors, performing, as one observer put it, "far above the expectation of the world"; in later years, he competed in two more tournaments, winning each time.

At twenty-one, Oxford had taken the royal court by storm. His stature at this point irresistibly recalls Ophelia's description of Hamlet:

> The courtier's, soldier's, scholar's, eye, tongue, sword, . . .
> The glass of fashion and the mold of form,
> The observed of all observers.

He had made a brilliant beginning. Nobody could have suspected how far he would later decline.

In the summer of 1571, a courtier wrote a letter to the Earl of Rutland with the latest news at court:

> The Earl of Oxford hath gotten him a wife—or at the least a wife hath
> caught him; this is Mistress Anne Cecil; whereunto the queen hath given
> her consent, and the which hath caused great weeping, wailing, and sor-
> rowful cheer of those that had hoped to have that golden day. Thus you
> may see whilst that some triumph with olive branches, others follow the
> chariot with willow garlands.

If Oxford was regarded as a prize, so was Anne Cecil. Rutland had
been among her suitors; so had young Philip Sidney. Little Anne, nicknamed "Tannikin" by her family, was only fifteen when she was married
to Oxford—pretty, well-educated, and sweet. Cecil wrote to Rutland
that the match was made at Oxford's initiative. The wedding, held in
December, was a huge social event, with the queen, the French ambassador, and other dignitaries attending. But though Oxford had been
caught, he had by no means been tamed, as poor Anne was to learn.

That same year, Oxford was suspected of plotting to rescue his relative Thomas Howard, Duke of Norfolk, who was under arrest and sentence of death. Norfolk had been implicated in the Ridolfi conspiracy
to overthrow Elizabeth and restore a Catholic monarchy. But any escape
plan came to naught, and Norfolk was beheaded in June 1572. Cecil
himself had prosecuted him for treason in the Ridolfi plot, and Oxford
and his father-in-law quarreled hotly, not for the last time. Norfolk was
then the only remaining duke in England, and Cecil's class were now in
the ascendant at court.

In 1572 we find Oxford writing to Cecil, now Lord Burghley, in a
respectful and even affectionate vein—a fact worth noticing, in view of
the often tense relations between the two men. The letter remarks on
some grim news from France: the St. Bartholomew's Day massacre:

> I would to God your Lordship would let me understand some of your
> news which here doth ring dolefully in the ears of every man, of the mur-
> der of the Admiral of France, and a number of noblemen and worthy
> gentlemen, and such as greatly have in their lifetime honoured the
> Queen's Majesty our Mistress; on whose tragedies we have a number of
> French Aeneases in this city that tell of their own overthrows with tears
> falling from their eyes, a piteous thing to hear but a cruel and far more
> grievous thing we must deem it them to see.

The mention of Aeneas in this context, as we shall see in a later chapter, has important Shakespearean echoes. The letter also makes hostile mention of "the papists," implying that Oxford, like his father-in-law, was at this time firmly on the Protestant side.

At about this time also, Oxford began to leave his own mark on literature. Castiglione's *The Courtier,* translated into Latin by Bartholomew Clerke, Oxford's tutor from Oxford University, was published under Oxford's sponsorship in 1572. (Sir Thomas Hoby's English version had appeared in 1561.) The book bore a preface, also in Latin, by Oxford himself, praising the eloquence of "my friend Clerke" and celebrating "our most illustrious and noble queen, in whom all courtly qualities are personified, together with those diviner and truly celestial virtues . . . to whom alone is due all the praise of the Muses and all the glory of literature."

By now Oxford was writing poems of his own, in English and Latin. Only a few of the English poems survive, most of which can't be dated with any precision. Some are brief love poems; some are maudlin and self-absorbed. One complains bitterly (and with extravagant alliteration) of the loss of his reputation, a complaint not explained in the poem itself; some think it was occasioned by Oxford's marital crisis in 1576. It begins:

> Fram'd in the front of forlorn hope past all recovery,
> I stayless stand, to abide the shock of shame and infamy.
> My life, through ling'ring long, is lodg'd in lair of loathsome ways;
> My death delay'd to keep from life the harm of hapless days.
> My sprites, my heart, my wit and force, in deep distress are drown'd,
> The only loss of my good name is of these griefs the ground.

But this vein was more typical:

> The lively lark stretch'd forth her wing,
>   The messenger of Morning bright;
> And with her cheerful voice did sing,
>   The Day's approach, discharging Night;
> When that Aurora blushing red,
> Descried the guilt of Thetis' bed.

Three other poems are worth quoting in full.

If women could be fair and yet not fond,
　　Or that their love were firm not fickle, still,
I would not marvel that they make men bond,
　　By service long to purchase their good will;
But when I see how frail those creatures are,
I muse that men forget themselves so far.

To mark the choice they make, and how they change,
　　How oft from Phoebus do they flee to Pan,
Unsettled still like haggards wild they range,
　　These gentle birds that fly from man to man;
Who would not scorn and shake them from the fist
And let them fly fair fools which way they list.

Yet for disport we fawn and flatter both,
　　To pass the time when nothing else can please,
And train them to our lure with subtle oath,
　　Till, weary of their wiles, ourselves we ease;
And then we say when we their fancy try,
To play with fools, O what a fool was I.

A sonnet is in the Shakespearean form created by his uncle Surrey:

Who taught thee first to sigh, alas, my heart?
　　Who taught thy tongue the woeful words of plaint?
Who filled your eyes with tears of bitter smart?
　　Who gave thee grief and made thy joys to faint?
Who first did paint with colours pale thy face?
　　Who first did break thy sleeps of quiet rest?
Above the rest in court who gave thee grace?
　　Who made thee strive in honour to be best?
In constant truth to bide so firm and sure,
　　To scorn the world regarding but thy friends?
With patient mind each passion to endure,
　　In one desire to settle to the end?
Love then thy choice wherein such choice thou bind,
　　As nought but death may ever change thy mind.

His shortest poem suggests the soliloquies of various Shakespearean kings:

> Were I a king I might command content;
> Were I obscure unknown would be my cares,
> And were I dead no thoughts should me torment,
> Nor words, nor wrongs, nor love, nor hate, nor fears;
> A doubtful choice of these things which to crave,
> A kingdom or a cottage or a grave

By his young manhood Oxford was a favorite of the queen, who nicknamed him "my Turk." One contemporary, Gilbert Talbot, wrote privately of him: "My Lord of Oxford is lately grown into great credit; for the queen's Majesty delighteth more in his personage, and his dancing and valiantness, than any other. I think Sussex doth back him all that he can; if it were not for his fickle head, he would pass any of them shortly." Burghley disagreed about his "fickle head," remarking, "There is much more in him of understanding than any stranger to him would think. And for mine own part I find that whereof I take comfort in his wit and knowledge grown by good conversation."

Burghley's wife was alarmed for her daughter's sake at the warmth of the forty-year-old Elizabeth's favor for her son-in-law; Burghley himself tactfully ignored such things. Talbot observed, "At all these love matters my Lord Treasurer winketh and will not meddle in any way. . . . [He] dealeth with matters of the state only." Court gossip had it that Elizabeth and Oxford were lovers.

All through his youth, Oxford was the subject of startling rumors and accusations, matching the wildness of his headlong and headstrong personality. No extreme of either sweetness or arrogance seems to have been beyond him.

Oxford's considerable charm, as well as his rank, helped rescue him from many scrapes and win forgiveness for his frequent insolence. Part of that charm was his natural gift for performance. There is a vivid account of his staging a spectacular mock battle for public entertainment at Warwick Castle in 1572, as part of the queen's annual summer progress around the country. On another occasion, it is reported that he declined

Elizabeth's request to dance before the French ambassador, which suggests that he wasn't ordinarily averse to exhibitions of his talent—or to making scenes when out of humor. To the queen's request "he replied that her Majesty would not order him to do so, as he did not wish to entertain Frenchmen. When the Lord Steward took him the message the second time, he replied that he would not give pleasure to Frenchmen nor listen to such a message. And with that he left the room."

One court observer ranked Oxford very highly as a poet and author of comedies and interludes; perhaps he performed with his own acting companies, too. His appearances in the lists at royal tournaments were accompanied by his own speeches.

B.M. Ward thinks Oxford was behind an elaborate literary prank at the expense of one of his court rivals, Sir Christopher Hatton. In 1573, Thomas Twyne dedicated his *Breviary of Britain* to Oxford. In that same year, Thomas Bedingfield offered him his translation of *Cardanus Comfort,* a meditation on death by the great Italian mathematician Geronimo Cardano. Bedingfield affected to be too bashful to publish his work, but Oxford wrote a warm prefatory letter in which he sweetly chided the author for wanting to withhold his virtues from the world. The letter shows Oxford in his happiest and most benevolent mood. In publishing the book against Bedingfield's wishes, he says, he is merely playing the role of a "physician,"

> who, although his patient in the extremity of his burning fever is desirous of cold liquor or drink to qualify his sore thirst or rather kill his languishing body, yet for the danger he doth evidently know by his science to ensue, denieth him the same. So you being sick of so much doubt in your own proceedings, through which you are desirous to bury and insevill your works in the grave of oblivion: yet I, knowing the discommodities that shall redound to yourself thereby (and which is more unto your countrymen) as one that is willing to salve so great an inconvenience, am nothing dainty to deny your request.

The whole letter, which especially foreshadows the Sonnets, is of the utmost importance to the authorship question (see Appendix 3).

In May 1573, three of Oxford's men were accused of attacking two of their former associates on the road between Gravesend and

Rochester, even firing calivers at them. The victims complained vehemently to Burghley, charging that the three, whom they named, had had "full intent to murder us," and pointing an apologetic finger at "our late noble lord and master [Oxford], who with pardon be it spoken, is to be thought of as the procurer of that which is done."

More serious charges were leveled against Oxford the following year. He was long suspected of harboring Catholic sympathies, of which the Spanish ambassador took hopeful note, describing Oxford as "a very gallant lad" with "a great following in the country." In January 1574, Ralph Lane, who had been linked to Oxford in the scheme to rescue Norfolk, apparently accused him of complicity with a Spanish agent named de Guaras. In July, Oxford suddenly left England without royal permission and fled to Brussels, where he was reported to be conferring with exiled English rebels against the queen. Elizabeth was furious, and dispatched Bedingfield to fetch him home. He readily returned, contrite, with his wife and father-in-law pleading for him to the queen; he was quickly forgiven and restored to favor.

In 1575, Oxford, now twenty-five, set out on a long tour of Europe, this time with Elizabeth's consent. Accompanied by a retinue of eight men, he stopped first in Paris for two months; the English ambassador there reported to Burghley that "indeed he was well liked of, and governed himself very honourably while he was here." While in Paris, Oxford received word from Burghley that Anne was pregnant. He wrote back joyfully:

> My Lord, Your letters have made me a glad man, for these last have put me in assurance of that good fortune which you formerly mentioned doubtfully. I thank God therefore, with your Lordship, that it hath pleased Him to make me a father, where your Lordship is a grandfather; and if it be a boy I shall likewise be the partaker with you in a greater contentation.

He exuberantly had his portrait painted and sent it, with two horses, as a gift to Anne.

From Paris he went to Strasburg, where he called on the great scholar Johannes Sturm, renowned as Sturmius, who later recalled him favorably in a letter to Burghley; Oxford himself had a "most high opinion" of Sturm, according to one of his companions. In May, Oxford reached

Padua; in September, Venice. There he learned that Anne had given birth to his first daughter, Elizabeth, in July. By now he was forced to borrow money, having outspent his budget: he had estimated the cost of his travels at a lavish 1,000 pounds, but finally spent nearly four times that amount. Meanwhile, he had great debts at home, and he wrote to Burghley asking him to "stop my creditors' exclamations—or rather, defamations I may call them" by selling some of his lands. He also asked Burghley to send him more money, and was irritated that Burghley failed to meet his needs. (A book published in Italy in 1699 recalls an Earl of Oxford clowning in a mock tilt in Venice. This may, however, refer to Oxford's son, the eighteenth and last earl of his line, who lived some years in Italy a generation after him.)

Of the rest of Oxford's tour we have only scattered indications. He went to Florence and Siena and on to Sicily; presumably, he would not have omitted Rome and Naples, though no proof is extant of his having been in either city. We are told by another account that in Palermo he issued a general challenge to all comers to meet him in single combat for the honor of England, "for which he was very highly commended, and yet no man durst be so hardy to encounter with him, so that all Italy over he is acknowledged the only Chevalier and Nobleman of England. This title they give unto him as worthily deserved." The following March he was in Lyons, then back in Paris before coming home in April. Like Hamlet, Oxford was briefly captured by pirates in the Channel; nevertheless, he arrived with his arms full of gifts, including a pair of perfumed gloves with tufts of colored silk that would delight the queen and set a new fashion in England. A perfume he brought back was named after him. He also brought from Venice a boy singer named Orazio Cogno, whose parents had given their permission for him to spend a year in England.

Oxford's return was poisoned by an ugly rumor about Anne and young Elizabeth: gossip had reached him in France insinuating that the child might not be his. Burghley, greatly agitated by the rumor, had been unable to contain his consternation and had blabbed the matter about, aggravating the scandal. Infuriated, Oxford refused to land at Dover, where Thomas Cecil, Burghley's son, had come to welcome him. Instead, he sailed right into the Thames and disembarked in London,

Martin Droeshout Sculpsit London.

William Shakespeare, or Mr. Shakspere, as shown in the 1623 Folio. The Folio editors are remarkably vague about him, offering no helpful details about his life (such as the dates of his birth and death) or mentioning his supposed patron, Henry Wriothesley, Earl of Southampton. *(By permission of the Folger Shakespeare Library)*

Elizabeth I. Oxford was a favorite of hers; she nicknamed him her "Turk," and in 1572 they were rumored to be lovers. *(By permission of the Folger Shakespeare Library)*

Edmund Spenser,
with Sidney the leading poet of the age in
the eyes of their contemporaries.
He and Oxford paid tribute to each other's
poetic genius. *(By permission of the
Folger Shakespeare Library)*

EDMUND SPENCER.

Ben Jonson, poet, playwright, and friend of Shakespeare.
His tantalizing remarks about his friend combine high praise, criticism,
and cryptic reminiscence. *(By permission of the Folger Shakespeare Library)*

Sir Philip Sidney,
the most admired of Elizabeth's
court poets. He and Oxford had
a noted quarrel over a tennis
court. *(By courtesy of the
National Portrait Gallery, London)*

Henry Wriothesley, Earl of Southampton. Like Oxford, he was a ward of Lord Burghley, who pressed him to marry his granddaughter and Oxford's daughter. He is the reluctant "lovely boy" the Sonnet urges to marry, but also the subject of the poet's passion: "O know, dear love, I always write of you." "Be thou the tenth Muse." *(By permission of the Folger Shakespeare Library)*

Edward de Vere, Earl of Oxford, as a young man was a courtier, poet, athlete, scholar, patron, and dandy. *(Painting by Rob Day)*

Henry Howard, Earl of Surrey.
Oxford's uncle by marriage
created the Shakespearean
sonnet form and introduced
blank verse into English.
(By courtesy of the
National Portrait Gallery, London)

William Cecil,
the great Lord Burghley.
He was the queen's chief
minister, Oxford's guardian
and father-in-law, and
Southampton's guardian.
(By courtesy of the
National Portrait Gallery, London)

William Herbert, third Earl of Pembroke. The Folio is dedicated to him and his brother Philip. During his youth, his parents, Burghley, and Oxford had discussed marriage between him and Oxford's daughter Bridget *(By courtesy of the National Portrait Gallery, London)*

Philip Herbert, brother of William and fourth Earl of Pembroke after William's death. In 1605, while he was Earl of Montgomery, he married Oxford's daughter Susan. *(By courtesy of the National Portrait Gallery, London)*

By the time of this portrait, Oxford was probably, as he describes himself in his letters, "lame." He was also "in disgrace with fortune and men's eyes." *(Copyright © 1975 Duke of St. Albans)*

without a word to Burghley and the unhappy Anne, who were there to greet him. In his rage and agitation he wrote to Burghley that he would not see Anne, putting much of the blame on Burghley himself:

My Lord, although I have forborne, in some respect, which should [be] private to myself, either to write or come unto your Lordship, yet had I determined, as opportunity should have served me, to have accomplished the same in compass of a few days. But now, urged thereto by your letters, to satisfy you the sooner, I must let your Lordship understand this much:

That is, until I can better satisfy or advertise myself of some mislikes, I am not determined, as touching my wife, to accompany her. What they are, because some are not to be spoken of or written upon as imperfections, I will not deal withal. Some that otherways discontent me I will not blaze or publish until it please me. And last of all, I mean not to weary my life any more with such troubles and molestations as I have endured; nor will I, to please your Lordship only, discontent myself. Wherefore, as your Lordship very well writeth unto me, that you mean, if it standeth with my liking, to receive her into your house, these are likewise to let your Lordship understand that it doth very well content me; for there, as your daughter or her mother's, more than my wife, you may take comfort of her; and I, rid of the cumber thereby, shall remain well eased of many griefs I do not doubt but that she hath sufficient proportion for her being to live upon and to maintain herself.

This might have been done through private conference before, and had not needed to have been the fable of the world if you would have had the patience to have understood me; but I do not know by what or whose advice it was to run that course so contrary to my will or meaning, which made her so disgraced to the world, raised suspicion openly, that with private conference might have been more silently handled, and hath given me more greater cause to mislike.

Wherefore I desire your Lordship in these causes—now you shall understand me—not to urge me any further; and so I write unto your Lordship, as you have done unto me, this Friday, the 27th of April.

Your Lordship's to be used in all things reasonable.

—*Edward Oxeford*

The rumor was almost certainly false and malicious—Oxford later accepted the child as his own—and the question of who may have started it has been a matter of much speculation. Moore doubts that Oxford really believed it himself; he argues that Oxford was enraged at Burghley, and especially at Lady Burghley, for their meddling. Lady Burghley had tried to instigate a servants' revolt in Oxford's household and did succeed in taking his wife with her to London. It may be that Oxford, feeling the disgrace and ridicule his supposed cuckoldry had occasioned, wanted riddance of the whole family. In any case, he refused Anne's pitiful entreaties to see him.

It would be more than five years before Oxford would relent and take Anne back, after he had incurred disgrace by his own fault. At all times she stood ready to forgive him, without even implying that he had wronged her, although Oxford's cruel treatment of her sprang more from a sense of his own injured dignity than from any misconduct on her part.

However maddening his in-laws may have been—and this rift was made more bitter by his suspicion that Burghley had held back the money he had requested—Oxford's behavior toward Anne is hard to excuse or even to understand. He had not doubted her fidelity at the time he learned of her pregnancy or again when he got the news of the child's birth; but any threat to his honor, his "good name," put him in a towering passion, and the fury of honor often leads men to dishonorable conduct, as witness the Shakespeare plays themselves. It was enough for him that Anne, however blameless, was "disgraced to the world." He would later blame his own cousin Henry Howard for spreading the rumor that the child was not his. For the time being, he refused to see either Anne or little Elizabeth.

In 1577, Oxford's sister Mary became engaged to a Protestant, Peregrine Bertie, later Lord Willoughby. Oxford violently opposed the match; Bertie said Oxford had sworn to kill him. Bertie's mother, the Duchess of Suffolk, opposed the union too, and named Oxford himself as one of the reasons: "If she [Mary] should prove like her brother, if an empire follows her I should be sorry to match so. She said that she could not rule her brother's tongue, nor help the rest of his faults." But the marriage proceeded, and a few years later we find Oxford dining amicably with his brother-in-law.

Now in his midtwenties, Oxford began to feel the financial pinch brought on by his prodigality. He was deeply in debt—to the tune of 6,000 pounds, by his own estimate. In 1577, he sold five estates to pay off the expenses of his tour. Selling off the lands he had inherited was to become a habit: in a single year not long after this, he sold thirteen estates. He also tried to augment his dwindling fortune by investing heavily in the voyages of Martin Frobisher and others to North America. Oxford was an enthusiast for the discovery of a Northwest Passage. But the only result of these ventures—more gambles than investments—was that he lost 3,500 pounds more and fell deeper into debt.

In July 1578, Elizabeth and her entire court visited Cambridge University, where the scholar Gabriel Harvey delivered a series of addresses, in Latin, honoring her leading courtiers. Harvey praised Oxford in particular for his many English and Latin verses (only a few of which are known to us), but urged him to put his pen and books aside and take up arms; war with Spain loomed, and Harvey even suggested that the Turks might invade England.

In 1579, it is recorded that Oxford and three other lords entertained the queen by performing a "device," probably a masque—the earliest known indication of his interest in drama, which would become more consuming in the next decade. By 1579, John Lyly, playwright and author of fashionable prose fictions, was Oxford's secretary. Lyly's novella *Euphues* had created a vogue for fantastically ornate rhetoric. Lyly dedicated a sequel, *Euphues and his England,* to Oxford, as did Anthony Munday, also a retainer, with his *Mirrour of Mutabilitie.* Even when he fell from favor at court, Oxford would maintain his high stature in literary circles.

The year 1579 also saw Oxford's famous tennis-court quarrel with Sir Philip Sidney, courtier, poet, soldier, and popular hero. Oxford and Sidney belonged to rival factions at court, with Oxford favoring a match between Elizabeth and the French Duke of Alencon, son of Catherine de Medici, while Sidney, following his uncle the Earl of Leicester, opposed it; the two men were also poetic rivals. (One of Sidney's extant poems is a reply to Oxford's *Were I a King.*) The origin of the tennis-court spat is unclear; apparently it was a quarrel over who had held the court first, in the course of which Oxford called Sidney a "puppy." Even the accounts of Sidney's friends imply, in spite of themselves, that

Oxford was in the right. Sidney issued a challenge to Oxford, but Elizabeth forbade the two men to duel. She ordered Sidney to apologize to Oxford as his social superior (Sidney refused and withdrew from the court); she meanwhile urged on Oxford the duties of his rank: quarreling with a knight was beneath his dignity. For all that has been made of this incident by Sidney partisans, there is no evidence of lasting rancor between Oxford and Sidney.

The Elizabethans were not shy in seeking social status, or in asserting it once they had attained it. Democratic notions of equality were to come centuries later. Mr. Shakspere himself sought a modest title, which appears wherever his name is recorded in legal documents after 1599. Oxford's extravagances, his quarrels, and his sheer arrogance were unusual, certainly, but they were also very typical of a time when people assumed that differences of degree were to be accentuated, not minimized. Such egalitarian sects as the Levellers were still regarded as cranks, the wild fringe of Protestantism, throughout the 1600s and even in Samuel Johnson's time.

The year 1580 bequeathed us a verse portrait of Oxford. Harvey caricatured him, though not with admiration, in an odd poem titled *Speculum Tuscanismi* ("The Mirror of Tuscanism"). Though the poem does not name Oxford, he was understood to be the target. Harvey lampoons his vanity, Italian affections, outlandish dress, and "womanish" works in contrast to his "valorous" words; but it also credits him with eloquence, wit, wisdom, might, bounty, and "all gallant virtues." The poem, written privately to the poet Edmund Spenser, was somehow published. Lyly apparently made an uproar about it, and Harvey was charged with libel. He apologized and protested that he had meant no offense to Oxford, blaming Lyly for creating that impression. Harvey, forgiven, praised Oxford, "not disposed to trouble his Jovial mind with such Saturnine paltry," for refusing to take Lyly's bait.

By the summer of 1580, in the judgment of B.M. Ward, Oxford, in spite of his break with his wife and his mighty father-in-law, was enjoying the peak of favor at Elizabeth's court. But by the end of the year, his downfall had begun.

In 1576, on his return from the Continent, Oxford had privately embraced the Catholic faith in company with his friends Lord Henry

Howard (also his cousin, and the brother of the beheaded Duke of Norfolk), Charles Arundel, and Francis Southwell, courtiers all, who had favored the queen's marriage to a French suitor. Now, in December 1580, Oxford openly broke with the three and denounced them as traitors conspiring for the Catholic powers. Placed under arrest, all three denied the charges (which were essentially true); two of them, Howard and Arundel, retorted by vilifying Oxford with accusations, many of them suspiciously wild. Howard accused Oxford of conspiring with the Spanish to overthrow Elizabeth, calling him "a shameless liar" and "an habitual drunkard." He added that Oxford had vowed to punish the queen for calling him a "bastard," an allusion to his youthful difficulties over his title. He went so far as to charge Oxford with swearing that Elizabeth had a miserable singing voice. Arundel added that Oxford had blasphemed and denied the divinity of Christ, "perjured himself a hundred times and damned himself to the pit of hell," was "a most notorious drunkard and very seldom sober," committed "all acts of cruelty, injury, and villainy, sparing no woman be she never so virtuous, nor any man, be he never so honourable," and so on. "To record the vices of this monstrous earl were a labour without end." One wonders how his horrified accusers could have kept company with him for so long. One of the charges is especially notable. Arundel accused Oxford of "buggering a boy that is his cook and many other boys." He added:

> I will prove him a buggerer of a boy that is his cook, by his own confession as well as by witnesses. I have seen this boy many a time in his chamber, doors closed locked, together with him, maybe at Whitehall and at his house in Broad Street, and finding it so, I have gone to the back door to satisfy myself: at the which the boy hath come out all in a sweat, and I have gone in and found the beast in the same plight. But to make it more apparent, my Lord Harry saw more, and the boy confessed it unto Southwell, and himself confirmed it unto Mr. William Cornwallis.

In a garbled memorandum that is hard to read, Howard named three of the alleged catamites: the boy singer Oxford had brought from Venice, Orazio Cogno, who had long since returned home (his name is spelled "Auratio" and "Orache"); a Henry McWilliams (spelled "Mackwilliams"); and a boy surnamed Power or Powers. He described the boys as complaining and weeping, and named witnesses who, he said, were distressed by these goings-on. He also said that Oxford spoke to Cornwallis of desiring "a priest to whom he must confess buggery."

Southwell, a more temperate accuser than the other two, wrote to them: "I cannot particularly charge my lord with pederastism but with the open lewdness of his own speeches, neither with Tom Cook, nor Powers, nor any else." Apparently, he did not think the accusation would be credited, and apparently it was not. Oxford's lewd speeches allegedly had to do with jocular suggestions about the uses of sheep, mares, and similar matters.

Oxford himself confined his charges against the three men to treason. Howard and Arundel were clearly libeling him extravagantly in most of their assertions; their backs were to the wall. They did claim to have witnesses, including the boys themselves, and some of their details sound plausible, as when Howard speaks of a "salve" that Oxford applied to his legs (he had injured a leg on his Italian journey). Though the queen seems not to have taken the buggery charges seriously at the time, they may have dogged Oxford afterward—especially if there was any grain of truth in them. This possibility, obviously, has some bearing on the Sonnets, the great majority of which are without question love poems addressed to a young man.

This bitter quarrel left incidental details of some interest. The salve Oxford used may point to the "lameness" the poet refers to in himself on two occasions. His accusers' accounts include many stories that he had told of his days in Italy. Readers of Shakespeare will take note of Oxford's passing references to "the Jews of Italy," most likely in Venice or Rome, and to a feud between two families in Genoa. Among the "lies" that were said to leave his auditors laughing was a description of St. Mark's Cathedral paved with rubies and diamonds, along with wild boasts of his own heroics—military, oratorical, and amatory. Oxford may have meant these yarns more to entertain than to deceive these men, with whom he was on friendly terms at the time and whom he probably did not consider simpletons. Moore notes that such inventions strikingly match Ben Jonson's brief memoir, in which "Shakespeare" is described as a conversationalist of uncontrollable fantasy.

Oxford's three antagonists received a few months' imprisonment; Howard convinced the queen that he had attended mass only because of certain scruples about the sacraments. At about this time, tensions with the Pope and the Catholic powers were coming to a head; Elizabeth, tolerant of Catholics as long as their religion did not seem politically subversive, began a harsh crackdown against "papists."

At the same time, Oxford faced another personal crisis—brought on, like most of his crises, by himself. He was having an affair with one of Elizabeth's ladies in waiting, Ann Vavasor. The liaison is recorded in a poem, "Ann Vavasor's Echo," which plays on the name "Vere" at the end of every line:

> On heavens! who was the first that bred in me this fe*ver*? Vere.
> Who was the first that gave the wound whose fear I wear for e*ver*? Vere.
> What tyrant, Cupid, to my harm usurps thy golden qui*ver*? Vere.
> What wight first caught this heart and can from bondage it deli*ver*? Vere.

Whether she or Oxford wrote it is in some doubt, but Oxford is more likely, for she is not known to have written any other verses. In March 1581, Ann Vavasor gave birth to a son by him. The queen, who took lax morals among her courtiers as an affront to her majesty, was furious: she sent father, mother, and infant to the Tower of London. Oxford was released after a few weeks but remained under house arrest for months.

In December, his wife Anne wrote him a moving letter pleading for reconciliation. She referred to his having recently shown her some "favour," which "made me assured of your good meaning, though you seemed fearful how to show it by open address." Apparently a meeting between them had been arranged, and he had seen his little daughter for the first time since infancy. With sad dignity, and without recrimination, Anne said she had now been informed that

> your Lordship is entered into for [sic] misliking of me without any cause in deed or thought. And therefore, my good Lord, I beseech you in the name of God which knoweth all my thoughts and love towards you, let me know the truth of your meaning towards me; upon what cause you are moved to continue me in this misery, and what you would have me do in

my power to recover your constant favour, so as your Lordship may not be led still to detain me in calamity without some probable cause whereof, I appeal to God, I am entirely innocent.

This time Oxford relented. It is a pity that his reply to her has been lost, but we gather from the grateful tone of Anne's response a few days later that he had written a kind but guarded letter offering to make peace with her, provided he could do so without exposing himself to the malice of her family and certain other courtiers. She expressed sympathy for his plight, hinting with delicate irony that she might claim a bit of sympathy too: "[I] am most sorry to perceive how you are unquieted with the uncertainty of the world, whereof I myself am not without some taste." She nevertheless thanked him "heartily," expressed her eagerness to help him and share his troubles, and tried to reassure him that her father meant him well. (As to her mother, she was silent.) She had been caught in the middle of a nasty fight among strong personalities, and had suffered deeply; yet her unimpaired sweetness shines through: "Good my Lord, assure yourself it is you whom only I love and fear, and so am desirous above all the world to please you."

From this point on, their marriage seems to have been peaceful at least; they had three more daughters (and an infant son who died) before Anne's death in 1588.

Others were less disposed than Lady Oxford to forgive. In March 1582, a well-connected courtier named Thomas Knyvet, apparently a kinsman of Ann Vavasor, attacked Oxford with a sword, gravely wounding him before receiving a wound himself. Knyvet's followers and Oxford's brawled in the streets of London for a year; four men died in their frays (one thinks of Tybalt and Mercutio). Oxford seems not to have participated; one senses that he was mellowing during these years.

By 1583, Oxford had lost Elizabeth's favor, and Burghley, while vainly pleading to the queen on his behalf, privately described him as "ruined." Oxford's chief ally at court, the Earl of Sussex, also died that year. Meanwhile, Anne bore him a son who died soon after birth in May. A few weeks later, after what one observer called "some bitter words and speeches," the queen pardoned Oxford and he was allowed to return to court. Whether his earlier Catholic leanings survived all this we are left to guess.

In 1585, Thomas Vavasor, evidently Ann Vavasor's brother, wrote to Oxford challenging him to a fight:

> If thy body had been as deformed as thy mind is dishonourable, my house had been yet unspotted, and thyself remained with thy cowardice unknown. I speak this that I fear thou art so much wedded to that shadow of thine, that nothing can force to awake thy base and sleepy spirits. Is not the revenge taken of thy victims sufficient, but wilt thou yet use unworthy instruments to provoke my unwilling mind: Or dost thou fear thyself, and therefore hast thou sent thy forlorn kindred, whom as thou hast left nothing to inherit so thou dost thrust them into thy shameful quarrels? If it be so (as I too much doubt) then stay at home thyself and send my abuses; but if there be yet any spark of honor left in thee, or iota of regard for thy decayed reputation, use not thy birth for an excuse, for I am a gentleman, but meet me thyself alone and thy lackey to hold thy horse. For the weapons I leave them to thy choice for that I challenge, and the place to be appointed by us both at our meeting, which I think may conveniently be at Nunnington or elsewhere. Thyself shall send me word by this bearer, by whom I expect an answer.
>
> —*Tho. Vavasor*

Apparently nothing came of it, but the letter tells us something of Oxford's "decayed reputation" in court circles by 1585. Vavasor addresses the great earl with a contemptuous "thou"—the familiar second-person pronoun, to a social superior, was a deliberate insult—and no sore point is left untaunted. The letter is also notable for Vavasor's tantalizing reference to "that shadow of thine." Nobody knows what he meant by this odd phrase. At any rate, the letter's fearless insolence implies that Oxford by now commanded little respect or fear. Vavasor obviously assumes that court opinion is on his side.

Oxford was now in his midthirties. He was no longer young, and no longer a star at court, despite a final triumph in the royal tournament of 1584. His private life was beginning to settle down into something like normality, but his finances reached their embarrassing nadir: during this year he was forced to sell seven more of his estates. According to

Burghley, who sometimes exaggerated such things, Oxford and Anne were reduced to four servants—a tiny retinue for an earl. It may not have been quite that bad, but Oxford was unable to shake off the aura of disgrace and disfavor, and he must have felt it deeply. So far, life had failed to keep the brilliant promise it had held out to him, and he himself was largely to blame.

Of all the letters Oxford wrote, nearly all that remain are addressed to Burghley and his son Sir Robert Cecil (they were preserved in the Cecils' state papers). These letters account for much of what we know of him. His relations with Burghley ranged from bitter to warm. Most of the letters are equable enough, respectful and businesslike, with many expressions of Oxford's gratitude. Thus, we find him thanking Burghley in 1583 for "your Lordship's friendly usage and sticking by me in this time wherein I am hedged in with so many enemies." As late as 1590, he speaks of Burghley as being "more fatherly than friendly with me," though he never calls him anything more intimate than "your Lordship." But in a postscript to a letter of 1584, when Oxford was thirty-four, he complains of Burghley's meddling with his servants:

> And I think very strange that your Lordship should enter into that course towards me whereby I must learn that I knew not before, but of your opinion and good will towards me. But I pray, my lord, leave that course, for I mean not to be your ward nor your child. I serve Her Majesty, and I am that I am, and by alliance near to your Lordship, but free, and scorn to be offered that injury, to think I am so weak of government as to be ruled by servants, or not able to govern myself. If your Lordship take and follow this course, you deceive yourself, and make me take another course than yet I have thought not of. Wherefore these shall be to be desire your Lordship, if that I may make account of your friendship, that you will leave that course as hurtful to us both.

Still, Oxford depended on his father-law. He had long since ceased to be the glass of fashion and the mold of form; he had lost ground at court to more ambitious, more calculating, less impulsive men. Oxford by now had little power of his own, but he had the queen's favor again and he could usually call on Burghley—the most powerful man in England, even if Oxford far outranked him in nobility of blood—for support and assistance when he needed them, as he often did. Of course, Burghley also had his long-suffering daughter and his three granddaughters' welfare to think of.

More than ever, Oxford in the 1580s was devoting his time to literature, and especially to the theater. In 1580, Anthony Munday had dedicated his book *Zelauto* to him, its dedication identifying him with Lyly's character Euphues. Munday also dedicated several later books to him and to his son Henry, the eighteenth Earl of Oxford. That same year, despite his shrinking fortune, Oxford took over the Earl of Warwick's acting company; he soon added another company of boy actors, which performed at court for Elizabeth on one occasion. In 1582, Thomas Watson dedicated his book of sonnets, *Hekatompathia,* to him; Watson is thought to have influenced Shakespeare, though it is possible that the real influence was in the other direction. Robert Greene dedicated *Greene's Card of Fancy* to Oxford in 1584, and John Soowthern wrote an ode in his praise. In yet another dedication, Angel Day called Oxford one "whose infancy from the beginning was ever sacred to the Muses." William Webbe, in *A Discourse of English Poetry,* named him "the most excellent" of the court poets. In 1584, Oxford acquired a sublease of the Blackfriars Theater, which he transferred to Lyly. He had his own company of actors at this time (their tours took them to Stratford-upon-Avon, among other towns).

In 1583, Oxford's brother-in-law Peregrine Bertie, Lord Willoughby, was sent on a diplomatic mission to Denmark. He returned with a vivid description of the royal court at Elsinore, including a feast given by the Danish king at which the visitor was saluted with fireworks and a great discharge of ordnance.

In late August 1585, after pleading with the queen and Burghley to give him military employment against Spain, Oxford went to the Continent to take command of a cavalry regiment as part of the English attempt to prevent a Spanish takeover of the Netherlands after the assassination of William the Silent. But court intrigue supervened, and he was replaced by the young Earl of Essex in early October. (He sent his baggage ahead to England, but it was captured by pirates on the way.)

In 1586, the queen granted Oxford a huge annual pension of 1,000 pounds. Burghley himself, with a household of eighty, received only twice that amount per year. Oxford, now sad and subdued, was back in the queen's good graces in spite of everything. But it must have seemed that his future was behind him. The world of affairs was passing him by; he had few friends left at court; his "good name" was now the "decayed reputation" Thomas Vavasor had dared to jeer at. All the old avenues to the glory he had once aspired to now appeared closed to him. Though he retained his hereditary status, he was never again able to gain advancement or exert much influence at court.

As England's foremost earl by birth, Oxford that year sat on the tribunal that convicted Mary, Queen of Scots, of treason, a verdict that ensured her beheading. But he held no appointive office, despite his many attempts to get one. He angrily blamed Burghley for his inability to gain "preferment," once reducing Anne to tears with his complaints about her father. Burghley denied the charge, saying he simply lacked the power to secure a position for Oxford; in fact, Oxford had so many enemies at court that he was unable to get more than a few votes in the annual election to the Order of the Garter. Over the years, he would continue to sue to Elizabeth, Burghley, and Burghley's son Sir Robert Cecil for some lucrative post or prerogative—trading monopolies, the governorship of Jersey, the presidency of Wales—but always in vain.

During these years, Oxford suffered personal losses. Two of his children died, one an infant son who would have become the eighteenth earl of his line, the other a young daughter named Frances. Anne herself died in June 1588, a few months after giving birth to another daughter, Susan. Oxford was absent from Anne's funeral; probably he was away at the time, preparing for war with Spain.

Burghley took charge of raising the three surviving daughters. He, not Oxford, is mentioned in Anne's elaborate epitaph—and with justice, it would seem. (An unpublished elegy by one Wilfred Samonde described her as "another Grissel for her patience." Recall Petruchio's words about Kate: "For patience she will prove a second Grissel.") Burghley must have deeply resented Oxford's treatment of his beloved "Tannikin"; a year earlier, he had written to the queen, "No enemy I have can envy me this match." Burghley cared nothing for the theater and regarded Oxford's association with theater folk as mere slumming, disgraceful to a gentleman, let alone a great lord. From his point of view,

Oxford had never grown up. It must have chagrined him that he had arranged such a marriage for Anne thinking it would be to her advantage. And yet there is no trace of ill feeling in Burghley's surviving communications with Oxford after Anne's death. Perhaps Oxford regretted the misery he had caused her.

Outrageous as Oxford's behavior often was, something about him could induce those who knew him best to forgive him seventy times seven. He was fiery, but never underhanded; at a court full of cunning schemers, his true emotions were always on the surface. If he was willful and self-centered, he could also be charming, warm, and generous. His loyalty, when he bestowed it, was deep, and he attracted loyalty in return. Above all, his brilliance made him a magnet even to other brilliant men; it is striking how ardently he was admired by writers as talented as Spenser.

In July 1588, Oxford set out, in a ship he had furnished at his own expense, to fight the Spanish Armada. But the queen again recalled him, for unknown reasons, shortly after the fighting began, thereby depriving him of a share in one of England's most glorious triumphs. He did take part in the November victory celebration at court, but from this time forth he seems to have taken little part in public affairs or court life and, despite his great pension, to have lived modestly, without the extravagance and display of his youth.

During this year, Anthony Munday dedicated several more works to Oxford. Unlike Lyly, who seems to have left Oxford's service around 1594, Munday remained close to his patron and wrote of him with devotion long after his death. The play *Sir Thomas More,* passages of which are now widely ascribed to Shakespeare, is by general scholarly agreement largely written in Munday's hand.

The brilliant pamphleteer and playwright Thomas Nashe was also a friend of Oxford. He made a punning reference to *Hamlet's* "tragical speeches" in a preface to Greene's *Menaphon* in 1589 (long before the date most scholars assign to the play—see chapter 6 for a discussion of the dating of the plays). He feuded with Harvey and, early in his pamphlet *Strange News,* clearly alluded to Oxford as "that lord thou libeledst," though without using Oxford's name. Nashe also defended Greene against Harvey's attacks. Addressing Harvey directly in *Strange*

News, after the allusion to Oxford he wrote, "I and one of my fellows, Will. Monox (hast thou never heard of him and his great dagger?), were in company with him [Greene] a month before he died, at that fatal banquet of rhenish wine and pickled herring. . . ." Who was "Will. Monox"? Monox, evidently a false name, suggests Oxford. Someone, at any rate, seems to have been in the company of these "university wits" under a pseudonym with the first name William. That this was Oxford is made more probable by the circumstance that Nashe, when he clearly does mean Oxford earlier in the pamphlet, avoids using his name. Nashe elsewhere refers to *1 Henry VI,* whose author, like *Hamlet*'s, he does not identify.

Other references to Oxford at about this time place him in the world of letters. Harvey, whose satirical poem *Speculum Tuscanismi* had described Oxford as affected and "womanish," in a peculiar phrase called Lyly Oxford's "minion secretary." In one of his dedicatory sonnets to *The Faerie Queen,* Edmund Spenser calls Oxford "most dear" to the Muses. The anonymous book *The Art of English Poesie* (1589), probably written by George Puttenham, tells us:

> Among the nobility or gentry as may be very well seen in many laudable sciences and especially in making poesy, it is so come to pass that they have no courage to write and if they have are loath to be known of their skill. So as I know very many notable gentlemen in the Court that have written commendably, and suppressed it again, or else suffered it to be published without their own names to it: as if it were a discredit for a gentleman to seem learned.

Later the book offers a remarkable example. It speaks specifically of

> Noblemen and Gentlemen of Her Majesty's own servants, who have written excellently well as it would appear if their doings could be found out and made public with the rest, of which number is first that noble gentleman Edward Earl of Oxford.

The modern reader finds it hard to understand the stigma the old gentility (and especially the nobility) attached to appearing in print, but the reason was simple. People of rank thought it undignified to submit one's efforts to the applause of the rabble or even the literate public.

They would have looked with especial horror on a nobleman who performed on the stage of a public theater, as Oxford, if he was Shakespeare, almost certainly did. (This may account for the poet's lament in Sonnet 110 that he has made himself "a motley to the view.")

By early 1590, Burghley was putting pressure on another of his many wards, Henry Wriothesley, the seventeen-year-old third Earl of Southampton, to marry Elizabeth Vere, Oxford's eldest daughter (who was then fifteen). Southampton, like Oxford, had lost his father in boyhood and had come under Burghley's power and tutelage. Like the young Oxford, he was a rising star at court, and was considered a great catch for any woman; he was very handsome, in a somewhat feminine way, with long, silken hair and intense brown eyes—to say nothing of his title and fortune, which were of greater interest to the practical, ambitious, and unromantic Burghley.

But Southampton resisted marriage more stubbornly than Oxford had. Burghley's secretary John Clapham wrote a Latin poem titled "Narcissus" to nudge him toward the altar with galling hints that the youth might be lacking in manliness; this approach did not succeed. Neither did a series of more flattering sonnets urging the "beauteous and lovely youth" to marry and carry on his "house." (Those sonnets, discussed in chapter 9, bear detailed similarities to Oxford's 1573 letter to Thomas Bedingfield.)

Southampton stalled for a couple of years, pleading his youth, then declined the match; he was fined heavily by Burghley for his refusal, such being the prerogative of the Master of the Wards. The Jesuit Henry Garnet recorded the amount: 5,000 pounds. Next, Burghley tried to marry his granddaughter to the Earl of Northumberland, but she did not fancy him. In time she would marry another earl, while Southampton went his own way as the friend, follower, and eventually kinsman by marriage of Robert Devereux, second Earl of Essex.

After 1590, Oxford's life becomes harder to trace. Few letters he wrote over the next five years survive. As it happens, this is the period when "William Shakespeare" first appeared in print, first with two long poems dedicated to Southampton, then as a dramatist. Was Oxford busy becoming Shakespeare? Burghley had earlier complained of Oxford's "lewd [i.e., common or vulgar] friends," a hint that Oxford's behavior was seen as *déclassé* by his peers. Now Oxford seems to have withdrawn from court life. He had interests in the theater and dealt with theater folk; he had leased the Blackfriars and had two acting companies: the playwright John Lyly was his secretary and friend; his figure lurks in Thomas Nashe's cryptic gossip; Puttenham placed him foremost among those noblemen who wrote "excellently" under other names. In these same years, the Lord Chamberlain's Men were organized, with William Shakespeare among the original partners. In short, Oxford appears fleetingly and almost furtively in the very theatrical and literary milieu in which Shakespeare thrived, and yet eludes all attempts to pin him down.

In 1591, Oxford made Hedingham over to Burghley in trust for his daughters; meanwhile, he was receiving his huge annuity from the queen. At about the same time, he married Elizabeth Trentham, a maid of honor at Elizabeth's court and daughter of a wealthy knight; described as "fair," she may have offered him financial security as well as beauty. In 1593, they had a son, Henry, who inherited Oxford's title but died childless in 1625. None of the Veres had ever been named Henry; it may be significant that this was Southampton's first name. (Oxford's natural son by Ann Vavasor, Edward Vere, eventually became a lieutenant colonel and was knighted.)

Throughout the 1590s, we find Oxford continually seeking favors and considerations from the queen, usually without success. On one occasion, in 1593, he was humiliated at being "browbeaten" by "bitter speeches" from her. A 1595 letter to Burghley says: "I most heartily thank your L[ordship] for your desire to know of my health, which is not so good, yet as I witness, I find comfort in this air, but no fortune at the court." His letters frequently complain of Elizabeth's delays in answering his requests or in keeping her promises. In 1600, he wrote to Sir Robert Cecil:

> Although my bad success in former suits to her Majesty have given me cause to bury my hopes in the deep abyss and bottom of despair, rather than now to attempt, after so many trials made in vain, and so many opportunities escaped, the effects of fair words and golden promises, yet for that I cannot believe but there hath always been a true correspondence of

word and intention in her Majesty, I do conjecture that with a little help, that which of itself hath brought forth so fair blossoms will also yield fruit.

After asking his brother-in-law to nudge the queen on his behalf, he added: "If she shall not deign me this in an opportunity of time so fitting, what time shall I attend which is uncertain to all men unless in the graves of men there were a time to receive benefits and good turns from princes."

In 1595, Elizabeth Vere found a husband: William Stanley, the very rich sixth Earl of Derby. Derby himself was a poet and a patron of the theater; such information as we have suggests that he and Oxford became close. Like Oxford, Derby lived in something like seclusion, away from the court. In 1599—during which year Derby visited Oxford at his suburban London residence at least twice—we find this tantalizing report in a letter by one George Fenner of June 30, 1599: "The Earl of Derby is busied only in penning comedies for the common players." But like Oxford, Derby left no play with his name on it.

In 1597, Lord and Lady Pembroke sought the hand of Oxford's daughter Bridget for their son, William Herbert, later to become the Earl of Pembroke, who appears as a dedicatee in the 1623 Folio of the Shakespeare plays. Oxford wrote to Burghley saying he was pleased by the prospect of the match, "for the young gentleman, as I understand, hath been well brought up, fair conditioned, and hath many good parts in him," adding his regret that he had not an "able body" and could not attend Her Majesty. But the marriage between Bridget and William never came off, though her sister Susan would later marry his brother Philip.

Oxford's letters during the 1590s often refer to his bad health; several times he describes himself as "lame," as in a letter to Burghley dated March 25, 1595: "Wherefore when your Lo[rdship] shall have best time and leisure if I may know it I will attend your Lordship as well as a lame man may at your house." The cause of this lameness cannot be gleaned from the record.

Burghley died in 1598. He had served Elizabeth for more than forty years, during which period, thanks largely to his statecraft, England became a great European power for the first time. We have no record of

Oxford's reaction, but his relations with Burghley's son and successor, Sir Robert Cecil, appear to have been cordial. The old man had dominated his life, and Oxford would outlive him by only six years.

During this period, Oxford continued to sponsor a troupe of actors, and we also find him mentioned as a playwright: in *Palladis Tamia* (1598), Francis Meres ranks him among "the best [playwrights] for comedy." In 1602, by the queen's permission, Oxford's players and those of the Earl of Worcester combined into one company; they performed at one of London's several inns named the Boar's Head. In 1603, Oxford's friend Sir George Buc became Master of the Revels, the officer under the Lord Chamberlain directly in charge of theatrical affairs. (This office is not to be confused with the Lord Great Chamberlain, one of Oxford's titles. The Lord Great Chamberlain was occasionally referred to as the Lord Chamberlain, leading some of Oxford's partisans to argue that he was the real sponsor of the Lord Chamberlain's Men, but this is impossible to prove.)

In 1601, once more in his capacity as England's senior earl, Oxford was in effect foreman of the jury of twenty-five noblemen who tried the earls of Essex and Southampton for high treason after their fizzled uprising against Elizabeth. The guilty verdict and death sentences were a foregone conclusion. But though Essex was duly beheaded, Southampton's execution was delayed indefinitely and he lived for two years in the Tower, surviving the queen.

The conspirators had hoped to spur sedition by commissioning a performance of *Richard II*. Elizabeth later fumed about the use of this play for subversive purposes; its deposition scene was deemed so inflammatory that it had been omitted from printed texts. Yet no action was taken against its author, and he was never even mentioned during the Essex uproar—even though the name William Shakespeare had appeared on the title page of a new quarto edition only three years earlier. Augustine Phillips, an actor in the Lord Chamberlain's Men, was called to answer for the company. Why the playwright himself was not called, we are left to wonder. Phillips explained in his deposition that the company had not really intended to perform this play, because it was "so old and so long out of use" that it would have drawn only a small crowd. This suggests that *Richard II* was older than the conventional dating, which puts it around 1595.

An anecdote from shortly after Essex went to the block illustrates something of Oxford's feelings about this whole episode. Oxford blamed his former friend Sir Walter Raleigh for Essex's fall; once, when Raleigh entered the queen's privy chamber while she was playing the virginal (a sort of small harpsichord) for Oxford and others, Oxford quipped bitterly: "When Jacks start up, heads go down"—a pun on the jacks that strike the keys of the virginal and on Jack, a common fellow.

The old queen died in 1603. Oxford was probably one of the six earls who carried the canopy over her bier. (Sonnet 125 begins: "Were't aught to me I bore the canopy . . .") He felt her loss deeply. In a letter to Sir Robert Cecil, he apologized for his inability to visit him as often as he would have wished, "by reason of my infirmity." He continued sadly:

> I cannot but find a great grief in myself to remember the mistress which we have lost, under whom both you and myself from our greenest years have been in a manner brought up; and although it hath pleased God after an earthly kingdom to take her up into a more permanent and heavenly state, wherein I do not doubt but she is crowned with glory, and to give us a prince wise, learned, and enriched with all virtues, yet the long time which we spent in her service, we cannot look for so much left of our days as to bestow on another, neither the long acquaintance and kind familiarities wherewith she did use us, we are not ever to expect from another prince as denied by the infirmity of age and common course of reason. In this common shipwreck, mine is above all the rest, who least regarded, though often comforted, of all her followers, she hath left to try my fortune among the alterations of time, and chance, either without sail whereby to take the advantage of any prosperous gale, or with anchor to ride till the storm be overpast.

In his last ceremonial act as Lord Great Chamberlain, Oxford officiated at the coronation of James I in 1603, bearing the sword of state. James's accession was fortunate for Oxford; the new king held him in high regard, and showed him favor. Oxford was immediately appointed to the Privy Council; in addition, his pension was renewed and his petition granted for custody of the Forest of Essex and the Keepership of Havering House (both of which, though he regarded them as his property by ancient hereditary right, had been withheld from both him and his father). Later this king would refer casually to "great Oxford"—a reference to his status, not an encomium. James, who shared Elizabeth's love of literature and drama, also elevated the Lord Chamberlain's Men: under his direct patronage, they became the King's Men.

Southampton fared even better under the new monarch. Three weeks after Elizabeth's death, he was released from the Tower after only two years' confinement. Soon afterward, he was officially pardoned and his title and lands restored to him. James made him a Knight of the Garter and bestowed other honors and favors on him and even on his mother and his followers. (James went out of his way to favor Elizabeth's enemies: he also pointedly held and kissed Essex's small son, praising his father as the noblest knight England had produced.)

Oxford had been ailing for a long time. From 1590 on, his letters often refer to his ill health and some unspecified disability. Around June 1604, he contracted the plague. Feeling his death imminent, he transferred custody of the Forest of Essex to his favorite cousin, Sir Francis Vere, and to one of his sons-in-law.

On June 24 he died, at the age of fifty-four. Of his end we know only that a note beside the record of his death says simply, "Plague." An anonymous comment on his death survives: "Of [him] I will only say what all men's voices confirm: he was a man in mind and body absolutely accomplished with honourable endowments."

On the night of June 24, 1604—the day Oxford died—James suddenly had Southampton and several of his followers arrested. Nobody knows why. No official record was kept, and the incident is known mostly because the French ambassador sent a detailed report of it to Henri IV. Southampton was released a day later, and the following month James resumed heaping favors on him, adding several large estates to his fortune.

After 1604, there are hints that Shakespeare is already gone. His name appears in a roster of players in March, three months before Oxford's death, but is not mentioned in a similar list in August. Beginning in 1605, other men's plays are published under his name with apparent impunity. William Barkstead pays tribute to him in the past tense in 1607. A poem in his honor by John Davies in 1610 has a similarly memorial ring. His intimate sonnets appear in 1609, published without his cooperation but without his protest; the publisher, not the poet, supplies the dedication. The 1609 quarto of *Troilus and Cressida* contains a preface by someone else, who refers to him guardedly as "this author" and hints that he will soon be "gone, and his comedies out of sale." In 1616, when Mr. Shakspere of Stratford dies, there is no recorded notice of the event in London.

In 1604, Oxford's daughter Susan married Philip Herbert, soon to be the new Earl of Montgomery. He was the brother of the William Herbert whom Oxford had hoped would marry one of his other daughters; in 1615, William, now Earl of Pembroke, became Lord Chamberlain, assuming charge of the English theater.

In 1607, Oxford's natural son by Ann Vavasor, Edward Vere, was knighted, having distinguished himself as a captain under Sir Francis Vere. In 1612, Oxford's widow died. In 1625, his son and heir Henry de Vere, eighteenth Earl of Oxford, died of a fever after leading an assault in battle; the earldom then fell to another branch of the family, which continued it until 1703.

Oxford was not forgotten with his death. That he left an imposing memory is clear from several posthumous tributes. In *The Revenge of Bussy d'Ambois,* published in 1613, George Chapman has a character speak the following lines:

> I overtook, coming from Italy,
> In Germany, a great and famous Earl
> Of England; the most goodly fashion'd man
> I ever saw: from head to foot in form
> Rare and most absolute; he had a face
> Like one of the most ancient honour'd Romans
> From whence his noblest family was deriv'd;
> He was beside of spirit passing great,
> Valiant and learn'd, and liberal as the sun,
> Spoke and writ sweetly, or of learned subjects,
> Or of the discipline of public weals;
> And 'twas the Earl of Oxford.

And in 1619, Anthony Munday wrote a moving dedication to Oxford's son, the eighteenth Earl, praising his father's "famous and desertful memory" and "matchless virtues." In a book on education published in 1622, Henry Peacham made a list of poets, including Sidney and Spenser, who had made Elizabeth's reign "a golden age" for poetry. The list began with "Edward Earl of Oxford." It made no mention of William Shakespeare, despite his popularity.

In 1623, the First Folio of Shakespeare's plays was published. It was dedicated to "the incomparable pair of brethren," William and Philip Herbert, now earls of Pembroke and Montgomery. Both men had known Oxford through their parents' friendship with him. In addition, as we have seen, Montgomery was married to Oxford's daughter Susan Vere, while Pembroke had been considered as a match for his other daughter, Bridget, with Oxford's warm approval.

Pembroke gave Ben Jonson generous patronage and no doubt did a good deal to arrange his appointment as poet laureate; he of all men was in a position to secure Jonson's cooperation in the fiction that William Shakspere was William Shakespeare.

With remarkable frequency, then, Oxford's life touches the lives of personalities familiar to students of Shakespeare: Elizabeth I, Golding, Burghley, Harvey, Lyly, Sidney, Watson, Greene, Nashe, Southampton, Spenser, Munday, Derby, Chapman, Meres, Raleigh, Essex, James I, Pembroke, Montgomery. Of course, it was a smaller world: London, including the suburbs, contained only 200,000 people. The world of the theater, with no more than four licensed acting companies existing at a time, was even smaller—which only makes it extremely incongruous that this great patron of the theater, living in London from the 1590s to his death in 1604, never seems to have crossed paths with William Shakespeare.

Chapter 6

1 6 0 4 : T h e   C r i t i c a l   Y e a r

*E*dward de Vere died in June 1604, an undisputed fact that
for most scholars is enough to eliminate him as a possible
author of Shakespeare's plays, ten of which are usually dated after that
year. If even one of the plays can be proved to have been written as late
as 1605, the whole case for Oxford collapses.

So it would seem that the dozen years between Oxford's death and
Mr. Shakspere's can disprove the Oxford theory, but not the traditional
view. It is probably impossible to prove that each play was written before
1604. And even if it were, Mr. Shakspere still could not be absolutely
ruled out as the real author. That could only be done if it were shown
that one or more of the plays dated from after 1616—which of course
would rule out Oxford, too. And yet close study of the years between
the two men's deaths actually bolsters the case for Oxford.

In the dozen years between 1604 and 1616, we have several hints
that Shakespeare was already known to be dead, whatever the public

fiction may have been. A poem titled *Mirrha the Mother of Adonis* by William Barkstead appeared in 1607, containing these lines (in the original spelling):

> His Song was worthie merrit (Shakspeare hee)
> sung the fair blossome, thou the withered tree
> Laurell is due to him, his art and wit
> hath purchast it, Cypres thy brow will fit.

Was worthy merit? Why is "Shakspeare," in 1607, already being spoken of in the past tense? Mr. Shakspere was then only forty-three, with many years to live. The cypress was a symbol of mourning; is this stanza a salute to a poet whom Barkstead expects his readers to understand is deceased? The passage can only embarrass the mainstream biographers, and it does. In spite of the severe shortage of records of Shakespeare's literary career, they rarely cite this item. Lee, Adams, Chute, Bentley, Quennell, Halliday, Rowse, Schoenbaum, Levi, Fraser, Kay, and O'Connor all fail to mention Barkstead's tribute.

There are other clues that Shakespeare was gone sooner than the standard story would have it. The 1609 quarto of *Troilus* begins with a strange anonymous preface, headed "A Never Writer, to an Ever Reader. News." We have no convincing explanation for this cryptic epistle. Oxfordians have made much of it, and with reason. Although the title page bears the name William Shakespeare, the preface guardedly calls him "this author," praising him in terms that sound almost memorial: "And believe this, that when he is gone and his comedies out of sale, you will scramble for them. . . ." Why "when he is gone"? Mr. Shakspere was only forty-five, and if his biographers are to be believed, still active. The "Never Writer" goes on to tell his readers they should "thank heaven for the scape it [this play] hath made amongst you, since by the grand possessors' wills I believe you should have prayed for them rather than been prayed."

The Never Writer is holding something back, and affecting a coy tone appropriate for his knowing audience—his "Ever Reader." Certain "grand possessors"—not the author, not the King's Men—apparently held Shakespeare's manuscripts.

The preface begins to make sense if we assume that the real Shakespeare was *already* dead, and that the Never Writer is telling readers in the know that *Troilus* was somehow obtained from those who control his literary remains—people of high rank, from the sound of it. But the most intriguing note of this preface is something more impalpable: its very subtle manner of talking about "this author" as we always speak of someone who is absent, and absent for good. He is spoken of with respect, but not as if the words could reach his ear. What is said about him belongs to a conversation of which he himself is no longer a part.

In the same year, *Shake-speares Sonnets* appeared, with another mysterious preface: the dedication by "T.T.," the publisher Thomas Thorpe. Why did Shakespeare not write his own dedication, as he had for *Venus* and *Lucrece*? The standard explanation is that the Sonnets were published without his permission or cooperation. But in that case, why did he fail to protest? And would a rogue publisher be so impudent as to write the dedication himself, as if on behalf of the poet whose work he was stealing?

Only, I submit, if the poet was dead. The respectful phrase "everliving" suggests this. We do not customarily ascribe immortality to those who are still alive, unless their careers are pretty surely complete (Joe DiMaggio, say). Again, Mr. Shakspere was only forty-five and, if the standard biography is correct, still in full possession of his genius. He would have seemed to all about him able to continue writing plays and poems for many years to come. There was no known indication that he was about to "retire," as the scholars would have it. Writing is not an activity you retire from, especially at forty-five.

Shake-speares Sonnets would not have been the poet's title. Writers do not ordinarily speak of themselves in the third person. Other sonneteers of the time called their works *Delia, Astrophel and Stella, Amoretti, Idea, Diana, Fidessa, Zepheria, Chloris, Phyllis,* and the surefire *Parthenophil and Parthenophe;* none puts his own name in the title. The phrase "Shakespeares Sonnets" has a kind of finality: it implies that there will be no more sonnets by this poet. Otherwise, the publisher might have called the collection "*Sonnets,* by William Shake-speare."

This is one more clue that Shakespeare had no part in the publication of the Sonnets; if he had given them a title, it would presumably have been the name of the youth he promises to immortalize. We may also have here a further clue that the poet was dead by 1609. Both the title and the dedication, like the preface to *Troilus,* seem to refer to him with the kind of objectivity we assume in discussing those who are absent. Again, it seems, the poet is not expected to hear what is being said about him. Both T.T. and the Never Writer give the impression of alluding to some open secret.

Shakespeare seems to have ceased writing the Sonnets at about the time Oxford died. Sonnet 107, one of the later numbers, seems to be referring to Elizabeth's death in 1603 in the line, "The mortal moon hath her eclipse endur'd." Why should Mr. Shakspere, assuming he was the poet, have abandoned the sonnet—a simple and congenial form—at just that time? It seems more likely that, unless the urge to write had completely left him, he would have kept writing sonnets privately after he had stopped writing plays for the public.

According to the standard view, the period from 1604 to 1612 should have been Shakespeare's peak years in the great city, years of glory, prosperity, and popular acclaim—with every advantage accruing to a great and recognized genius. Schoenbaum assures us that Shakespeare during these years enjoyed "celebrity"; but in fact these are the years of Shakespeare's most unaccountable invisibility. Mr. Shakspere is visible enough during this time, but only in Stratford, where we find him buying property, marrying off a daughter, becoming a grandfather, and engaging in a lawsuit. In London we find no trace of him between 1604 and 1612, when he returns to testify in the Mountjoy lawsuit. His testimony itself suggests a rather tentative presence in the city: he said he had taken rooms with the Mountjoy family between about 1602 and 1604, which confirms that he never had a permanent residence in London, even after supposedly achieving great success as a playwright. Needless to say, nothing in the testimony suggests that he was an author. We are left to wonder why he left London in 1604.

Shakespeare's plays were so popular that several plays he did not write, far inferior to his authentic work, were passed off as his by rogue publishers. In 1605, *The London Prodigal* appeared under the name "William Shakespeare." In 1608, *A Yorkshire Tragedy* was printed as the work of "W. Shakspeare." In 1611, *The Troublesome Reign of King John,* first published in 1591, reappeared in print ascribed to "W. Sh."—clearly an attempt to sell the play as Shakespeare's *King John* (which had not yet been published).

It is obviously risky to pass off a spurious play as the work of a living playwright; any author would denounce such an abuse of his name. What is significant about these plays is that they began appearing the year after Oxford's death. Mr. Shakspere, of course, was still alive; if he had been believed to be the author, the impostures would hardly have been perpetrated. The scholars have uniformly failed to notice anything odd about a living author passively allowing others to exploit his name and reputation fraudulently—especially one given to lawsuits.

From 1598—the year when William Shakespeare makes his debut as a playwright in print—to 1604, a series of authentic Shakespeare plays came forth in quarto form. By 1604, a dozen of the plays had been offered for sale in rapid succession. Then, for no apparent reason, they stopped. No more new plays appeared until 1608, when quartos of *Lear* and *Pericles* (an extremely popular play) were published, followed by *Troilus* in 1609—and then none until *Othello* in 1622. In 1623, the Folio presented the world with twenty new plays—some of which, as far as we can tell, had never even been performed—and affirmed that Mr. Shakspere was Shakespeare.

Why did the flood of quartos dry up in 1604? Perhaps for the same reason Shakespeare's Sonnets end in about 1604; it was the year of Oxford's death.

Shakespeare speaks publicly in the first person only twice, in the dedications to *Venus* and *Lucrece,* and never again. Both these poems were written before Shakespeare was known as a dramatist. As the inexhaustibly inventive and eloquent plays pour out, the author leaves the paradoxical impression that he himself is remote and taciturn—if, that is, we take the documented life of Mr. Shakspere as the record of the playwright.

The scholars fail to ask another obvious question. After scoring two great triumphs in the poems dedicated to Southampton, why does Shakespeare never make another bid for noble patronage? Would not many noblemen—including Oxford himself—have eagerly sought to enlist and support his talent? Ben Jonson wrote a good deal of occasional verse for various lords. It was an easy way to supplement his income from the theater. Why did Shakespeare not do likewise, especially if he was so eager for gain that as late as 1613, when Mr. Shakspere was a wealthy man, he would supply the Earl of Rutland with an "impreso" for 44 shillings?

The year 1604 clearly marks some important break in Shakespeare's career. Mr. Shakspere abruptly absents himself from London—at least we find no further trace of his presence there until 1612, when he testifies in the Mountjoy lawsuit. No play of Shakespeare's is based on any source later than 1603. The last of the Sonnets also seem to date from about this time. Several references to Shakespeare after 1604 hint that he is already dead. Others write prefatory matter for two of his works published in 1609. The series of authentic quarto editions of his play come to an end for several years; but apocryphal plays bearing the name of Shakespeare begin to appear in 1605.

The simplest explanation of these facts is that the Earl of Oxford, who died in 1604, was William Shakespeare, and that William Shakspere, a member of his acting company, was fronting for him. This would also explain why, in 1616, the literati utterly ignored Mr. Shakspere's death.

The conventional dating of the plays, which is widely held to rule out Oxford's authorship, is based, we have seen, on the assumption that Mr. Shakspere was Shakespeare, so that the plays must have been written between 1590 and 1612 (give or take a year). In explaining his method of dating, Edmond Malone, the father of modern Shakespeare scholarship, wrote in 1778 that "the plays which Shakespeare produced before the year 1600 are known, and are 17 or 18 in number. The rest of his dramas, we may conclude, were composed between that year and the time of his retiring to the country" (around 1610, according to Malone's own estimate). More recently, Edmund Chambers said of his own method of dating: "The total result is certainly not a demonstration, but in the logical sense a hypothesis which serves to colligate the facts and is consistent with itself and with the known events of Shakespeare's external life." That is, with Mr. Shakspere's external life.

The standard dating schedule has not changed radically since Malone. If we assume Mr. Shakspere's authorship, this schedule is reasonable enough, though it presents a few problems. If we suspend that assumption, the difficulties loom larger, most notably for *Hamlet,* and the plays may be dated very differently.

There is little within the plays themselves to tell us when they were written. Shakespeare makes few references or unequivocal allusions to current events and persons. The chief exception is *Henry V,* which pretty clearly alludes to Essex's expedition to Ireland in 1599. At the beginning of Act V the Chorus says:

Were now the general of our gracious empress—
As in good time he may—from Ireland coming,
Bringing rebellion broached on his sword,
How many would the peaceful city quit
To welcome him!

This sounds as if it were written during the expedition, which lasted from March to September. The expedition ended so badly that it would have been embarrassing to mention it afterward; these cheerful lines can hardly have been written once the mission had failed. So the play, or at least this chorus, can be pretty firmly dated at 1599. But the choruses before each act do not appear in the 1600 quarto of the play, which may have been reconstructed from actors' memories rather than from a text; the lines in question were not printed until the 1623 Folio. Possibly the play was written *before* 1599 and the choruses inserted later, just after Essex set out. Nothing else in any of the plays dates them with even this moderate certainty.

Henry VIII and *The Two Noble Kinsmen* (which was not included in the Folio) not only exemplify Shakespeare's late style, but show the hand of a second author. From this, most scholars infer that Shakespeare at the end of his career had taken to "collaborating" with another writer, usually thought to be John Fletcher. But it seems odd that such a master, at the height of his powers, would split his labors with an inferior playwright, however competent. Many have found the Shakespearean passages of *The Two Noble Kinsmen* exceptionally beautiful. If he had written these plays himself, they might have been as lovely as *Cymbeline* or *The Winter's Tale.*

Another possibility is that Shakespeare left a few plays incomplete when he died, and that Fletcher and others were brought in to finish them. The first two acts of *Pericles* (also omitted from the Folio) are in a very different style from the last three; the play we have was probably an early one, incompletely revised late in the author's life. *Timon of Athens,* of which there is no mention anywhere before its appearance in the Folio, looks unfinished, and this may be true of *Macbeth,* too; though it is in Shakespeare's late style and contains some of his most magical poetry, it is very short, with loose ends and evident interpolations.

Macbeth does seem to reflect current events: Banquo's line was to produce James VI of Scotland, who became James I of England when Elizabeth died in 1603. If Oxford was Shakespeare, he may have written the play in James's honor, dying before he could put the final touches on it. The scholars usually interpret the Porter's jokes immediately after the murder of Duncan, about equivocation leading to damnation, as a hit at the Jesuits' role in the Gunpowder Plot of 1605, which would mean that Oxford could not have written the Porter scene or, by extension, the rest of the play. But the popular association of Jesuits with the devious arts of equivocation—paltering in a double sense, deceiving without actually lying—began long before 1605; Edmund Chambers dates it to the sensational trial of the Jesuit Father Robert Southwell in 1595. The supposed allusion to the Gunpowder Plot is, after all, only a guess.

Still, the old notion dies hard. In his recent book, *Witches & Jesuits: Shakespeare's Macbeth,* Garry Wills takes it further than most scholars: he contends that the whole play, and not just the Porter scene, is shaped by an awareness of the Gunpowder Plot, and that even the play's general vocabulary is colored by that recent event. Unfortunately, as Wills admits, there is little in the play to support this notion. In order to explain the deficit, he is forced into circular reasoning, positing that most of the evidence for his thesis must have been removed from the text after its first performance by revision and censorship. So his case for dating the play in 1606 rests on the assumption that it was altered *after* 1606. Wills comes close to arguing that his case is proved by the very absence of proof. Nevertheless, he contends that "some traces [of Gunpowder language] remain" in *Macbeth*. His chief example is the word "blow"—as in "blow up." "Words like 'train' and 'blow,'" he insists, "could no more be used 'innocently' in the aftermath of the Powder Plot than could 'sneak attack' or 'grassy knoll' in the aftermath of Pearl Harbor or John Kennedy's assassination." But the phrase "grassy knoll" is not analogous, because it was not in everyday use before November 1963. Shakespeare uses the word "blow" hundreds of times, and its several occurrences in *Macbeth* do not evoke the plot or even the image of an explosion. They clearly mean either the blowing of winds ("trees blown down") or the sort of blows struck by a fist or club ("blows and buffets").

We happen to have a detailed contemporary account by the astrologer Simon Forman of a 1611 performance of *Macbeth*. It mentions nothing suggesting the Gunpowder Plot in any way. If the play made any allusion to the most famous conspiracy of the age, it was totally lost on Forman, an alert observer, even though the plot was still a recent and vivid memory.

Wills inadvertently raises a point almost opposite to the one he intends. If *Macbeth* had been written shortly after the Gunpowder Plot, it would likely have reflected that fact in its treatment of regicide against a Scottish monarch. But it does not. The natural inference is that the play was written well before the plot, and was never even revised to include allusion to it.

Most scholars sense something wrong with the surviving text of *Macbeth*. Aside from its evident interpolations, corrupt passages, and marginal incoherence, it is shorter than any other Shakespeare play except *The Comedy of Errors*. Some surmise that the play was mutilated by its first editors. But if Mr. Shakspere was Shakespeare, he would have written *Macbeth* around 1606, ten years before he died. This would have left him plenty of time to revise and perfect it, as Shakespeare apparently revised *Hamlet* and *Lear*, judging by the differences between the quarto and Folio texts of these plays. Why would the playwright leave such a magnificent piece of work in such a sorry state? The most likely answer is that he did not live to finish it himself.

By all indications, Shakespeare's first editors respected his work profoundly. Far from mutilating *Macbeth*, they probably did their best to assemble it from the fragments Shakespeare left when he died—before the

Gunpowder Plot of 1605. Thus the problematic text of *Macbeth* is one more piece of circumstantial evidence for Oxford's authorship. If this is correct, the editors may have done for *Macbeth* what they did for *Henry VIII* and *The Two Noble Kinsmen* (and possibly other plays): they called in some posthumous assistance—in this case, Thomas Middleton, who drew in a few places on his own work (the play as we have it includes a song from Middleton's play *The Witches*). Even if Shakespeare did write *Macbeth* in 1606, it is hard to explain how he could have borrowed bits of it from a play apparently written after 1609.

As Chambers acknowledges, the later plays—those usually dated after 1603—are harder to date than the earlier ones. There are fewer quartos of them, fewer records of their performance, fewer contemporary references to them, and more textual problems. Their verse is more ragged, and they often bear signs of incompletion, a second author, or editorial additions and deletions. All this is consistent with the possibility that Shakespeare did not live to finish them.

The dating of the plays is sometimes based in part on the dates of their sources, since Shakespeare took plots, ideas, and various incidentals from contemporary books. Tom Bethell and Peter Moore have noticed that the plays use *no source dated later than 1603*. Geoffrey Bullough's eight-volume edition of Shakespeare's sources enumerates dozens printed during the 1580s and 1590s, but few after 1603 (Bullough further deems most of the latter only "possible" sources).

Why did Shakespeare suddenly cease drawing on new books? Oxford died in 1604 (when Mr. Shakspere was only forty). This would explain why Shakespeare, indebted to so many books, owes no debt to any book published after 1603.

Most scholars (though Chambers is an important exception) infer a late source for *The Tempest*. Mostly because Ariel speaks of "the still-vex'd Bermoothes," they have generally agreed that the play is based on William Strachey's account of the 1609 shipwreck of the *Sea-Venture* off the coast of Bermuda (the ship was bound for Virginia). The style of the verse places *The Tempest* among Shakespeare's late works; the play is often read as his "farewell to the theater." And the year 1609 fits nicely into the conventional dating scheme. All this, of course, would make Oxford's authorship untenable.

One immediate problem with this theory is that Strachey's letter, dated July 15, 1610, was not published until 1625—two years after the Folio, and well after Shakespeare's death, whether he was Mr. Shakspere or Oxford (Francis Bacon died in 1626). The scholars surmount this problem by positing that Shakespeare may have read the long letter in manuscript. But that is only a guess.

Despite what so many of the scholars repeat, however, Bermuda was not discovered by the crew of the *Sea-Venture*. It was well known to English and Spanish soldiers long before 1609. The island is surrounded by a vast maze of reefs, and it has seen more than six hundred shipwrecks. In 1600, Richard Hakluyt described one that had happened in 1595. We tend to forget that shipwrecks, now rare, were common occurrences in those days, as common as plane crashes are today, and the shipwreck in *The Tempest* bears no specific resemblance to that of the *Sea-Venture*. Strachey's account conspicuously lacks any magician with a daughter, or any creatures corresponding to Ariel or Caliban; these are figures from traditional tales of desert islands. The dating of *The Tempest* has to rest on better grounds than Strachey's letter.

The merits of the conventional view may be judged by Chambers' cautious speculation about the play's origin: "Sylvester Jourdan's *A Discovery of the Bermudas,* containing an account of the shipwreck of Sir George Somers in 1609, was published about October 1610, and this *or some other contemporary narrative* of Virginian colonization *probably* furnished the *hint* of the plot" (my emphasis) Why "Virginian"? Everything about the play smacks of Italy and the Mediterranean; more recent scholarship has suspected its inspiration may be a type of Italian pastoral tragicomedy, usually set on an enchanted island and dominated by a benevolent magician resembling Prospero in many details.

There is another strong reason to doubt that Strachey provided the source of *The Tempest*. Scholars have reached a general consensus about the chief sources of Shakespeare's plays; but they have failed to notice that the publication dates of these sources form a distinct pattern: most were published after 1550, the year of Oxford's birth, and all were published by 1603, the year before he died. Strachey's letter, which until 1625 existed only in manuscript, falls seven years outside this span. If we accept Strachey's letter as the source of *The Tempest,* we find ourselves left with an anomalous pattern: Shakespeare using a modern published source every year or two until 1603, then using only a single unpublished source seven years later.

If only one indisputable source of an undisputed Shakespeare play had been published after 1604, of course, Oxford would have to be ruled out as the author of any of the plays. If, on the other hand, none of the plays was based on a source published after 1603, Mr. Shakspere could not be logically excluded as the author, but it would appear odd that he should suddenly stop reading in 1604. Some of Shakespeare's sources (the classics, Chaucer, Boccaccio) were widely available before 1500. Among those published after 1500, we find one from 1516, one from 1529, two from the 1530s, three each from the 1540s and 1550s, nine from the 1560s, seven each from the 1570s, 1580s, and 1590s—and two from the year 1603 (see table on pp. 156–157).

The plays' sources, then, are concentrated within Oxford's lifetime, and cease abruptly at about the time of his death. Moreover, a half-dozen of them existed only in Italian, French, and Spanish. In two cases, the scholars believe, Shakespeare used the originals rather than English translations already available. Oxford was fluent in Italian and French, and Spanish would have been easy enough for him to read. We have no indication that Mr. Shakspere knew any foreign languages.

One of the acknowledged sources furnishes another clue. *The Winter's Tale* was taken from Robert Greene's novella *Pandosto*. The play was licensed for performance in 1610, and the conventional dating puts its composition at about that year. But Shakespeare evidently used the 1588 edition of the novella, though it had been reprinted in 1607. A minor point, but it illustrates the way the evidence never links Shakespeare's work with anything written, published, or reprinted after Oxford died.

We have seen that Oxford's death in 1604 by no means rules him out as the author of the Shakespeare works. It merely calls into question the standard method of assigning dates to the plays. Can the dating of Shakespeare's works cast doubt on Mr. Shakspere's authorship?

On New Year's Day of 1577, a play called *The Historie of Error* is recorded as having been presented at Hampton Court by a troupe of boy actors called the Children of Paul's. Since "history" often meant "story" rather than a factual chronicle of real events, this play may have been the one we know as *The Comedy of Errors.* If so, we can rule out Mr. Shakspere, then twelve years old, as the author.

But do the two titles refer to the same play? Charlton Ogburn considers it "highly likely"—and so it may be, if Oxford was Shakespeare. We have too little evidence to be sure. But this example shows that, just as Oxford can be ruled out as the author of any play written after 1604, Mr. Shakspere can be ruled out as the author of any play written much before 1590. None of the plays can be dated with precision. Yet several data suggest that Shakespeare was flourishing well before Mr. Shakspere could have established himself as a poet and playwright. The scholars are forced to belittle or ignore these troublesome data in order to preserve the orthodox dating schedule.

If any play is synonymous with Shakespeare, it is *Hamlet.* The scholars almost unanimously date the play around 1601. This suits the supposed dates of Mr. Shakspere's career and puts this masterpiece around the middle of it; the first quarto of the play, a crude one, appeared in 1603, and a much better one in 1604. So 1601 seems at first glance a reasonable guess.

Yet there is a problem. Thomas Nashe, as we have seen, makes a punning mention of "whole Hamlets, I should say handfuls, of tragical speeches" as early as 1589. The diary of William Henslowe records a performance of a play called *Hamlet* on June 11, 1594. And in 1596, Thomas Lodge mentions "the visard of the ghost which cried so miserably at the Theatre like an oyster-wife, 'Hamlet, revenge.'" So a play about Hamlet, known for its "tragical speeches" and a ghost crying for revenge, was familiar to the public long before 1601. The problem for the mainstream scholars is that the only extant play meeting this description is Shakespeare's. How could Mr. Shakspere have written it before 1589?

The scholars have solved this problem by positing an earlier play as the chief source of Shakespeare's version. They call this supposed lost play the Ur-*Hamlet,* and they assign its authorship (on evidence it would be hyperbolic to call slender) to Thomas Kyd. In this way a difficult fact has been disposed of with an ingenious inference, and the inference itself is treated as fact. Scholars have seriously debated whether the gar-

Sources of Shakespeare's Plays

YEAR	SOURCE	PLAY OR PLAYS
1516	Fabyan, *Chronicle*	*1 Henry VI*
1529	More, *Dialogue*	*1 Henry VI*
1532	Gower, *Confessio Amantis*	*Pericles*
1534	Polydore, Vergil *Anglica Historia*	*Richard III*
1542	Montemayor, *Diana Enamorada**	*Two Gentlemen*
1548	Halle, *Union of York and Lancaster*	English history plays
1549	Thomas, *History of Italy*	*Tempest*
1557	More, *Richard III*	*Richard III*
1558	Fiorentino, *Il Pecarone**	*Merchant of Venice*
1559	*Mirror for Magistrates*	English history plays
1562	Brooke, *Romeus and Juliet*	*Romeo*
1562	Secchi, *Gl'Ingannati**	*Twelfth Night*
1563	Foxe, *Martyrs* (1583 ed.?)	*1 Henry VI*
1565	Cinthio, *Hecatommithi**	*Othello, Measure*
1566	Painter, *Palace of Pleasure*	*All's Well*
1567	Golding, *Metamorphoses*	general
1567	Fenton's *Bandello**	*Much Ado*
1569	Grafton, *Chronicles*	*1 Henry VI*
1570	Foxe, *Acts and Monuments*	*Henry VIII*
1573	Gascoigne, *Supposes*	*Shrew*
1576	Belleforest, *Histoires Tragiques**	*Hamlet*
1576?	Twine, *Painful Adventures*	*Pericles*
1577	Holinshed, *Chronicles*	English history plays
1577	Eden, *History of Travel*	*Tempest*
1578	Whetstone, *Promos and Cassandra*	*Measure*
1579	North's Plutarch	*J.C., A.&C., Coriolanus, Timon*

continued

1582	Bretin's Lucian	*Timon*
1582?	*Rare Triumphs*	*Cymbeline*
1587	Holinshed, *Chronicles* (revised)	English history plays
1588	Greene, *Pandosto*	*Winter's Tale*
1590	Sidney, *Arcadia*	*King Lear, Pericles*
1590	Spenser, *Faerie Queene*	*King Lear*
1590	Lodge, *Rosalind*	*As You Like It*
1591	*Troublesome Reign of King John*	*King John*
1591	Harington's Ariosto	*Much Ado*
1592	*Second Part of Cony-Catching*	*Winter's Tale*
1594?	*King Leir*	*King Lear*
1595	Daniel, *Civil Wars*	*Henry IV*
1598	*Famous Victories*	*Henry IV, Henry V*
1598	Chapman's Homer	*Troilus*
1603	Harsnett, *Popish Impostures*	*King Lear*
1603	Florio's Montaigne	*Tempest*
1610	Strachey's Bermuda letter	*Tempest*

*Source Shakespeare is believed to have read in Italian, French, or Spanish.

bled 1603 quarto of *Hamlet* is an amalgam of Shakespeare's *Hamlet* and the Ur-*Hamlet,* and *The Reader's Encyclopedia of Shakespeare* says flatly: "In *Hamlet* Shakespeare adopts some of the devices that Kyd exploits in his famous work," adding, "From available evidence it appears that Shakespeare followed the plot of his source fairly closely."

The scholars often forget that there is no evidence that an Ur-*Hamlet* ever existed. It is only their own hypothesis, devised to save their dating system—and the more fundamental premise of Mr. Shakspere's authorship. The play as we know it appears to be based on François de Belleforest's *Histoires Tragiques,* published in France in 1576; the play requires no other source, since many of Shakespeare's plays are based on much slighter tales than Belleforest's. Lodge's reference to the play's performance at the Theatre, where the Lord Chamberlain's Men played until

1596, is a further indication that the *Hamlet* he has in mind is Shakespeare's.

Recall that Nashe had made a cryptic mention of a "Will. Monox" in *Strange News,* published in 1593. We also owe to Nashe what seems to be the earliest mention of the first part of *Henry VI,* in 1592—though this, unlike his reference to *Hamlet,* is at least consistent with the scholars' dating scheme. These mysterious allusions, coupled with Nashe's familiarity with at least one or two of the Shakespeare plays, leads us to another mysterious allusion to a similar name.

In 1591, Edmund Spenser published *The Teares of the Muses* (in a volume of poetry titled *Complaints*), a series of short poems lamenting the low state of learning and the arts in his day. Most of these poems deprecate the age in general terms. But in the third complaint, Thalia, Muse of Comedy, cries that "the comick stage" has sunk to "scoffing Scurrilitie," "scornful Follie," and "shameless ribaudrie" during, *and because of,* the recent absence of a single excellent playwright, whom she calls only "our pleasant Willy":

> And he, the man whom Nature self had made
> To mock her selfe, and truth to imitate,
> With kindly counter under mimick shade,
> Our pleasant Willy, ah! is dead of late:
> With whom all joy and jolly meriment
> Is also deaded, and in dolour drent.

Note that *all* joy and jolly merriment have departed with Willy. None of the other poems in *The Teares of the Muses* singles out an individual for praise this way, except the queen herself, and in her case no doubt is left as to her identity: "Divine Elisa, sacred Emperesse." Who can this imposing playwright be? And why is he identified only by a nickname? This coyness about naming him matches the evasive way Shakespeare is often alluded to—as when, in 1603, Henry Chettle refers to him as "Melicert" with his "honeyed muse." Chettle's 1603 poem, *England's Mourning Garment,* also implies that Melicert is ungrateful for failing to mourn the dead queen, implying some personal relation between the poet and Elizabeth: she had "graced his desert" and "to his lays open'd her royal ear."

Two stanzas later, after describing the sort of "idle wit" that has filled the void left by the absent Willy, Thalia makes it clear that his death "of late" is only a figure of speech for his current retirement from the stage, which she hopes will soon end:

But that same gentle spirit, from whose pen
Large streams of honnie and sweete nectar flowe,
Scorning the boldnes of such base-borne men,
Which dare their follies so rashlie throwe,
Doth rather choose to sit in idle cell,
Than so himselfe to mockerie to sell.

For many generations, beginning with John Dryden, it was taken for granted that "our pleasant Willy" could be nobody but Shakespeare—whom early eulogists had described as "honey-tongued," "honey-flowing," "sweet," "gentle," and "a happy imitator of nature," also associating him with the Muses. Many words in Ben Jonson's 1623 tribute to Shakespeare also seem to echo Spenser's praise of Willy.

But recent scholars have abandoned this identification because it cannot be reconciled with their own chronology of Mr. Shakspere's career. He would barely have begun to write plays by 1591, and would have had no time to make his mark, let alone retire temporarily. After all, the standard view insists that *Greene's Groatsworth* proves that Shakespeare was a mere "upstart" as of 1592. Once more, Mr. Shakspere proves too young for an apparent salute to Shakespeare.

Oxford, however, might well have retired from writing comedies during the 1580s, when he was distracted by personal scandal, quarrels, debt, military affairs, and his wife's death. Moreover, Spenser's contrast between Willy's "gentle" spirit and that of "base-borne men" also hints that Willy is a man of some social rank, which may explain why he is not more explicitly identified. By praising Oxford, Spenser might also have been bidding for his patronage; *The Teares of the Muses* is partly a complaint that the nobility is not supporting the arts as generously as it should.

Yet another dating problem arises in 1594, when a verse *roman à clef* titled *Willobie his Avisa* makes the first printed reference to "Shakespeare," who is casually mentioned as the author of *The Rape of Lucrece*.

The problem lies not in the use of Shakespeare's name, but in the poem's deliberately puzzling narrative. The story concerns a lady called Avisa and her several suitors. Avisa is apparently a code name for Queen Elizabeth; at least the censors seem to have thought so, since they eventually suppressed the popular book. One of the suitors in the tale is a youth identified as "H.W.," who is befriended by an "old player," identified as "W.S.," who not long before had been one of Avisa's suitors himself. W.S. counsels his young friend in lines that have at least four Shakespearean echoes:

> She is no saint, she is no nun;
> I think in time she may be won.

Compare these lines from *Titus Andronicus, 1 Henry VI, Richard III*, and Sonnet 41, respectively:

> She is a woman, therefore may be woo'd;
> She is a woman, therefore may be won.

> She's beautiful and therefore to be woo'd'
> She is a woman, therefore to be won.

> Was ever woman in this humour woo'd?
> Was ever woman in this humour won?

> Gentle thou art and therefore to be won,
> Beauteous thou art, therefore to be assail'd.

The scholars are divided over whether W.S. is Shakespeare; but again, the chief difficulty is their own chronology, based as it is on the assumption that Shakespeare was Mr. Shakspere of Stratford, who could hardly have progressed from "upstart crow" to "old player" by 1594. Mr. Shakspere would also have been an improbable suitor for a queen. Oxford, however, had been a favorite as well as a rumored lover of Elizabeth. He also had a link to a prominent young "H.W.," a new favorite of the aging queen: Henry Wriothesley, Earl of Southampton.

The dating problem recurs in the Sonnets, which were probably begun in the early 1590s and whose author keeps describing himself as "old." As we have seen, the usual solution is to argue that the Sonnets may be at least partly fictional, or that it was conventional for the sonneteer to adopt the persona of an aged man. I hope I have shown that such explanations are unconvincing.

We are left with several strong indications that Shakespeare was composing poems and plays earlier than the scholars can plausibly argue that Mr. Shakspere was writing. Among individual plays, as we have seen, there is reason to believe that *The Comedy of Errors, Hamlet,* and *Macbeth* (which must have been written before the Gunpowder Plot, and not, as most scholars assume, after it) existed well in advance of the dates conventionally assigned to them.

The same may be true of *As You Like It.* The play makes three veiled allusions to Marlowe, two of which imply that he is dead. The scholars usually date the play around 1600, when we first hear of it, but Marlowe was killed in May 1593. A fellow poet and playwright would naturally refer to his sudden death shortly after the event, while it was still fresh news, rather than seven years later.

In his introduction to the 1614 edition of *Bartholomew Fair,* Ben Jonson speaks of *The Spanish Tragedy* and *Titus Andronicus* as having been in vogue "these five and twenty, or thirty years." It is hard to know just how to take these words, but they may mean that *Titus* was on the boards a decade before it was entered in the Stationer's Register and sold as an anonymous quarto in 1594.

The standard dating schedule not only postulates Mr. Shakspere's authorship but is necessitated by that postulate. We can question it on many grounds, and it is important to notice a general pattern. The evidence against that dating system is not randomly distributed. It consistently points to earlier dates than conventional scholarship agrees on—never to later ones.

These earlier dates for five very diverse plays mean that all the plays could have been written by 1604, the year of Oxford's death. We have indications that *The Comedy of Errors* existed by 1577, *Titus Andronicus* by 1584, *Hamlet* by 1589, *As You Like It* by 1594, and *Macbeth* before—perhaps some years before—1605. So the dates of the plays seem to move back several years, without doing violence to their apparent sequence; *Errors* and *Titus,* judging by their style and quality, are early plays, *Hamlet* and *As You Like It* belong to the poet's urbane maturity, and *Macbeth* is written in his concentrated "late" style, when his verse achieved a unique freedom and density.

This would put the plays within Oxford's life span. It would do so even without assuming his authorship. It also accords with signs that the author later known as Shakespeare was flourishing by the 1580s (a period for which we have few records about English drama) and could be described as "old" by the early 1590s.

Chapter 7 ∼ↄ

Oxford's Milieu

The Shakespeare plays point to Oxford in two ways. First, they are written from the vantage point of a nobleman. Second, they echo many details of Oxford's own life. In neither respect do they suggest Mr. Shakspere at all. As the son of a small-town tradesman, he would have had a profoundly different social perspective, and his life offers few if any notable parallels with the plays.

Nearly all of Shakespeare's heroes belong to the upper and ruling classes. Of course, this was true of many Elizabethan plays, but not as many as most readers may assume. Some of the most popular plays of the age feature common people—not only comedies like *The Shoemaker's Holiday* and *Gammer Gurton's Needle,* but such tragedies as *A Woman Killed with Kindness* and *Arden of Faversham.* Moreover, Shakespeare shows the ruling classes with the insight born of intimacy. He is keenly aware of their manners, their feelings, their special problems, their temptations, and their habits of thought. We never feel that he is guessing or speculating about their inner lives from afar.

One way to account for this is to ascribe a convenient "universality" to him. He has rare empathy for the whole human race, including kings. Nothing human is alien to him.

The trouble with this explanation is that it is not true. Shakespeare typically makes his common characters buffoons. He presents them in an entirely different way from his noble characters. They are usually illiterate and illogical. They speak in malapropisms and mangled classical references. Their inmost thoughts are preposterous. My point is not that he is hostile to them, but that he sees them from outside—and above. He looks *down* on them, however benignly and affectionately. They are inherently ridiculous. When they form a mob, they are also dangerous, but still ridiculous. When a yokel rebel says, "The first thing we do, let's kill all the lawyers," he is not speaking for Shakespeare, as most people who quote his famous line assume, but revealing his own comic unfitness to form a new social order. Shakespeare is clearly *pro-lawyer.*

More often Shakespeare's common characters are harmless, even likable butts: Bottom, Launce, Launcelot Gobbo, Dogberry, Pompey, Mistress Quickly, Stephano and Trinculo, Sampson and Gregory, Ancient Pistol, Macbeth's Porter, Juliet's Nurse, Hamlet's gravediggers, and assorted nameless clowns and citizens. Sometimes they are allowed shrewd comments on their betters; a few are given their own humble dignity. But as a class, their chief distinguishing trait is that they *talk funny.* They are victims of a language they cannot master. Their own native tongue continually betrays them. Shakespeare gives them a monopoly on bad English.

We may, if we like, accuse Shakespeare of snobbery. The point is that he shows by his consistent distribution of linguistic blunders that he is not one of the common people himself. He shows verbal ineptitude as a class trait, like a white man making fun of black speech.

This suggests that the playwright himself was in all likelihood not one of the common people. We see members of our own class as individuals, and we barely notice the traits—notably speech habits and accents—we share with them. But we see members of other classes primarily as types, marked by the externalities that make them conspicuously different from ourselves.

Shakespeare is no exception to this rule. He portrays the nobility and gentry as individuals, because he is one of them; he portrays the lower classes as types, even as stereotypes, because he is remote from them. The inferior nature of the common people is not asserted but assumed. Shakespeare feels no hostility toward ordinary folk, any more than most whites felt hostility toward the blacks who were made subjects of mirth in *Amos 'n Andy.* He merely takes his own superiority as a given, not something to be proved. And though few other writers could approach him in endowing every character with a special voice, he does not distinguish very sharply among his common characters. In his imagination, they form a single mass, with a collective voice.

As Bernard Shaw and many other modern egalitarians have noticed, speech snobbery can be so profound as to be almost unconscious most of the time.* But the author reveals his own class implicitly by accepting distinctive class speech forms as departures from a tacit norm, defined by orthographic convention. Had *Huckleberry Finn* been published anonymously, we would still catch on that the author, whoever he was, did not talk like Huck or Jim.

Speech patterns are one of the chief ways in which we type people as members of a class. Stereotypes express our sense of the comic predictability of those we perceive as "others." If Shakespeare laughs at the illiterate speech of the lower classes, he also lampoons the affected speech of upwardly mobile commoners like Malvolio and Osric who, in trying to talk like their betters, overdo it to comic effect. They are fancy without finesse. Their creator was not, we may infer, of their element.

---

* Such snobbery is evident in the pages of Victorian fiction, which, as Hugh Kenner writes in *The Mechanic Muse,*

> had worked out elaborate codes for exhibiting what always preoccupies a British reader, the social class of the characters. The principle is easily stated. You commence with a "neutral," literate idiom, called the narrator's. That is the idiom the writer shares with the reader. In itself it is not noticeable at all, but other idioms become visible by deviating from it. Deviations of diction and syntax are common, also deviations of rhythm. Any of these signals the presence of a "character," and repeating the pattern makes the character recognizable. To indicate oddities of pronunciation you deviate systematically from standard spelling: an elementary instance is the Cockney's dropped aitch.

Not that Shakespeare lacks all sympathy for common people. Far from it. It is instructive to contrast his treatment of Dogberry with Dickens' portrait of Mr. Bumble. Both characters are ignorant and self-important minor officials. For all Dogberry's absurdities, Shakespeare views him benignly as a harmless little prop of social order. Dickens, who knew what it was to be at the mercy of such officials, portrays Bumble as he might be seen from below: as a petty tyrant, fully capable of hurting innocent people.

Shakespeare's aristocratic perspective is most evident when he shows his ideal of the common man: the faithful servant who sacrifices himself for his master. We may think of the old Adam in *As You Like It,* whose loyalty evokes Orlando's warmest praise:

> O good old man, how well in thee appears
> The constant service of the antique world,
> When service sweat for duty, not for meed!
> Thou art not for the fashion of these times,
> Where none will sweat but for promotion,
> And having that do choke their service up
> Even with the having.

Timon of Athens, cursing the entire human race, is forced to make a single exception for his servant Flavius, who has selflessly followed him into the wilderness to comfort him. *King Lear* offers several examples of the type: Lear's Fool, Kent (disguised as a servant), even Goneril's Oswald, an evil functionary whose dying devotion to his mistress troubled Dr. Johnson's sense of fitness: "I know not well why Shakespeare gives to Oswald, who is a mere factor of wickedness, so much fidelity."

Few scenes are more moving than the one in *Lear* in which Cornwall's servant dies while trying to prevent his master from blinding Gloucester:

> Hold your hand, my lord.
> I have serv'd you ever since I was a child,
> But better service have I never done you
> Than now to bid you hold.

Note the tone of duty even in the act of defiance. Even in this moment of extremity, the rightness of the social order remains unquestioned. There is no suggestion that the servant is released from his bond by the master's depravity; instead, he is pushed to a final act of self-sacrifice. This is the feudal ideal par excellence. Burke would understand; Tom Paine would violently disapprove.

Sometimes, even when the common people form a mob, Shakespeare allows them to express justified grievances. If Shakespeare ever takes the side of plebeians against patricians, it is in *Coriolanus,* whose hero is guilty of insufferable pride and insolence in denying that anything in his own nature is "common"; the play may serve as a test case of the playwright's class attitude. Yet even here the common people remain beneath the dignity of tragedy, and Coriolanus alone, repellent as he may be even to Shakespeare, merits tragic attention. In Shakespeare the tragic hero may be, morally speaking, the worst man in the play; but his social rank is essential to his tragic stature. Even the warrior Othello, a racial alien in Venice, can boast of possessing the royal blood of his own country.

Whitman was right to detect in Shakespeare basic prejudices "non-acceptable to Democracy." In Shakespeare, he complained, "common blood is but wash"—the hero is always of high lineage. He called such works "poisonous to the idea of the pride and dignity of the common people, the life-blood of Democracy." This aristocratic prejudice is so deeply ingrained that noble blood asserts itself even in characters who do not realize they have it. The princess Perdita in *The Winter's Tale* is a case in point. Raised by a shepherd and unaware that he is not her real father, she still talks and behaves according to her "nature"—so much so that she enchants a prince who happens to meet her. Frank Kermode has noted "the magic of nobility" that runs through Shakespeare's romances; but it is not confined to the romances. It amounts to a patrician mystique that is taken for granted in all the plays.

Shakespeare believes that the common people have a right to be well ruled; he clearly does not believe that they have any right, or capacity, to rule themselves, and their occasional attempts to do so are always disastrous. He regards rebellion as downright evil; when it becomes necessary, it must be undertaken by the nobility themselves, as in *Richard III* or *Macbeth*. Not that he is uncritical of the ruling classes. When they fail—and many of the plays are studies of their failures—there is no remedy, certainly not in democratic reform (a concept that never even occurs to Shakespeare). The tragic's hero's stature means that his faults, his crimes, and his fall reverberate through the whole social order. Lesser people perish with him: "Some innocents 'scape not the thunderbolt."

A passage of *Sir Thomas More,* widely accepted as Shakespeare's, in which More quiets a rebellious mob, expresses the same social conservatism we find elsewhere in the plays: in Ulysses' speech on degree in *Troilus,* in the speeches of Menenius and Marcius to the mob in the first scene of *Coriolanus,* in the speeches of Rosencrantz and Guildenstern to Claudius in the prayer scene of *Hamlet.* More warns the rebels that their success would mean their destruction; if the likes of *you* achieved power, he tells them sternly.

> You had taught
> How insolence and strong hand should prevail,
> How order should be quell'd, and by this pattern
> Not one of you should live an aged man,
> For other ruffians, as their fancies wrought,
> With self-same hand, self reasons, and self right,
> Would shark on you, and men like ravenous fishes
> Would feed on one another.

Scolding them for the sin of disobedience to lawful authority, More adds:

> Why, even your hurly
> Cannot proceed but by obedience.
> What rebel captain,
> As mutinies are incident, by his name
> Can still the rout? Who will obey a traitor?
> Or how can well that proclamation sound
> When there is no addition but a rebel
> To qualify a rebel?

Such words express the angle of vision and habit of authority of the feudal nobility. The first duty of common people is obedience to their betters. Mr. Shakspere, the small-town burgher, might well have agreed with these sentiments, but they are more typical of Oxford's class. Shakespeare also believes that the nobility has duties to the common people, and that all classes are bound together by reciprocal obligations. Moreover, he considers it fatal arrogance for the highest to forget their human kinship with the lowest. Time and again his tragic heroes learn the hard way that they are neither gods nor angels, but belong to the same natural order as ordinary people. This is not democracy, however; it is feudalism.

Shakespeare's philosophy is thoroughly feudal. He puts a premium on fealty and what used to be called "knowing one's place." He is keenly interested in all the technicalities of "place," and L.G. Pine, an authority on heraldry, remarks: "Most of the notable English writers are at sea on the subject of heraldry, though William Shakespeare is a great exception." His villains are often social malcontents who resent their assigned station in the hierarchical system of society: "Take but degree away, untune that string,/And hark, what discord follows!" The great untuners are malicious men like Macbeth, Richard III, Henry IV, Claudius, Edmund, Cassius, and Iago. Shakespeare has some sympathy for the alienated, and he gives them their say by way of explaining their motives, sometimes so eloquently that we may wonder whose side he is on (as with Shylock). But he never doubts that the order is essentially good, and that its disturbance—by rebellious, subversive, or ambitious subjects or by tyrannous, weak, or abdicating rulers—is bad. Cassius is bad in one way, but Antony's rabble-rousing is also, by his own admission, "mischief." Not the least part of Shakespeare's greatness lies in our sense that he always sees the commonwealth whole, and never becomes a mere partisan of any of his contending characters. He may even allow evil to consume innocence; but he never allows usurpation to succeed indefinitely.

In Shakespeare's most serene tragedy, the wonderfully ripe and relaxed *Antony and Cleopatra,* we find, manifest but unassertive, his sensual conservatism and his aversion to the purposeful ambition of Octavius. Shakespeare understands fully that Octavius is bound to defeat the lovers, and he accepts this. But the lovers are still more admirable to him than their victorious opponent. They have a touch of the infinite that even Octavius recognizes and honors. They represent the careless, even reckless greatness of a passing order; he represents only the future. Antony announces his generous but self-destructive philosophy in the opening scene: "There's beggary in the love that can be reckoned."

Here there is no doubt which side Shakespeare is on. For him as for Burke, an age of chivalry is yielding to one of calculators, sophists, and economists. He is thinking not of Rome but of England, where upstarts, Puritans, and businessmen are taking over, and the old nobility may soon be extinct. The play may be read as a kind of elegy for Oxford's class and the people it could produce. It is not an argument; it does not aim to convert anyone. It merely displays the splendor of the lovers' "sovereignty of nature" and lets it speak for itself. Yet it also recognizes the practical superiority of Octavius, whose virtues suit the time better than theirs.

Shakespeare's habitual language is the idiom of the courtier, not the peasant or burgher. It is the language we find in Oxford's letters, but not in Mr. Shakspere's documents: *majesty, sovereignty, lords, ladies, reign, rule, degree, condition, place, highness, greatness, name, rank, title, claims, rights, interest, nobility, embassies, ambassadors, baseness, honour, dishonour, attainder, chivalry, dignity, command, countermand, decree, obedience, duty, faithfulness, bonds, privilege, prerogative, tribute, salutation, peers, prelates, heralds, pursuivants, courts, courtiers, courtesans, masters, lieges, liegemen, followers, knights, squires, chamberlains, statists, gentlemen, scholars, pensioners, subjects, attendants, vassals, servants, servitors, sentries, guards, stewards, posts, messengers, grooms, fools, pages, liveries, castles, palaces, presence, monarchy, empire, supremacy, thrones, sennets, drums, trumpets, crowns, coronets, diadems, robes, gowns, canopies, ceremony, coronations, pomp, processions, rites, balm, anointings, obsequies, realm, dominion, commonwealth, state, government, sway, kingdom, council, counsellor, possession, dispossession, seals, signets, orbs, scepters, armour, mail, helmets, visors, shields, bucklers, champions, banners, devices, standards, coursers, lances, rapiers, falchions, foils, poniards, halberds, truncheons, carriages, gages, gauntlets, leisure, sport, falcons, tennis, royalty, authority, tyranny, usurpations, deposings, elections, ambition, upstarts, preferment, advancement, enfranchisement, employment, promotion, consent, permission, allowance, rising, falling, conspiracy, faction, offices, commissions, policy, thralldom, loyalty, fealty, constancy, fickleness, oaths, vows, swearing, promises, perjury, treason, flattery, fawning, time-servers, insults, suits, entreaties, grace, disgrace, law, legitimation, patrimony, inheritance, succession, dowry, precedent, reversion, estate, lands, rents, revenues, levies, proportions, moieties, monopolies, parks, blood, birth, primogeniture, ancestry, pedigree, descent, progenitors, predecessors, forefathers, posterity, bastardy, houses, lineage, kinship, alliance, league, treaties, compacts, contracts, covenants, amity, enmity, adversaries, rivals, competitors, confederates, pride, humility, contentment, malcontents, insolence, revolt, rebellion, defiance, parley, truce, commendation, report, reputation, fame, praise, defamation, proclamation, blazon, publishing, slander, scandal, rumour, desert, merit, worthiness, manners, courtesy, challenges, power, might, puissance, pardon, clemency, interdiction, imprisonment, banishment, ransom, execution, wealth, treasure, jewels, ornament, tombs, monuments,* and so on. (Shakespeare's feudal preoccupation with kinship and lineage is wittily caught in Kenneth Tynan's capsule parody of the history plays: "And dost thou now presume, base Leamington,/To scorn thy brother's cousin's eldest son?")

This is very much Shakespeare's language, and he constantly puts it into the mouths of his chief characters. We never feel that these words, as he uses them, are being parroted or have been conned from a dictionary or from observation. They have real and personal associations for their author. They are not abstractions for him; they are the integers of his own experience, and they summon up for him the "swarms of inarticulate feeling" T.S. Eliot spoke of as the characteristic of Shakespeare's supremely articulate language. He feels strongly about the world of the courtier, whether he is idealizing it, laughing at it, or moralizing against it. It is his element. Even when he shows us life in a forest or on a desert island, it is *court* life in the forest or on the island. It is striking how many of the later plays are about men angrily tearing themselves away, or being violently driven, from court and city.

There is an undeniable sense in which Shakespeare is a "universal" author. The whole world loves him, and he himself tells us that "one touch of nature makes the whole world kin." The Folio calls him "a happy imitator of nature"; Dr. Johnson said apropos of him that "nothing can please many, and please long, but just representations of general nature." But the vehicles of Shakespeare's universality deserve closer inspection. He clearly writes in the language of a particular time, place, and class; and that highly local language—feudal, aristocratic, courtly— is the medium through which he achieves his own specific kind of universality.

Oxford was a playwright himself, and Francis Meres, writing in 1598, ranks him "among the best for comedy" among the Elizabethans. But no play bearing his name survives, and Meres does not cite a single title of an Oxfordian comedy.

Oxford was also a leading patron of the London theater, and we have already seen several of his associations in that world. He employed the playwrights John Lyly and Anthony Munday as his personal secretaries, both of whom dedicated works to him. "The original copy of the manuscript *Sir Thomas More* (*c.* 1596) was written by Munday," writes F.E. Halliday, "but that he was the author is another matter." The play is widely accepted as Shakespeare's, at least in part; the passage quoted above sufficiently explains why. We also have records of Oxford's friendship with the writers Nashe and Greene. Yet no link has been found between the leading patron and the leading playwright of the age, though it would seem inevitable that their paths should cross.

We have seen that Oxford was well acquainted with Edmund Spenser, who addresses a warm salute to him in one of the 1590 prefatory sonnets to *The Faerie Queene,* calling him "most dear" to the Muses. And of course Spenser, in *Teares of the Muses,* pays tribute to a playwright, "our pleasant Willy," whose absence Thalia, the Muse of comedy, weepingly laments. Since Spenser praises "Willy" in the very terms that soon became standard in praising Shakespeare ("the man whom nature self had made/To mock her self, and truth to imitate . . ."), we may reasonably suspect that later eulogists were taking their cue from Spenser.

The orthodox scholars, realizing that Willy can hardly be Mr. Shakspere, have been unable to explain who, in that case, Willy could have been; some are driven to argue that Willy was probably only a fictional character. The denial that Willy was Shakespeare stands in amusing contrast to the scholars' adamant insistence that the "upstart crow" of *Greene's Groatsworth* could have been nobody else. In neither case can we claim absolute certainty, but the terms in which Spenser describes Willy, unlike the *Groatsworth* invective, are at least consistent with the way others spoke of Shakespeare.

Moreover, there appears to be another bridge connecting Spenser, Oxford, and Shakespeare: one of the commendatory poems in *The Faerie Queene,* signed "Ignoto" ("Anonymous"). It reads:

To look upon a work of rare device
The which a workman setteth out to view,
And not to yield it the deserved price
That unto such a workmanship is due,
   Doth either prove the judgment to be naught,
   Or else doth show a mind with envy fraught.

To labour to commend a piece of work
Which no man goes about to discommend,
Would raise a jealous doubt that there did lurk
Some secret doubt whereto the praise did tend.
   For when men know the goodness of the wine,
   'Tis needless for the host to have a sign.

Thus then, to show much judgment to be such
As can discern of colours black and white,
As all's to free my mind from envy's touch,
That never gives to any man his right,
   I here pronounce this workmanship is such
   As that no pen can set it forth too much.

And thus I hang a garland at the door,
Not for to show the goodness of the ware,
But such hath been the custom heretofore,
And customs very hardly broken are.
   And when your taste shall tell you this is true,
   Then look you give your host his utmost due.

Ogburn and others remark that this sounds very much like Shakespeare, and Ben Jonson paraphrases it, with deliberate echoes, in the opening lines of his 1623 Folio eulogy:

> To draw no envy (Shakespeare) on thy name,
>   Am I thus ample to thy book and fame.
> While I confess thy writing to be such
>   As neither Man nor Muse can praise too much.
> 'Tis true, and all men's suffrage. But these ways
>   Were not the paths I meant unto thy praise:
> For seeliest Ignorance on these may light,
>   Which, when it sounds at best, but echoes right;
> Or blind affection, which doth ne'er advance
>   The truth, but gropes, and urgeth all by chance;
> Or crafty malice might pretend this praise,
>   And think to ruin, where it seem'd to raise.
> These are as some infamous bawd or whore
>   Should praise a matron. What could hurt her more?
> But thou are proof against them, and indeed
>   Above th'ill fortune of them, or the need
> I therefore will begin. . . .

Jonson's sixteen-line exordium is little more than a paraphrase of the rest of Ignoto's poem, which likewise treats of the way "envy" can creep into seeming praise. Again, the early date—1590—deters modern scholars from recognizing Shakespeare as the author. But Jonson's readers, if they were alert to such clues, might find them in the introductory matter of *The Faerie Queene,* an immensely popular poem that any purchaser of the First Folio could have been expected to own. Some scholars are willing to grant that Aetion, in Spenser's 1595 poem *Colin Clouts Come Home Again,* is Shakespeare:

> And there, though last not least, is Aetion;
> A gentler shepheard may no where be found,
> Whose Muse, full of high thoughts invention,
> Doth like himselfe heroically sound.

Spenser's dedicatory sonnet to Oxford in *The Faerie Queene* is of further interest, especially in its reference to the Muses as the "Heliconian imps":

Receive, most noble Lord, in gentle gree
    The unripe fruit of an unready wit,
    Which by thy countenaunce doth crave to bee
    Defended from foule Envies poisnous bit:
Which so to doe may thee right well befit,
    Sith th'antique glory of thine auncestry
    Under a shady vele is therein writ,
    And eke thine owne long living memory,
Succeeding them in true nobility;
    And also for the love which thou doest beare
    To th'Heliconian ymps, and they to thee,
    They unto thee, and thou to them, most deare.
Deare as thou art unto thy selfe, so love
That loves and honours thee, as doth behove.

Coming from Spenser, this is high praise: Oxford, like Willy, is a darling of the Muses. This sonnet is echoed in a tribute to Shakespeare, published in 1614, by one "C.B.," often identified as Christopher Brooke, who puts these lines into the mouth of the ghost of Richard III:

To him that imp'd my fame with Clio's quill;
Whose magic rais'd me from Oblivion's den;
That writ my story on the Muses' hill,
And with my actions dignifi'd his pen;
He that from Helicon sends many a rill,
Whose nectar veins are drunk by thirsty men;
Crown'd be his style with fame, his head with bays,
And none detract, but gratulate his praise.

We have seen that many tributes to Shakespeare sound like Spenser's praise of Willy, and that Ben Jonson's praise of Shakespeare sounds like Ignoto's praise of Spenser. Here we find a tribute to Shakespeare that sounds like Spenser's praise of Oxford.

What shall we make of all this? Possibly that many of those who praised Shakespeare used Spenserian allusions to tip off their sophisticated readers that they were really speaking of Oxford.

The orthodox scholars dismiss any seeming allusion to Shakespeare that cannot be assimilated to their dating system or that challenges their conviction that Shakespeare was Mr. Shakspere. And so Shakespeare comes to seem oddly isolated from his contemporaries. The man Jonson hailed as the "Soul of the Age" appears to have been something of a recluse.

But if Oxford is the subject of these allusions, we need not assume that there was any great conspiracy to conceal Shakespeare's identity. It was probably one of those open secrets that elites share among themselves and even discuss publicly in coded language.

Several other men whose names are familiar to students of Shakespeare touch Oxford, as relatives, acquaintances, and influences. In fact, most of them appear to have been closer to Oxford than to Shakespeare, even if we accept the traditional identification of Shakespeare with Mr. Shakspere.

First among these is Henry Howard, Earl of Surrey (1517–1547). Surrey was Oxford's uncle by marriage, though as a result of enmities incurred in court intrigues, he was beheaded by Henry VIII in his thirtieth year, three years before Oxford's birth. In his short, turbulent life, Surrey established himself with Sir Thomas Wyatt as one of the two leading court poets of Tudor England. He observed the nobleman's code by publishing none of his verse except a brief tribute to Wyatt; the rest of his poetry appeared in print posthumously.

Surrey was the victim of bad luck. He ran afoul of Henry at the very end of that irritable monarch's life; had the king died a few days sooner, Surrey might have lived. The reason for his execution remains somewhat clouded, but it occurred only a week before Henry's death.

In his reputation as a poet, too, Surrey was somewhat unlucky. Both of his literary innovations are chiefly associated not with him, but with the poet who became their supreme master. He and Sir Thomas Wyatt originated the verse form we know as the Shakespearean sonnet, consisting of three quatrains whose alternate lines rhyme and closing with a final couplet. He also introduced blank verse into English. Shakespeare echoes Surrey's poetic version of Psalm 8 (a free rendition rather than a translation) in *Hamlet*.

Surrey adopted blank verse first in his translation of the second and fourth books of the *Aeneid*. As it happens, these are also the books Shakespeare cites most often, especially the second, in which Aeneas recounts for Dido the fall of Troy. For Shakespeare, this event, as described by Virgil, is the archetype of tragedy, and he refers to it over and over again. It forms the setting of *Troilus and Cressida;* a long passage in *Lucrece* recounts the terrible story as a parallel with Lucrece's rape; he refers many times to the fate of Priam and his sons; and the plays make frequent brief references to Troy's destruction and the emotions it stirs. Shakespeare often mentions Aeneas' tale to Dido, the Trojan horse and Sinon's cunning, the slaughter of Priam and his sons, Hecuba's grief, Aeneas carrying his father Anchises from the burning city. Of the characters Virgil mentions by name in Book Two, Shakespeare mentions Achilles, Aeneas, Ajax, Anchises, Andromache, Ascanius, Calchas, Cassandra, Diomedes, Hector, Hecuba, Helen, Laertes, Menelaus, Paris, Priam, Pyrrhus, Sinon, Thersites, and Ulysses; the only characters in the story he never refers to are Astyanax, Creusa, and Laocoon.

Troy is Shakespeare's favorite emblem of suffering, loss, and unbearable grief, especially the everlasting grief of surviving witnesses—chief among whom is Aeneas. In September 1572, we find Oxford writing to his father-in-law Lord Burghley about meeting refugees from Paris who described to him the recent St. Bartholomew's Eve massacre, in which "a number of noble men and worthy gentlemen" were murdered, "on whose *tragedies* we have a number of French *Aeneases* in this city, that tell of their own *overthrows* with *tears falling from their eyes, a piteous* thing to hear" (my emphasis). One of his poems also refers to "Paris, Priam's son."

Shakespeare makes eight references to Aeneas (who is also a character in *Troilus*). Most of these are to the passage of the *Aeneid* in which he tells Dido the calamities he witnessed in Troy's final hours. In his letter, Oxford likewise invokes Aeneas less as hero than as a witness to Troy's "tragedies." In *Hamlet,* the prince asks the Player King, one of the "tragedians of the city" newly arrived at court, to recite "Aeneas' tale to Dido, and thereabout of it especially where he speaks of Priam's slaughter." The Player King delivers Aeneas' speech with heartfelt passion, whereupon Hamlet and Polonius remark on the "tears in his eyes." Shakespeare's brief mentions of Aeneas in *Titus Andronicus, 2 Henry VI,* and *Julius Caesar* all derive from the same "tale to Dido." (The proximity of "overthrows" and "piteous" in Oxford's sentence also recalls Romeo and Juliet's "piteous overthrows.")

Shakespeare's favorite classical poet is not Virgil, however, but Ovid. It is a commonplace of scholarship that he draws on the *Metamorphoses* in both the original Latin and Arthur Golding's translation. *Venus and Adonis* is drawn from the *Metamorphoses, The Rape of Lucrece* from Ovid's *Fasti.* Again we find a strong link to Oxford: Golding, who lived from about 1536 to 1605, was the half-brother of Margaret Golding, Oxford's mother. A distinguished scholar and Calvinist theologian, he seems to have been employed by Burghley, to whom he dedicated one of his books. He served as Oxford's tutor and was extremely fond of him, dedicating several books to him. Oxford's known poems abound in classical references, most of them to stories from Ovid, whom he knew in part, no doubt, via Golding.

For his part, Burghley, Oxford's guardian and father-in-law, appears prominently in *Hamlet,* one of Shakespeare's greatest plays. There is little doubt that he is the model for Polonius, as we shall see in detail in chapter 8.

More than one critic has sensed an obscure allusiveness in *Hamlet.* T.S. Eliot judged the whole play "most certainly an artistic failure," mostly because, as he thought, Shakespeare had not disciplined the emotion he put into it. We need not agree with his judgment to see his point. Part of the richness of *Hamlet* lies in the sense that its characters are somehow larger than their roles in the story. The playwright may reveal himself most in passages that seem dramatically gratuitous: Hamlet is captured by pirates in the English Channel, just as Oxford was on his return from his European tour. Claudius may be based on Elizabeth's sometime suitor, the Earl of Leicester, who was rumored (probably falsely) to have poisoned his wife in order to free himself to marry the queen. Leicester also blocked Oxford's receipt of his full inheritance of entailed lands, somewhat as Claudius prevents Hamlet's succession.

Oxford was also well acquainted with Shakespeare's supposed patron, Henry Wriothesley, third Earl of Southampton. Like Oxford, Southampton lost his father early in life and became a ward of Burghley. When Southampton reached his late teens, Burghley exercised his prerogative of choosing a bride for the handsome and eligible youth committed to his care. Burghley selected his own flesh and blood for the match: Elizabeth Vere, his granddaughter and Oxford's daughter. When Southampton resisted the match, Burghley finally exercised another prerogative of his position: he fined Southampton a stiff 5,000 pounds.

It is hard to doubt that this doomed match forms the story behind the first seventeen of Shakespeare's Sonnets, which prod a fair youth to marry, reproduce, and carry on his "house."

Shakespeare's two long poems, *Venus and Adonis* and *The Rape of Lucrece,* are dedicated to Southampton. *Venus* repeats the theme of the early Sonnets when Venus lectures Adonis on his duty to beget, as he himself was begotten; the story is from Ovid, but the theme is the poet's own. (Ovid's comically lust-crazed Venus is not much concerned with posterity.)

After Oxford's death, his son Henry and Southampton became friends and political allies; a woodcut from the period portrays them together on horseback, with their coats of arms and mottoes. Nobody has ever succeeded in establishing any connection between Mr. Shakspere and Southampton; the presumption that they knew each other at all is an inference from the dedications to the two long poems.

Likewise, we have no grounds for believing that Mr. Shakspere knew the "incomparable pair of brethren," the Herbert brothers—William and Philip, earls of Pembroke and Montgomery—to whom the 1623 Folio is dedicated; we have only the word of the dedication itself that these patrons showed him "favor" while he lived. But Oxford knew both men well. William Herbert, later Pembroke, had in 1597 been proposed as a match for Oxford's daughter Bridget; Oxford wrote warmly of the lad to Burghley, but the marriage never came off. Philip Herbert, who was to be Montgomery, did marry Oxford's daughter Susan in 1605, a year after Oxford's death.

In short, Oxford seems to have known everyone Mr. Shakspere *should* have known if he was Shakespeare. But in London Mr. Shakspere can be definitely linked only to a handful of actors and shareholders in the theater; to his one-time landlord and his family; and to four others in-volved in a minor dispute in 1596. We can name more of his acquain-tances in his hometown than in the teeming city where, during his lifetime, the name of William Shakespeare was honored and where, in 1616, the death of William Shakspere was ignored.

Connections to the Plays

*M*r. Shakspere's biographers, as we have seen, have been unable to find convincing traces of his life and person ality in the plays. However, Oxfordians from Looney to the Ogburns have remarked on the many parallels between Oxford's life and Shakespeare's plays. And the plays do seem to reflect Oxford's varied experience.

Shortly after his father's death, Oxford's half-sister Katherine, his father's daughter by his first marriage, and her husband Edward, the third Baron Windsor, tried to deprive him of his title, arguing (unsuccessfully) that his parents' marriage was legally invalid. If the court had accepted their argument, they would have received Oxford's enormous inheritance, and the noble Oxford would have become, technically, a bastard. In his society, this would have meant disgrace, poverty, and ruin.

A similar situation arises in *King John*. In the play's first scene, the king has to hear a suit over the legitimacy of Philip Faulconbridge, the elder son of the widow of Sir Robert Faulconbridge, brought by her younger son, who wants the lands accruing to his father's heir under the feudal principle of primogeniture. It turns out that Philip is indeed a bastard, conceived during Sir Robert's two-year absence from home, his real father being Richard the Lion-Hearted. Philip, identified in the text as "Bastard," not only accepts this verdict but rejoices in it. He says proudly that he would rather have Richard's blood than Robert's lands. And he mockingly congratulates his half-brother on his victory: "Your face hath got five hundred pound a year,/Yet sell your face for fivepence and 'tis dear." He even congratulates himself on his bastardy, since it is of Richard's blood:

> Brother by th' mother's side, give me your hand.
> My father gave me honor, yours gave land.
> Now blessed be the hour, by night or day,
> When I was got, Sir Robert was away.

And, "Near or far off, well won is still well shot,/And I am I, howe'er I was begot."

This belief in the superiority of noble and royal blood persists through Shakespeare's plays. For Shakespeare, it seems to be a matter of nature rather than mere arbitrary custom.

The Bastard is one of those robust Shakespearean creations—like Berowne, Mercutio, Benedick, Beatrice, Rosalind, Falstaff, Hamlet, Cleopatra, even Richard III—who seem to speak with so much of the humor and energy of their creator that in them we sometimes feel we are hearing Shakespeare's own voice. They have in common an enormous capacity for delight, spanning the sensuous and the ironical. Nothing is lost on them, and they face life with a kind of comprehensive wit. These characters are given great indulgence by their creator, who allows them unusual opportunities for expression, such as in Shakespeare's hallmark long soliloquies and set speeches.

When Oxford accused Howard, Southwell, and Arundel of conspiring with the Spanish against Elizabeth, they accused him in turn of being a drunkard and of having said he hated the queen for playfully calling him a "bastard." This may have been a lie; but even so, it suggests that the accusers knew the challenge to his legitimacy to be a sore point with Oxford, and that the queen was known to have teased him about it. The Bastard can be seen as expressing not only Oxford's contempt for those who tried to deprive him of his title, but also his joy in what he is in himself, apart from his title, his lands, his wealth—even apart from the question of his technical legitimacy.

Oxford's exposure of the three traitors has its own parallel in Act II, Scene 2, of *Henry V.* Just before embarking for France, Henry plays a feline game with the unsuspecting trio of Scroop, Cambridge, and Grey, who do not realize that he has learned of their plot to kill him for the French. He orders the release of a drunken man who has been arrested for railing against him. When the three plotters urge the sharpest penalty, Henry, pleading the man's remorse, says, "O let us yet be merciful!" He then springs his trap: with sudden fury, he hands his betrayers papers proving their conspiracy. When they beg for clemency, he tells them coldly that they stand condemned by their own counsel.

The scene is not strictly necessary to the flow of the action (Laurence Olivier cut it from his version), and fifty lines are given to Henry's diatribe against Scroop, his sometime intimate ("that knew'st the very bottom of my soul"), whose betrayal is far worse than that of Cambridge and Grey.

> Show men dutiful?
> Why, so didst thou. Seem they grave and learned?
> Why, so didst thou. Come they of noble family?
> Why, so didst thou. Seem they religious?
> Why, so didst thou.
> I will weep for thee,
> For this revolt of thine, methinks, is like
> Another fall of man.

Henry's long, unbroken speech is far longer than any other denunciation in Shakespeare. If Oxford wrote it, it would bear an obvious personal meaning, transferred unqualified from his life to the play. It might be a description of Howard, whom Oxford was reported to have called "the worst villain that lived in this earth" and his family "the most treacherous race under heaven." (Oxford probably also blamed Howard for planting his tortured but baseless doubts of his wife's fidelity just before his return from Paris in 1576.) In the play's historical source, Holinshed's *Chronicles,* Henry denounces the three traitors, but does not single out Scroop.

Oxford traveled for more than a year on the Continent, and his extravagant expenditures there forced him to sell several estates. Rosalind seems to glance at this in *As You Like It* when she tells Jacques: "A traveller! By my faith, you have great reason to be sad. I fear you have sold your own lands to see other men's. Then to have seen much and to have nothing is to have rich eyes and poor hands." A moment later she teases him, doubting that he has ever really been in a "gundello" (gondola); she knows something about Venice. So does her creator, who sets two plays there and refers to it in five others. We saw earlier that Shakespeare had close knowledge and experience of Italy. Of the dozen plays he sets in Italy, most are placed in cities Oxford visited: Venice (where he made his longest stay), Verona, Padua, Mantua, Siena, Palermo. *All's Well* refers to the broils between the Lombards and the Sienese of about 1575—the very time when Oxford was passing through Siena. It seems unlikely that Mr. Shakspere would have known or cared about this strife enough to mention it a generation later. Oxford wrote home to Burghley that he meant to avoid Milan, "the bishop whereof exerciseth such tyranny," but, having covert Catholic leanings, he may have gone there anyway. Presumably he did not skip Rome and Naples, though we have no record of his having visited them. As for Naples, the clown in *Othello* says, "Why masters, ha' your instruments been at Naples, that they speak i' th' nose thus?" How would Mr. Shakspere, who apparently never left England, have known the Neapolitan accent? An intelligent man might learn to read some Italian without leaving home, but it is another thing to be familiar with fine points of regional Italian accents. The joke certainly gives the impression that the author himself had been struck by such regional variations.

A slight but striking echo of Oxford's Italian travels occurs in *The Taming of the Shrew*. Kate's father is Baptista Minola of Padua, rich in "crowns." His name conflates the names of Baptista Nigrone, from whom Oxford borrowed 500 crowns in Venice, and Pasquino Spinola, through whom he received more money—in Padua. As Ogburn observes, this is one of those small biographical links a Stratfordian scholar would be overjoyed to find between Mr. Shakspere and the plays. We can find dozens for Oxford.

Earlier earls of Oxford are treated revealingly in Shakespeare's plays. One of the Veres—John de Vere, the thirteenth earl—appears as a hero in Part 3 of *Henry VI* for having supported the Lancasters in the Wars of the Roses. But Oxford's collateral ancestor Robert de Vere is not even mentioned in *Richard II*. This is a particularly notable omission: Robert was Richard's favorite, and their homosexual friendship enraged the other nobles and led to Richard's downfall. Shakespeare tactfully begins his play after Robert's death. Here one of the great disgraces of the de Vere line fails to appear where one would most expect it.

Some of the plays make use of this kind of court gossip, with which Oxford would have had far more acquaintance than Mr. Shakspere. *Love's Labour's Lost* uses actual names from the court of Henri of Navarre (where the play is set): Marshal Biron becomes Berowne, the Duke of Longueville becomes Longaville, and the Duke de Maine becomes Dumaine. The French ambassador de la Mothe Fenelon, whose name is borrowed for the play's Moth, was himself at the English court at the very time of Oxford's wedding and dined with Burghley during the month of the nuptials. Armado seems to be based on an eccentric Italian at the English court named Monarcho, who had died by 1580. The play also echoes a 1578 episode at the court of Navarre and a 1582 visit to Elizabeth's court by a Russian delegation, whose absurd conduct made them a joke among English sophisticates.

It is generally agreed that *Love's Labour's Lost* is both a fairly early work and the most topical of Shakespeare's plays—the one that seems to be based most directly on real contemporaries of the English and French courts. The scholars have been unable to identify the real models for some of its characters or to explain many of its inside jokes. As a court insider, Oxford had precisely the background suited to writing such a play. Mr. Shakspere, at the time the play is usually dated, was a young man from the provinces, not yet thirty. It is at least plausible to suppose that Shakespeare, like most writers, began by writing about what he knew best: court life. Besides, the known real-life models for the play belong to a period several years before Mr. Shakspere came to London. By the time of his arrival, it all would have been old stuff, too stale for a *pièce à clef.*

Measure for Measure seems to be based in large part on a source the mainstream scholars never cite: an affair in Paris around 1580. Georges Lambin, a French scholar, discovered the story and found that Shakespeare simply adapted the name Angenoust to Angelo in the play. The names of other characters also closely resemble those of figures in the Parisian episode: Claude Tonard to Claudio, de Vaux to Varrius, Saint-Luc to Lucio, and so on, right down to one Ragosin, who became the minor character of Ragozine the pirate. The young future Earl of Derby, destined to be Oxford's son-in-law, was in Paris at the time and may well have brought the story to England. Mr. Shakspere might have known of it too, but once more, his later arrival in London makes this seem less likely. Another similarity lay closer to home. Claudio's imprisonment for having impregnated Juliet, under a law rarely invoked, has its counterpart in Oxford's personal experience: the queen had sent him, Ann Vavasor, and their illicit infant to the Tower. The play centers around the hypocrisy of Angelo, the Duke's hypocritical deputy, who has revived the dormant law and turns out to be a worse sinner than the man he has sentenced to die. The play may be an indirect comment on the queen, whose own morals, as Oxford would have had reason to know, fell somewhat short of sanctity. Just as Elizabeth was known publicly as the Virgin Queen, Angelo is renowned for his austere virtue—until events expose him.

Antonio's venture in *The Merchant of Venice* is much like Oxford's investments in Frobisher's voyages, and he comes close to losing the sum Oxford did lose in one of them: Oxford lost 3,000 pounds on one of Frobisher's journeys; Antonio nearly loses 3,000 ducats. Shylock's name may be taken, a little punitively, from Michael Lok, who was accused of defrauding the investors in the enterprise after its failure.

The plots of three Shakespeare plays—*Othello, Cymbeline,* and *The Winter's Tale*—revolve around chaste wives whose husbands are taken in by slanders against them—a theme of Oxford's life as well. (*Much Ado About Nothing* has a similar subplot.) The theme of calumny, especially sexual calumny against chaste women, recurs remarkably often in Shakespeare; Hamlet raises it with no particular pertinence to the story when he warns Ophelia, "Be thou as chaste as ice, as pure as snow, thou shalt not 'scape calumny." As a young man, it will be recalled, Oxford had written a self-pitying poem on the loss of his "good name."

All's Well features a petulant youth who rejects a wife far beneath him in rank, though morally speaking, he himself is the undeserving one. Like Oxford, Bertram is a royal ward whose mate may be chosen for him by those he is subject to; he absents himself from the court after being denied permission to leave; and he refuses to live with his wife. Helena finally captures him by the device of the "bed trick": under the delusion that he is sleeping with another woman, he lies with her and begets a child. Thirty years after Oxford's death, a published rumor recalled that this had actually happened to him. His daughter Susan (who had married the Earl of Montgomery) was described as "the daughter of the last great Earl of Oxford, whose lady was brought to his bed under the notion of his mistress and from such a virtuous deceit she [the Countess of Montgomery] is said to proceed." This seems extremely improbable; if there were any truth in it, the story would probably refer to his first daughter, Elizabeth; a later version of the story has this "virtuous deceit" resulting in a son. But what is important is that this fable was associated with Oxford at all. It shows that early gossip had already linked him, somehow, to Shakespeare's highly contrived plot device, borrowed from the play's source in Boccaccio.

The ostensible source of *Timon of Athens* is Plutarch, but Timon's fate immediately reminds us of Oxford's. A rich and generous patron suddenly finds that his munificence has left him ruined and friendless. He bitterly denounces the human race, with one interesting exception: his steward. Timon's praise of his steward, in the midst of his railing against mankind, suggests Oxford's own praise of Robert Christmas, a faithful servant who apparently stayed with him during the hardships he inflicted on himself through his legendary prodigality.

Like *All's Well, Timon* was never acted in Shakespeare's time, as far as we can tell. It appears only in the Folio, and seems incomplete. Perhaps the author put it in a drawer and went on to make better dramatic use of its themes and sentiments in *Lear* and *Coriolanus.*

One recurrent feature of the plays has never been remarked on, as far as I know: the grieving, often remorseful widower or lover. Brutus, Antony, and Posthumus receive news of their wives' deaths while abroad, as Oxford did. Hamlet returns to Denmark to find Ophelia dead. Othello and Leontes, of course, are directly responsible for their

wives' deaths, and are justly guilt-stricken when they learn of their innocence. Claudio in *Much Ado* similarly blames himself for Hero's supposed death after his public insult to her chastity.

We have no record of Oxford's reaction to the news of Anne's death
in 1588, but it is likely that he realized with pain how much misery he
had caused her during her short life. Her letters of 1583, pleading her
innocence and begging for reconciliation, are reminiscent of Ophelia
and Desdemona, both of whom may be modeled on her (as may Vir-
gilia, the stormy Coriolanus' meek, patient wife). When Antony, ca-
vorting with Cleopatra in Egypt, is told of Fulvia's death in Rome, he
reflects with regret on his failure to value her properly while she lived:

> There's a great spirit gone! Thus did I desire it.
> What our contempts doth often hurl from us,
> We wish it ours again. The present pleasure,
> By revolution low'ring, does become
> The opposite of itself. She's good, being gone;
> The hand could pluck her back that shov'd her on.

This situation appears often in Shakespeare, and rarely in the work of
any other dramatist. He works many variations on it, but the motif is
the same: in Lear's piercing words of Cordelia, "I did her wrong." A
slightly different case is Pericles, whose wife, Thaisa, apparently dies
shortly after giving birth to a daughter—as Anne had died not long after
giving birth to Susan. One way and another, the Shakespearean male is
shown remarkably often as undeserving of the most precious woman in
his life. At his best, he says with Brutus: "O ye gods!/Render me worthy of this noble wife." More often, he fails her and even destroys her.

Shakespeare's plays follow a broad trajectory, moving from comedies
of high society to tragedies of isolated men—a progress that parallels
Oxford's disgrace at court and his removal to a more solitary life. Hamlet is alienated from his native environment; Othello and Macbeth by
their crimes isolate themselves within the societies in which they have
achieved high place as warriors; Lear, Timon, and Coriolanus go into
outright exile. We may add Prospero to this list, though the play in
which he appears is a comedy of sorts; he, like Oxford, is a nobleman of
literary tastes, whose "library/Was dukedom large enough."

Shakespeare is such a versatile writer that we should pay special attention to such repeated themes as disgust with court intrigue. Of the thirty-eight plays, at least twenty-eight refer to courts and courtiers, and many are set at court from the opening scenes. Often he observes court life and manners with amusement; more often, his exiled characters vent their hatred of court life, with all its flattery, treacheries, and slanders.

One of Oxford's angry letters to Burghley contains a pair of striking phrases: "I serve her majesty, and I am that I am." Oxford was reminding the great Burghley, with angry pride, that he too was a great man who answered only to the queen, not to the likes of Burghley. In *Lear*, Kent tells Cornwall and Regan, with similar defiance, "I serve his majesty." And in the same spirit of protest, Shakespeare, in Sonnet 121, uses Oxford's very words: "No, I am that I am, and they that level/At my abuses reckon up their own."

We may note many other suggestive details linking Oxford to the plays. The Gadshill robbery in Part 1 of *Henry IV* appears to be based on the assault some of Oxford's own men were accused of committing at the same site in 1573. The street feuding of the Montagues and Capulets in *Romeo and Juliet* recalls the brawls between Oxford's supporters and Anne Vavasor's. *Richard III* centers around the Tower of London, where Oxford himself, like so many errant noblemen, was confined for a time. It also features clashes between the established nobility and various "upstarts." A satire on Christopher Hatton, one of Oxford's upstart enemies at court, refers to him as "*Fortunatus Infoelix*"—an English rendition of which, "the Fortunate-Unhappy," is used to dupe the social climber Malvolio in *Twelfth Night*. The more we learn of Oxford's life, the more of such resemblances we find. But centuries of research have turned up virtually nothing of the kind about Mr. Shakspere.

No play bears more convincing witness to Oxford's life and personality than the one many think is Shakespeare's greatest: *Hamlet*. Hamlet himself reminds us of the youthful Oxford. He is the very model of the courtier described by Baldesar Castiglione, whose fashionable book *The Courtier* had been translated into Latin under Oxford's patronage.

Some scholars, including Lily B. Campbell and Hardin Craig, have long noted that Hamlet's most famous soliloquy seems to take its inspiration from *Cardanus Comfort*—the book translated in 1573 by Thomas Bedingfield with the encouragement and sponsorship of young Oxford, who also wrote a preface to it. Of course, similitudes between death and sleep or a journey are ancient, even archetypal. But Cardanus also gives expression to other themes in Hamlet's soliloquy. Here are some excerpts:

> Alas, what evil can it be to want hunger, thirst, grief, labor, sadness, fear, and finally the whole heap of evils, which, the soul being parted from the body, we must of necessity want?

> Therefore Socrates was wont to say that death might be resembled either to sound sleep, a long journey, or destruction, as is the death of brute beasts.

> For there is nothing that doth better or more truly prophesy the end of life than when a man dreameth that he doth travel and wander into far countries, and chiefly if he imagineth himself to ride upon a white horse that is swift, and that he travelleth in countries unknown without hope of return.

> Death doth take away more evils than it bringeth, and those more certain.

> Only honesty and virtue of mind doth make a man happy, and only a cowardly and corrupt conscience do cause thine unhappiness.

This book is full of somber themes that resound through Shakespeare, of which a few others are likewise detectible in *Hamlet*. When Cardanus says that "good or evil fortune importeth nothing to blessed life," we hear the overtones of Hamlet's praise of Horatio:

> For thou hast been
> As one in suff'ring all that suffers nothing,
> A man that Fortune's buffets and rewards
> Hath ta'en with equal thanks; and blest are those
> Whose blood and judgment are so well commingled
> That they are not a pipe for Fortune's finger
> To sound what stop she please.

Cardanus: A man is nothing but his mind: if the mind be discontented, the man is all disquiet though all the rest be well, and if the mind be contented though all the rest misdo it forseeth little.

Hamlet: O God, I could be bounded in a nutshell and count myself a king of infinite space, were it not that I have bad dreams.

Cardanus: Private calamities manifold we accompt those when a man by many mishaps at one instant is molested.

Hamlet: When sorrows come, they come not single spies,/But in battalions.

Another remark of Cardanus might almost stand as the basic principle of Shakespearean tragedy: "Whoso doth mark it well shall find that for the most part we are causes of our own evil."

Many readers have felt that *Hamlet* is Shakespeare's most Shakespearean play and Hamlet himself the most Shakespearean character—the creation into whom the great poet poured more of himself than into any other. Hamlet is the only one of Shakespeare's heroes we can imagine writing the Sonnets, with all their variety and depths of feeling. Hamlet is Shakespeare's most Oxfordian character—a Renaissance courtier of many accomplishments,

The courtier's, soldier's, scholar's eye, tongue, sword,
The expectancy and rose of the fair state,
The glass of fashion and the mould of form,
The observed of all observers.

Ophelia's words in Act III, Scene 1, might almost be a description of Oxford in his young manhood.

Yet, like Oxford, Hamlet becomes a misfit in the court where he had begun so brilliantly. Though "to the manner born," he does not really like court life; he finds its carousing distasteful. He has studied at Wittenberg and wants to return there; his best friend is his "fellow student" Horatio. Wittenberg's theological renown reminds us of Oxford's religious interests. Hamlet's "antic disposition," disguising his serious purpose, may also remind us of Oxford's "fickle head."

There are other telling details. Oxford's father, like Hamlet's, died prematurely; his mother, too, remarried so quickly it would be natural for her son to feel revulsion like Hamlet's. On his return from France in 1576, Oxford was captured by pirates in the English Channel, who, like Hamlet's "thieves of mercy," recognized him and spared his life. Hamlet, too, is a connoisseur of the theater who directs his actors in the fine points of their craft. He speaks of a company of boy actors; in the 1580s, Oxford sponsored such a company, named in one record as "the children of the Earl of Oxford."

Hamlet complains of being virtually disinherited by Claudius, who has murdered his father. When asked the cause of his discontent by Rosencrantz—who, knowing nothing of the murder, points out that the king has named Hamlet his successor to the throne—Hamlet replies, "Ay, sir, but while the grass grows—the proverb is something musty," an allusion to the saying, "While the grass grows, the silly horse starves." He implies that he cannot wait indefinitely for what is rightfully his.

This has a remarkably close parallel in Oxford's January 3, 1576, letter to Burghley from Siena. Pressed by debt, he complains that lands due to him by inheritance are being withheld when he needs to sell them. Like Hamlet, he cannot wait indefinitely, and he says with some asperity that he is being asked "to content myself, according to this English proverb that it is my hap to starve like the horse, while the grass doth grow." It is one thing for two men to use the same proverb, another for both to refer to it *as* a proverb, and to give it the same subtle twist. Both Oxford and Hamlet are saying that they are being forced, by others' interference with their rights, into the position of the proverbial horse who starves while waiting for the grass to reach full height.

Burghley himself appears in *Hamlet*. He is the model for Polonius. This is hardly deniable. It was acknowledged by scholars as early as 1869, long before Oxford was proposed as the author—just as Southampton was seen in the youth of the Sonnets long before anyone imagined that his connection to Oxford was significant. Edmund Chambers, foremost of modern Shakespeare scholars, agrees that Polonius appears to be based on Burghley. The *Reader's Encyclopedia of Shakespeare* says of Burghley: "A master of craft himself, he had a striking capacity to ferret out the conspiratorial designs of others. In the 1590s his chief opponent at court was Essex, whose faction Shakespeare is said to have supported." The *Reader's Encyclopedia* concludes:

As a result many scholars have argued that Burghley is being satirized as Polonius in *Hamlet*. Evidence of this view is believed to be found in Burghley's *Certaine Preceptes, or Directions* (1616), which he wrote for his son, Robert Cecil, and which Shakespeare may have seen in manuscript. Polonius' famous advice to Laertes (I, iii, 58–80) is strikingly similar to Burghley's precepts in this treatise. Hamlet's reference to Polonius as a "fishmonger" may also be an allusion to Burghley's attempt as treasurer to stimulate the fish trade.

The only thing amiss in this passage arises from the assumption of Mr. Shakspere's authorship. It makes the incongruous suggestion that Mr. Shakspere would not only have taken sides in a political rebellion, but, having gotten hold of Burghley's then unpublished precepts to his son, would dare to satirize Burghley on the stage. Oxford would obviously have been far more likely to have access to Burghley's precepts, and to have had both motive and liberty to lampoon them.

Polonius does not appear in the play's source. In Belleforest's account, Hamlet kills an unnamed "councillor" whom he catches spying on him. Shakespeare not only expands the part into one of the longest speaking roles in his play, but makes Polonius Hamlet's chief antagonist, albeit a relatively benign one, for the first three acts. The leisurely second act, in which the action pauses, digresses languidly, allowing a vivid portrait of Polonius to be drawn.

Like Burghley, Polonius is a garrulous royal minister with a penchant for spying. When we first meet him, his son Laertes wants to go back to France, where, we later gather, he has been living wildly. Burghley's son Thomas Cecil spent two years in France, causing his father great distress with his wayward life, as reported to Burghley by his spies. Shakespeare gives us a dramatically superfluous scene in which Polonius sends his servant Reynaldo to spy on Laertes, explaining to him the art of eliciting information without seeming to: "By indirections find directions out" (Act 2, Scene 1). Soon afterward, Polonius is spying on Hamlet; in 1584, Oxford was enraged to discover that Burghley had tried to use one of his (Oxford's) servants as an informant.

Incidentally, Polonius' phrase "falling out at tennis" (Act 2, Scene 1) may be a buried joke about Oxford's famous spat with Sidney, whose pedantic taxonomy of dramatic forms is also satirized through Polonius: "The best actors in the world, either for tragedy, comedy, history, pastoral, pastoral-comical, historical-pastoral tragical-historical, tragical-comical-historical-pastoral . . ." (Act 2, Scene 2).

Thinking that Hamlet is mad, Polonius asks, "Do you know me, my lord?" (Act 2, Scene 2) Hamlet, pretending to be mad, replies, "Excellent well. You are a fishmonger"—a gibe at Burghley's efforts, mentioned above, to promote the interests of fishermen in Parliament. In 1563, he had urged a bill imposing a second compulsory fish day every week, Wednesday as well as Saturday. In a surviving memorandum, we find him arguing that it is "necessary for the restoring of the Navy of England to have more fish eaten and therefore one day more in the week ordained to be a fish day and that to be Wednesday rather than any other." He sought, among other things, restrictions on the import of fish and the removal of restrictions on their export. Catholics called the result "Cecil's Fast." Nothing could better illustrate the difference between Oxford's temperament and his father-in-law's than Burghley's energetic pursuit of this mundane measure.

We feel the difference all through Hamlet's exchanges with Polonius, his almost-father-in-law. "Have you a daughter?" Hamlet asks. When Polonius says yes, Hamlet, still feigning insanity, warns: "Let her not walk in the sun. Conception is a blessing, but not as your daughter may conceive"—another allusion to the real-life relations between Oxford and Burghley, whose daughter's first conception resulted in such uproar.

Ophelia herself, sweet and innocent but unable to cope with the warring males in her life, strongly resembles the young Anne Cecil. Polonius is unable to believe that Hamlet loves Ophelia honorably, and his cynicism undermines their budding love, much as Oxford felt that his in-laws had blighted his marriage to Anne.

When the acting troupe arrives at Elsinore, Burghley's contempt for Oxford's "lewd friends" is evident in Polonius' disdain for the players Hamlet loves, whom Rosencrantz has announced as "those you were wont to take delight in, the tragedians of the city." While Hamlet is moved by the leading actor's recitation of Aeneas' speech on the fall of Troy, Polonius merely complains that the speech is "too long." He finds it unbearable that the actor shows emotion: "Look, whe'r he has not turned his color, and has tears in's eyes. Prithee no more!"—an unmistakable echo of Oxford's 1572 letter to Burghley, quoted earlier, describing Huguenot refugees from the St. Bartholomew's Eve massacre as "French Aeneases" recounting their "tragedies" with "tears falling from their eyes."

Hamlet advises Polonius to treat the players with respect, for they may have the last word about him: "Let them be well used, for they are the abstract and brief chronicles of the time. After your death you were better have a bad epitaph than their ill report while you live." The suggestion that the theater is topical surprises us if we assume that Shakespeare is writing "universally," with no special reference to his own time. But Hamlet himself tells us otherwise, and the play itself is the fulfillment of his warning. It gives us a fascinating glimpse of Oxford and Burghley.

When Hamlet stabs Polonius, the deed has to be covered up—as Oxford's stabbing of Burghley's undercook had been. The very phrase Burghley had used to excuse Oxford, *"se defendendo,"* is parodied in the gravedigger's blundering legal terminology, *"se offendendo."* Hamlet's grim pun that "politic worms" are making the dead Polonius their "diet" looks like another private joke: according to Gerald W. Phillips, Burghley liked to recall that he was born during the Diet of Worms.

Such personal touches offer a tantalizing intimacy with the playwright, and they have persuaded many of Oxford's authorship. In reconsidering the Sonnets, we shall see evidence both more intimate and more obvious.

Chapter 9 〜')

The Sonnets Revisited

My name be buried where my body is,
And live no more, to shame nor me nor you.

— Sonnet 72

The best key to the identity of our greatest playwright may not lie in his plays. Perhaps we need look no further than the little volume published in 1609 under the title *Shake-speares Sonnets*. These remarkable, though mysterious, poems contain self-revelations that make it hard to avoid the conclusion that Oxford wrote them. Yet Oxford's partisans, as well as Mr. Shakspere's, have failed to understand them because both sides, for the most part, have shrunk from facing the strong evidence that the poet and his young friend are homosexual lovers.

We have seen persuasive evidence that the young man is Henry Wriothesley, the third Earl of Southampton. Once this fact is accepted, we can draw several inferences about the poet. In every respect, these inferences match Oxford but not Mr. Shakspere.

The first seventeen sonnets, the "procreation" poems, give every indication of belonging to Burghley's campaign to make the boy marry his granddaughter, and Oxford's daughter, Elizabeth Vere. Obviously, Oxford would have known all three parties when the campaign began in 1590, when Henry was seventeen and Elizabeth was fourteen. It is hard to imagine how Mr. Shakspere could have known any of them, let alone have been invited to participate in the effort to encourage the match.

These sonnets, moreover, are written in the form we now know as Shakespearean, a form pioneered by Sir Thomas Wyatt and Oxford's uncle Henry Howard, Earl of Surrey. They also bear many resemblances to the "Phaeton" sonnet addressed to John Florio, Southampton's friend and tutor, in 1591. Despite its style, most mainstream scholars believe its date precludes Mr. Shakspere's having written it. But if Oxford was Shakespeare, it falls naturally into place as one of the "sugared sonnets" distributed among his "private friends" that Francis Meres referred to in 1598.

The poet, we have also seen, is clearly older than the youth, as he says repeatedly and as he assumes even when he is not saying it. Oxford was twenty-three years older than Southampton. The poet contrasts his age with the youth's, likening himself to a "decrepit father" delighting in his child. Mr. Shakspere was only nine years older—a fair difference in age, but not wide enough to warrant his speaking as if Southampton were a full generation younger.

It is clear, too, that the poet is of the same rank as the youth. He praises, scolds, admonishes, teases, and woos him with the liberty of a social equal who does not have to worry about seeming insolent. As mentioned earlier, his plea, "Make thee another self, for love of me," is impossible to conceive as a request from a poor poet to his patron; it expresses the hope of a father—or perhaps a father-in-law. And Oxford was, precisely, Southampton's prospective father-in-law.

In Sonnet 91 the poet writes:

> Thy love is better than high birth to me,
> Richer than wealth, prouder than garments' cost,
> Of more delight than hawks or horses be.

The lines imply that he is in a position to make such comparisons, and that the "high birth" he refers to is his own. The other topics he mentions are within Oxford's experience: wealth, rich garments, hawks, and horses. In Sonnet 125, he speaks of having "bor[ne] the canopy," an apparent allusion to a ceremonial function at court; as Lord Great Chamberlain, Oxford would probably have helped carry the royal canopy over Elizabeth I or James I on solemn state occasions such as the celebration of the victory over the Spanish Armada in 1588 or James' coronation in 1603. This phrase has never been explained by scholars who assume that the poet is Mr. Shakspere.

Scholars have largely ignored one of the chief themes of the Sonnets: the poet's sense of disgrace. This painful motif is one of our chief assurances that the Sonnets are autobiographical. The poet keeps referring, at unpredictable intervals, to his own notoriety. He is in "disgrace" (Sonnet 29), the subject of "vulgar scandal" (112), and "bewailed guilt" (36). He speaks of his "outcast state" (29), of "blots" (36) and "shame" (36,72); he is "despised" (37), "guilty" (111), and "vile esteemed" (121); his name has received a "brand" (111) and so forth. He expects and even hopes for "a common grave" (81) where "my name [may] be buried where my body is" (72). Why would Mr. Shakspere have felt so blue about his reputation and prospects at the very time when he was becoming a popular, critical, and financial success? Every public reference to "Shakespeare" in the 1590s was laudatory; none imputed anything shameful to him.

But there can be no doubt that the poet is referring to something real that he expects his friend to know about; in fact, he makes it clear that a wide public knows about it—good evidence that the poet is a public figure who has fallen into disrepute, not (as some scholars suppose) an obscure man who is beginning to achieve public esteem. Once again, the poet's situation matches Oxford's. We have seen that in 1584 a social inferior had taunted him about his "decayed reputation" and challenged him to fight. He had been a topic of scandal on several occasions, and his contemporaries saw the course of his life as one of decline from great wealth, honor, and promise to disgrace and ruin. This perception was underlined by enemies who accused him of every imaginable offense and perversion, charges he was apparently unable to rebut.

Mr. Shakspere, meanwhile, was prospering handsomely; in 1597, he bought New Place, one of the largest houses in Stratford, and soon he would apply for a title and coat of arms. Yet however prominent he became in Stratford, he remained obscure in London, where he left few traces and seems to have frustrated even the tax collectors who sought him.

The author of the Sonnets expects and hopes to be forgotten. While he is confident that his poetry will outlast marble and monument, it will immortalize his young friend, not himself. He says that his style is so distinctive and unchanging that "every word doth almost tell my name," implying that his name is otherwise concealed—at a time when he is publishing long poems under the name William Shakespeare. This seems to mean that he is not writing these Sonnets under that name. And in fact, the title *Shake-speares Sonnets* indicates that it was the publisher, not the poet, who attached the name to the 1609 edition. Note that the poet playfully says to his mistress in Sonnet 136 that "my name is Will," but he also seems in the previous sonnet to refer to his young friend as Will. It was apparently a shared nickname or alias. She may not have known either man's real identity.

The nature of the poet's disgrace was surely, at least in part, sexual. Sonnet 121 speaks angrily of his detractors, who have judged him "vile" for his unspecified "frailties" and "sportive blood." Whatever his imputed fault was, he seems loath to name it. Moreover, he keeps warning the youth to avoid public association with him, lest the disgrace taint him too. In Sonnet 36 he urges discretion:

> Let me confess that we two must be twain,
> Although our undivided loves are one;
> So shall those blots that do with me remain,
> Without thy help, be borne by me alone. . . .
> I may not evermore acknowledge thee,
> Lest my bewailed guilt should do thee shame,
> Nor thou with public kindness honour me,
> Unless thou take that honour from thy name.

In Sonnet 71, the youth is actually cautioned not to be observed mourning at the poet's death: "Lest the wise world should look into your moan,/And mock you with me after I am gone." This is not sentimentalism; it is practical advice. The "wise world" does not mock mourners ordinarily. The implication is highly specific: if the sophisticates observe you grieving over me, they will draw certain conclusions about us.

The poet's disgrace—*and the dangers it poses for the youth*—form an important clue to the real meaning of the Sonnets. What may otherwise sound like the poet's maudlin self-effacement is much more pointed and particular than scholars (mainstream or Oxfordian) have grasped. The youth is involved in an amour that could severely damage his good name. By contrast, the poet can be quite jaunty about his adulterous liaison with his mistress in Sonnets 127 through 152; he never frets that it will hurt either his own reputation or hers, such as it is. His scandalous "frailties" do not seem to be heterosexual.

Again, this seems to have no connection to Mr. Shakspere of Stratford; he is not known to have been notorious for anything, let alone sodomy (which was then a capital crime, though rarely punished). And he would hardly have had to warn a nobleman of Southampton's stature to avoid being associated with him.

But Oxford *was* notorious. He had every reason to caution his young lover. It would hardly have disgraced Southampton to be the known companion of a spendthrift, eccentric, or ordinary rake. To be known as the close friend of a reputed homosexual, once accused of "buggering boys," would have been an entirely different matter.

One remarkable general feature of the Sonnets is the evidence they provide of the poet's legal knowledge. They abound not only in legal terms—more than two hundred—but in elaborate legal conceits. Like many noblemen and gentlemen, Oxford was trained in the law: he was admitted to Gray's Inn, one of the Inns of Court, in 1567. (Justice Shallow reminisces about Gray's Inn in *Henry IV, Part 2*.) Oxford's letters, which deal extensively with legal matters, use many of the same terms the Sonnets do: *account, adversary, allege, appeal, auditor, bond, cause, charge, compounded, contract, count, counterfeit, debt, defects, defend, determination, due, exchequer, execute, forfeit, grant, heirs, impeach, inheritance, interest, issue, judgment, lawful, lease, moiety, mortgage, pardon, parties, patent, plead, possession, receipt, recompense, render, rent, revenues, seal, slanderously, statute, successor, suit, sum, sureties, tenants, title, treasons, usage, witness.*

A further detail is especially notable. The poet twice (in Sonnets 37 and 89) speaks of himself as lame. We have no record of whether Mr. Shakspere was lame in any way, and most commentators take the word to be figurative. But the once athletic Oxford, in a 1595 letter to Burghley, refers to himself as "a lame man." Two years later, he explains that he is unable to attend the queen because "I have not an able body." Letters to Robert Cecil written in 1601 and 1602 also speak of his "lame hand." We do not know the precise nature of his affliction, but it hardly matters: at about the time the poet describes himself as lame, Oxford describes himself with the same word.

So far, then, Oxford fits the profile of the poet on many counts. He was of the right age and rank. He would have known both Burghley and Southampton during Burghley's prolonged effort to marry Southampton off to a young lady, who happened to be Oxford's own daughter. He was the nephew of Henry Howard, Earl of Surrey, one of the pioneers of the Shakespearean sonnet form; one of Oxford's known poems—"Who taught thee first to sigh, alas, my heart?"—is written in this form. He had been educated in the law. He was a public figure, a leading courtier, and hereditary Lord Great Chamberlain. But he had fallen from favor at court, incurred notoriety, and become the subject of malicious sexual gossip. His health had declined, too, in that he was "lame." He may have felt his death approaching during the time the Sonnets were written; Sonnet 107, almost certainly written the year before Oxford died (scholars generally agree that it refers to the queen's death in 1603), suggests a recent brush with mortality ("death to me subscribes"). The poet implies that his published verse does not bear his real name; we saw earlier that Oxford was known to have written works to which his own name was not attached.

Not one of these details can be shown to describe Mr. Shakspere. Most of them cannot possibly refer to him. He was only nine years older than Southampton and of modest birth. He could hardly have known Burghley and Southampton soon after his arrival in London; even if he somehow made their acquaintance, it is incongruous to imagine him being engaged by Burghley to persuade Southampton to marry; it is equally incongruous to imagine him in a close friendship, let alone an erotic tangle, with a nobleman. (His will mentions no friend above the rank of knight, and no literary patron.) If he was educated at all it is extremely unlikely that he was trained in the law. We have no reason to doubt that he enjoyed health and prosperity in the 1590s. He was anything but a public figure; if he suffered some disgrace, he could easily have left London, but of course we have no indication that he had any personal reputation at all in the city, good or bad. If he was the author of the Shakespeare poems, it makes no sense for him to lament that his name must be "buried" while boasting that his verse will live forever. He simply could not have written these Sonnets. Oxford could.

We have seen that most mainstream scholars have given up the attempt to interpret the Sonnets as any sort of record of Mr. Shakspere's life. Yet those who insist that they are fictions argue from their inadequacy as autobiography, not from their success as fiction. Either the Sonnets must be autobiography because they cannot be fiction, or they must be fiction because they cannot be autobiography. Note that these arguments are negative. Scholars are trapped by their premise that Mr. Shakspere wrote the Sonnets, which makes it impossible to argue on positive grounds that the Sonnets are either fiction or autobiography. The way out of the difficulty, of course, is to recognize that the Sonnets are neither fictions nor *Mr. Shakspere's* autobiography.

Not only does Oxford seem to match the author of the Sonnets in many details, we also have striking positive evidence, from his own hand, that he was the author. His 1573 prefatory letter to Thomas Bedingfield's translation of *Cardanus Comfort,* written when he was twenty-three, employs much the same style of argument, imagery, and general vocabulary as the Sonnets, with a density that rules out any likelihood of coincidence. Just as the Sonnets argue that the youth has no right to withhold his beauty from the world, Oxford argues that Bedingfield has no right to withhold his book from his countrymen. Just as the Sonnets promise that they will be the youth's eternal "monument," Oxford assures Bedingfield that his book will be a "monument" after Bedingfield himself is "dead and gone." Just as Sonnet 31 tells the young man, "Thou art the grave where buried love doth live," Oxford affectionately scolds Bedingfield for seeming determined to "bury and insevil your work in the grave of oblivion." The Bedingfield letter uses images of roses, jewelry, and ornaments; medicine, fever, and salve; murder, imprisonment, and military spoils; so do the Sonnets. Detailed parallels are cited in Appendix 3.

The Shakespearean personality that Harold Bloom says "always evades us, even in the Sonnets," and that certainly evades us in the records of Mr. Shakspere's life can be found, vividly recognizable, in Oxford's letter to Thomas Bedingfield. This letter shows the same courtly eloquence and generosity we encounter in dozens of Shakespearean kings and heroes. It may be the strongest single proof of Oxford's authorship of Shakespeare's works.

Reinventing Shakespeare

M ainstream scholarship in the twentieth century has
added remarkably little to our picture of Shakespeare.
That, in fact, may be why it is known as "mainstream": it has been conventional, conservative, self-enclosed, slow to assimilate new information, and even slower to recognize shortcomings in its own composite image of the poet. At the same time, it can become unduly excited at the slightest addition to its body of knowledge.

In 1909, a Missouri-born scholar named Charles William Wallace, combing through the Public Record Office in London, found what he claimed was "the most important addition to our knowledge of Shakespeare's life which has been made in the past one hundred and fifty years." Later scholars have agreed with this assessment. F. E. Halliday calls Wallace's chief find "one of the most important of biographical discoveries," and even the usually reserved Samuel Schoenbaum hails it as nothing less than "the Shakespearean discovery of the century." What was this fantastic treasure? Mr. Shakspere's deposition, written in the third person by a legal clerk, in a 1612 lawsuit. The case involved a maker of women's headdresses named Christopher Mountjoy, with whom Mr. Shakspere had lodged around 1604. Mr. Shakspere seems to have helped encourage and arrange a marriage that year between his landlord's daughter, Mary, and an apprentice named Stephen Belott. When the son-in-law sued Mountjoy over an allegedly promised dowry that was never paid, other witnesses named Mr. Shakspere as the man who would have known the crucial details; but he was unable to remember the terms of the dowry. The trial had nothing to do with the theater and throws no light on the works of Shakespeare. The Mountjoy episode merely leaves us with one more barren legal record. Its flavor may be gathered from an excerpt summarizing part of Mr. Shakspere's testimony:

> To the fourth interrogatory this deponent saith that the defendant promised to give the said complainant a portion of money and goods in marriage with Mary his daughter, but what certain portion he remembereth not, nor when to be paid, nor knoweth that the defendant promised the plaintiff two hundred pounds with his daughter Mary at the time of his decease; but salts that the plaintiff was dwelling with the defendant in his house, and they had amongst themselves many conferences about their marriage which was consummated and solemnized. And more he can [not depose].

Wallace and his wife spent years reading, with truly extraordinary determination, similar documents—five million, as they calculated. They also found a few records of Mr. Shakspere's dealings, from late in his life, on the business side of the theater. Despite their heroic efforts, they turned up nothing that William Henry Ireland would have bothered to forge.

S.H. Burton, a recent biographer, sensibly admits that there is little to be gleaned from the episode: "His [Mr. Shakspere's] relationship with the Mountjoys (simply that of ordinary good neighborliness) reveals nothing of that 'inner life' which so many have tried to reconstruct." Other biographers have been less restrained. Beginning with Wallace, they have found Shakespearean intimations in the spare story Wallace himself wrote: "That Shakespeare lived with a hard-working family, shared in their daily life, and even lent his help with the hope of making two young people happy makes him as the world would gladly know him, an unpretentious, sympathetic, thoroughly human Man." Peter Alexander is equally grand: "This happy glimpse of the king of poets, moving familiarly among the humbler subjects of his art, not only confirms the reports of his urbane humanity, but suggests that Shakespeare, so far from being afflicted with the invincible repugnance to acquire any language but his own, may have gone to the Mountjoys partly to improve his French." Peter Quennell remarks: "Again, we recognize Shakespeare's native caution; he was not to be betrayed into a possibly inaccurate statement, but did his best by both parties." Rowse, as always, assumes intimacy with the story's hero: "When it came to the details of the portion promised or the legacy Mary Mountjoy should have from her father's will, Shakespeare could not remember. How like him!" Schoenbaum comments: "Of all the Shakespeare records, only the Belott-Mountjoy suit shows him living amidst the raw materials for domestic comedy The proceedings, for all their mercenary or sordid overtones, reveal the poet-dramatist as a somewhat baffled mortal." Peter Levi says hopefully that the documents of the case "do tell us he had some influence with the young, and that he was on the side of marriage and on the side of women." The popular biographer Robert Payne outdoes the professional scholars in extrapolation: "What attracted Shakespeare to the house may have been the mischief and the violence of the place where beautiful women were continually coming to buy wigs and jeweled tires. . . . We should not be surprised that Shakespeare would choose to live in a house like this. We sometimes imagine him to have been one of those men who live calmly above the tempest, remote from life while reflecting its infinite varieties. This is to forget the evidence of his passion, his piercing intensity, his fierce sensitivity, his almost unbearable openness to sensations. His mind worked with lightninglike speed and his senses were perpetually in motion. He would go wherever the excitement was, and when he had had enough he would shut the door and write his poetry. . . . In the Mountjoy house there was always as much excitement as he needed."

How did the Wallaces themselves feel about their great discovery? Wallace described their emotions at the moment they came upon it:

I asked her to come over and look at a document. We sat down together to read it, as we had done in hundreds of cases. We looked through it with about as much excitement as we do the morning paper. I saw by the look on her face that she felt as I did,—glad, but disappointed in a measure. We were aware of the bigness of what we had. But we were looking for bigger. We had searched at various periods for some years, always confident as we had long before announced to our friends, that we should get Shakespeare's signature and a personal expression from him. We had fixed our minds on the topic he should speak on,—one that would be finally thereby settled to all the world—and this was so much less than we had wished!

Wallace's remarks elsewhere show that the authorship question was very much on his mind. He contended that Mr. Shakspere's signature on the deposition, which he praised as "clearer, and more legible than that of the average modern university graduate," confuted "Shakespeare's enemies," who held "that he was an ignoramus who could not write his name legibly"—a clear reference to the anti-Stratfordians, who not only denied Mr. Shakspere's authorship but ridiculed him roughly. As far as the evidence goes, they may have been excessive; Mr. Shakspere might well have attended the Stratford grammar school and learned to read some Latin as well as English. We simply do not know. In the authorship debate it has become customary for each side to belittle the other's candidate, and even to defame his character, with all the bitter fervor and exaggeration of lawyers in a child custody fight. At any rate, Wallace's remark about Shakespeare's "enemies" shows that he thought of himself as belonging to one side in the controversy, and he had hoped that his Herculean labor would gain the final victory.

Actually, the signature on the deposition is very hard to read—it looks like "Willn Shandy," if it can be said to look like anything. This may not matter, since many highly literate people have poor penmanship. It does not appear to be the writing of a man who was used to clutching a pen, but this is only an impression. Anti-Stratfordians tend to insist that Mr. Shakspere's signatures prove his illiteracy. The orthodox scholars usually explain the three unseemly scrawls on his will by surmising that he was mortally ill when he made them. And it is possible that his surviving signatures, all of which date from the last five years of his life, owe their appearance to arthritis or some other condition of encroaching age. Still, no one argues that Mr. Shakspere's half-dozen known signatures prove he was an author.

Why did Wallace feel he must deny what is obvious to the naked eye? Only because he realized what was at stake. Doubts about Shakespeare's identity were at least as strong at the turn of the century as they are now. Wallace's fellow midwesterners Mark Twain and Ignatius Donnelly had recently given those doubts rowdy expression; so had titled Englishmen like Sir Edward Durning-Lawrence (forever associated with the word *honorificabilitudinitatibus*) and Sir George Greenwood. Meanwhile, Andrew Lang, J.M. Robertson, and others wrote books vindicating Mr. Shakspere. Controversy raged. What was needed was firm documentary proof. So, after checking millions of documents, the Wallaces had made no more than a mildly interesting addition to Mr. Shakspere's biography—leaving the case for his authorship, however, right where it had been since the publication of the First Folio in 1623.

The inquirer who studies the records of Oxford's life, in stark contrast, feels anything but disappointed. On the contrary, the experience is one of repeated shocks of recognition. The Wallaces showed how little can be found about Mr. Shakspere in London between 1604 and 1612. This was the period during which, by every orthodox assumption, he should have been a highly visible figure in the city. Up to the year when we lost track of him in London, he apparently never owned a residence, but kept moving from one address to another every year or two. The trial documents identify him, as of 1612, not as a London playwright, actor, or businessman, but as a "gentleman" of Stratford-upon-Avon, adding to the impression that he had not lived in the city for some time. As the name of Shakespeare becomes ever more imposing over the first decade of the century, Mr. Shakspere the man becomes all the more strangely invisible—unless we accept him as the small-town burgher he became.

As we have seen, most Shakespeare scholars scorn any suggestion that a nobleman wrote the canon of Shakespeare's plays. They find it absurd that his authorship could have been concealed, though there can be little doubt that it would have been easy to prevent publication of the truth in an age when everything printed had to be licensed. Noblemen and gentleman appeared in print, if at all, on their own terms. These scholars insist that the evidence of Mr. Shakspere's authorship is beyond question. Yet, given the circumstantial historical and literary evidence compiled in previous chapters, many readers will probably be ready to agree with Walt Whitman that the plays were indeed written by a nobleman.

As Oxford was a nobleman of high rank and ancient lineage, it would have been scandalous if he had been known to be slumming in the theater—not the sort of news that would be fit to print. It would have been the sort of unpublished but ubiquitous gossip of which the Sonnets complain. Muckraking journalism was not a Tudor genre. An attitude of respect toward the upper echelons of society prevailed, though gossip can be so widely shared as to be public without actually being published.

Sir Philip Sidney's sonnet cycle *Astrophil and Stella* was an allegorical work, published posthumously in 1591, about his own adulterous love for Penelope Devereux, and its actual referents were the kind of secret everyone is on to. The real identities of Astrophil and Stella were known at the time and for many years afterward, but they were never committed to print. The idealization of Sidney after his death prohibited any public mention of the scandalous liaison. He was the *beau ideal* of the courtier and the gallant poet, a young national hero who died in battle at thirty-two and whose funeral in 1586 all of London crowded the streets to witness. "For once dead," writes Roger Howell, "Sidney took on a fame far wider than he had enjoyed in life." Subsequently, his sonnet cycle was read for centuries as "pure"—that is, impersonal or fictional—just as many scholars still read Shakespeare's Sonnets. *Astrophil and Stella* was published five years after Sidney's death. The "stigma of print," as J.W. Saunders dubbed it, forbade him to allow its publication during his life, just as many other gentleman poets had refrained from publication, including Oxford's uncle, the Earl of Surrey. This taboo was by no means peculiar to Tudor England; it is common to aristocratic societies. The facts of his affair with Penelope Devereux were totally lost until rediscovered in the 1930s.

A germane case from the world of music has recently come to light. In 1979, the musicologist Albert Dunning discovered that six short concerti formerly ascribed to Giovanni Pergolesi were in fact composed by Count Unico Wilhelm van Wassenaer, a Dutch nobleman. Born in 1692, seven years after Bach (and more than a century after Oxford), Wassenaer, the son of a diplomat, studied law and took up his father's career, serving as ambassador to Paris and Cologne. He was also a gifted composer but did not wish this to be known, since, as the conductor and scholar Roy Goodman puts it, "at that time [it would have been] far beneath the dignity of a true nobleman." Wassenaer's concerti were extremely popular in Holland and England; yet he never acknowledged them. He died in 1766.

After their enthusiastic public reception, the concerti were published anonymously in 1740 and mistakenly attributed first to Carlo Ricciotti, then to Handel, and later to Pergolesi. Those inclined to trust traditional ascriptions should consider Goodman's remark: "In fact, about ninety per cent of the 330 works bearing Pergolesi's name in the libraries of the world are not authentic. After all, he died at the age of 26 and his posthumous fame created an enormous demand for his music"—just as the demand for works by Shakespeare led to the publication of bogus plays beginning in 1605, the year after Oxford's death.

We have seen the difficulties of establishing authorship in Elizabethan times. The most popular play of the age, *The Spanish Tragedy,* is now universally assigned to Thomas Kyd; but his name appears on none of the title pages of its first ten editions. All we really know is that Thomas Heywood refers to him as its author in *Apology for Actors,* published in 1612, eighteen years after Kyd's death. Apart from one translated play, no other known work of Kyd's survives.

The leading poets of the late Elizabethan age were Sidney and Spenser, with Shakespeare ranking third. His fame and popularity were local; none of his works were translated until 1740. His genius was honored by all the great poets—Jonson, Milton, Dryden, Pope, Johnson— but in the seventeenth century, Shakespeare was not yet a name to conjure with. Oxford was cited as chief among the writers of rank who chose not to publish under their own names—this in *The Art of English*

Poesy (1589), whose author is himself anonymous. Oxford's prefatory letter to Thomas Bedingfield's translation of Cardanus Comfort underlines the same point: it purports to overrule Bedingfield's refined aversion to letting the book be printed.

Professor Gary Taylor's recent book *Reinventing Shakespeare* is a fascinating survey of changes in Shakespeare's image from the Restoration to the present. But it overlooks the first greatest reinvention of Shakespeare: the one wrought by the First Folio of 1623. Properly titled *Mr. William Shakespeares Comedies, Histories, & Tragedies,* the First Folio completely replaced Shakespeare the poet with Shakespeare the playwright—a change that has perdured through all other shifts of fashion. We still think of Shakespeare almost exclusively as a playwright. The full significance of this fact has eluded Oxford's partisans along with orthodox Stratfordians.

Modern readers seldom realize that for five years, from 1593 to 1598, William Shakespeare was identified in print not as a playwright, but exclusively as the author of two splendid and popular poems: *Venus and Adonis* (1593) and *The Rape of Lucrece* (1594). Both poems were regarded as masterpieces, especially *Lucrece,* and both went through many editions; *Venus* was reprinted at least ten times before 1623, *Lucrece* at least five—while only *Richard III* and *1 Henry IV,* among the plays, were reprinted as many as six times in quarto. Some idea of the change in taste between Shakespeare's day and ours can be gathered from the number of editions his individual works went through. *Richard II* had five editions before the Folio, *Romeo and Juliet* four, *Pericles* four, *Titus Andronicus* three. Of the tragedies we regard as supreme, *Hamlet* appeared only three times, *Lear* twice, *Othello* once, *Macbeth* not at all. However, it is clear that the two poems' high place in public esteem was fixed long before the Folio offered a full canon of Shakespeare's plays.

Thus, in his own day, the name Shakespeare was synonymous with *Venus* and *Lucrece.* The reason was less that these were his first published works than that they were, in general esteem, his greatest. Popular drama was considered an inferior genre, far below other forms of verse; Ben Jonson was mocked in 1616 for calling his collected plays his "works." To speak of Shakespeare chiefly as a playwright would have been to belittle him. The gross misconstruction of *Greene's Groatsworth* has created the false impression that Shakespeare was known as a play-wright by 1592—an impression the record belies. To every literate Londoner, Shakespeare, from his first public notice in 1593, was a poet. When his name began appearing on printed plays in 1598, that name meant "by the author of *Venus and Adonis* and *The Rape of Lucrece*." Needless to say, nobody in his own time ever referred to *Greene's Groatsworth* in connection with Shakespeare; nobody quoted it, whether in agreement, refutation, or irony, as being a reflection on him.

Venus, which had appeared in six editions by 1599 (and then appears to have been suppressed for nearly twenty years), was especially popular—and a bit scandalous—for its lighthearted sensuality. Not everyone approved. In 1622, one Thomas Robinson referred to it as a "scurrilous book"; as late as 1631, Richard Braithwaite could still admonish readers of his *English Gentlewoman,* a guide to genteel behavior, that "Venus and Adonis are unfitting consorts for a lady's bosom."

Lucrece, the "graver labour" the poet had promised Southampton in the dedication to *Venus,* is a longer and more serious poem than its predecessor. It was only slightly less popular, and far more highly rated for its somber moral power, redeeming its author from the charge of licentiousness to which the earlier poem had exposed him.

One of the earliest printed references to Shakespeare occurs in the anonymous *Willobie his Avisa* (1594), which contains the lines,

> Though Collatine have dearly bought
> To high renown a lasting life,
> And found that most in vain have sought,
> To have a fair and constant wife,
> Yet Tarquin pluck'd his glistering grape,
> And Shakespeare paints poor Lucrece' rape.

Apart from *Willobie his Avisa,* there are other mentions of *Lucrece* from as early as 1594, by Michael Drayton and "W. Har." (sometimes identified as Sir William Harbert). An obscure poem by Thomas Edwards, published in 1595, alludes to several poets by the names of their creations; Spenser is "Colleyn," Daniel is "Rosamund," Marlowe is "Leander," and Shakespeare is "Adon" ("Adon deafly masking through Stately tropes richly conceited"). A 1595 poem by Robert Southwell also alludes to *Venus;* the same year, William Covell has a muddled note in his *Polimanteia* referring to "sweet Shakespeare," "worthy Lucrecia," and "wanton Adonis" with "all praise." A 1600 poem by John Lane contains the lines,

> When chaste Adonis came to man's estate,
>
> Venus straight courted him with many a wile;
>
> Lucrece once seen, straight Tarquin laid a bait,
>
> With foul incest [sic] her body to defile.

Four of the short poems in *The Passionate Pilgrim* (1599), all ascribed by the publisher William Jaggard to Shakespeare, are about Venus (also called Cytherea) and Adonis; their authenticity is not settled, but it is clear that poems about Venus and Adonis could be passed off as Shakespeare's because those were the names popularly associated with him

Francis Meres' 1598 compilation, *Palladis Tamia: Wit's Treasury,* lists Shakespeare among recent poets by whom "the English tongue is mightily enriched": Sidney, Spenser, Daniel, Drayton, Warner, Shakespeare, Marlowe, and Chapman, in that order. Most of these were not dramatists at all (only Marlowe and Chapman wrote both lyric poetry and plays). A few paragraphs later, Meres lists Sidney, Spenser, Daniel, Drayton, Shakespeare, and Warner as the modern English poets whose works are likely to endure; then come Spenser, Daniel, Drayton, Shakespeare, and Breton as the best lyric poets in English. Even in his separate praise of Shakespeare, Meres begins with his *nondramatic* verse: "As the soul of Euphorbus was thought to live in Pythagoras, so the sweet witty soul of Ovid lives in mellifluous and honey-tongued Shakespeare, witness his *Venus and Adonis*, his *Lucrece,* his sugared sonnets among his private friends, etc." Only then does Meres turn to Shakespeare's plays, of which he names a dozen (citing *Titus Andronicus* as proof of his excellence in tragedy). He puts Shakespeare in his inventories of both "the best for tragedy" and "the best for comedy among us." His roll of "the best for comedy" begins with "Edward, Earl of Oxford," which some quote as proof that Oxford and Shakespeare could not have been the same writer. But this assumes that Meres must have known that Oxford, whose reputation had been established much earlier, was now writing as "Shakespeare," whose name was fairly new. Even if Meres did know, he might well have joined in the ruse by pretending that Shakespeare was a different writer; it would not have been up to a writer of his station to expose an earl.

This is the first known mention of Shakespeare as a playwright. Seven of his plays had already appeared in quarto editions anonymously—*after* the thoroughly successful publication of *Venus* and *Lucrece* in 1593. It would have been natural for profit-seeking publishers to use the name William Shakespeare on the title pages of his plays to attract readers. Yet from 1594 to 1598, *Titus Andronicus,* two parts of *Henry VI, Richard II, Richard III,* and *Romeo and Juliet* were all published anonymously. Why? Few scholars have asked this obvious question. The absence of Shakespeare's name on these quartos also further refutes the assumption that he was a well-known theatrical figure by 1592, the time of *Greene's Groatsworth*—or at least that Greene's supposed attack made him well-known (see chapter 2). Why not publish the author's name? One likelihood is that Shakespeare was at first only an ad hoc invention for Oxford's poems honoring Southampton, and that Oxford had not yet decided to attach it to his plays.

Finally, Meres adds yet another list of poets: "the most passionate among us to bewail and bemoan the perplexities of love: Henry Howard Earl of Surrey, Sir Thomas Wyatt the elder, Sir Francis Brian, Sir Philip Sidney, Sir Walter Raleigh, Sir Edward Dyer, Spenser, Daniel, Drayton, Shakespeare, Whetstone, Gascoigne, Samuel Page [sometimes fellow of Corpus Christi College in Oxford], Churchyard, Breton."

In 1598, Richard Barnfield, in *A Remembrance of Some English Poets,* was already predicting immortality for Shakespeare, but not because of his plays:

> And Shakespeare, thou whose honey-flowing vein,
> Pleasing the world, thy praises doth obtain,
> Whose Venus and whose Lucrece, sweet and chaste,
> Thy name in fame's immortal book have plac'd;
> Live ever you!—at least in fame live ever;
> Well may the body die, but fame dies never.

Gabriel Harvey, in marginal notes he wrote sometime during the same period, refers to three of Shakespeare's works: "The younger sort take much delight in Shakespeare's *Venus and Adonis,* but his *Lucrece,* and his *Tragedy of Hamlet, Prince of Denmark,* have it in them to please the wiser sort." Gabriel's own list of "flourishing metricians"—foremost among them "Dyer, Raleigh, Spenser, Constable, France, Watson, Daniel, Warner, Chapman, Sylvester, Shakespeare"—are, except for Chapman and Shakespeare, exclusively nondramatic poets.

The antiquarian William Camden's *Remains* (1605) names recent English poets of distinction "Sir Philip Sidney, Ed. Spenser, Samuel Daniel, Hugh Holland, Ben. Jonson, Th. Campion, Mich. Drayton, George Chapman, John Marston, William Shakespeare, and other most pregnant wits of these our times, whom succeeding ages may justly admire."

Only three of these poets wrote plays, but all wrote nondramatic verse. Nobody's list of the age's leading poets included names of men who were strictly playwrights.

Even those tributes that acknowledge Shakespeare's plays honor him chiefly for his poems. The satirical *Parnassus* plays of about 1600 glancingly mention some of the plays, but quote extensively from *Venus* and ridicule the craze for it among "the younger sort" by having one character pledge, "Let this duncified world esteem of Spenser and Chaucer, I'll worship sweet Mr. Shakespeare, and to honour him will lay his *Venus and Adonis* under my pillow." "I never read anything but *Venus and Adonis,*" says a character in Thomas Heywood's comedy *The Fair Maid of the Exchange,* published in 1607. The humor of such casual references tells us how familiar the topic was.

John Weever's 1599 sonnet illustrates the general order of esteem in which the works were held:

> Honey-tongu'd Shakespeare, when I saw thine issue,
> I swore Apollo got them and none other;
> Their rosy-tainted features, cloth'd in tissue,
> Some heaven-born goddess said to be their mother:
> Rose-cheek'd Adonis with his amber tresses,
> Fair, fire-hot Venus charming him to love her,
> Chaste Lucretia virgin-like her dresses,
> Proud lust-stung Tarquin seeking still to prove her;

Romeo, Richard, more whose names I know not,
Their sugar'd tongues and pure attractive beauty
Say they are saints, although that saints they show not,
For thousands vow to them subjective duty.
They burn in love thy children. Shakespeare, let them:
Go, woo thy Muse more nymphish brood beget them.

Robert Allot's 1600 anthology, *England's Parnassus: or, The Choicest Flowers of Our Modern Poets,* included ninety-five extracts from Shakespeare: a total of thirty from five plays, twenty-six from *Venus,* and thirty-nine from *Lucrece.* Another anthology from the same year, John Bodenham's *Belvedere, or The Garden of the Muses,* had a similar proportion of quotations: eighty-eight from six plays (forty-seven from *Richard II* alone), thirty-five from *Venus,* ninety-two from *Lucrece.*

Even as Shakespeare the dramatist grew famous, Shakespeare the poet remained preeminent, with *Venus* and *Lucrece* continuing to sell in new editions. In 1614, long after many of the plays first appeared in print, Thomas Freeman addressed another sonnet to Shakespeare, still awarding pride of place to the two poems, twenty years after their first publication:

Shakespeare, that nimble Mercury, thy brain,
Lulls many hundred Argus eyes asleep,
So fit for all thou fashionest thy vein.
At the horse-foot fountain thou hast drunk full deep:
Virtue's or vice's theme to thee all one is.
Who loves chaste life, there's Lucrece for a teacher;
Who list read lust, there's Venus and Adonis,
True model of a most lascivious lecher.
Besides in plays thy wit winds like Meander,
Whence needy new composers borrow more
Than Terence doth from Plautus and Menander
But to praise thee aright I want thy store.
Then let thine own works thine own worth upraise,
And help t'adorn thee with deserved bays.

Both works inspired imitation. Thomas Middleton wrote a long poem called *The Ghost of Lucrece,* published in 1600. The same year brought forth a shorter poem, "The Shepherd's Song of Venus and Adonis," signed H.C. and imitating Shakespeare. A play by Thomas Heywood, *The Rape of Lucrece* (printed in 1608), was based on Shakespeare's poem; Heywood later claimed authorship of a poem titled *The Scourge of Venus, or The Wanton Lady* (featuring "The Rare Birth of Adonis"), published in 1613 and written in direct imitation of *Venus and Adonis,* even using the same stanza. William Barkstead's poem *Mirrha the Mother of Adonis* spoke of Shakespeare in the past tense: "His song was worthy merit (Shakespeare he)." The poem was published in 1607, when Oxford had been dead for three years.

So completely was the poet identified with his two great narrative poems that when Henry Chettle wanted to chide Shakespeare for his failure to honor the queen at her death in 1603, he had only to allude to one of them to make it clear whom he was talking about:

> Nor doth the silver-tongued Melicert
> Drop from his honey'd muse one sable tear
> To mourn her death that graced his desert,
> And to his lays open'd her royal ear.
> Shepherd, remember our Elizabeth,
> And sing her rape, done by that Tarquin death.

Modern Shakespeare scholars and critics treat *Venus* and *Lucrece* as works of apprenticeship. But Shakespeare's contemporaries at once recognized them for what they were: the debut of greatness. Not a rough, rustic, somewhat uncouth, "natural" greatness, but an achievement of high culture and classical learning. We are blinded to their merit by hindsight: we compare them, unfairly, with the greater works that were to come.

Despite the extensive evidence cited above, the Folio describes Shakespeare only as an actor and dramatist. It does not include *Venus* or *Lucrece*. None of its six generous prefatory tributes, though full of classical names, even mentions or alludes to either of the poems on classical myths that had made his towering reputation, and for which he had been primarily renowned for *thirty years.* Unlike all earlier eulogists, the Folio never so much as acknowledges that Shakespeare wrote any non-dramatic verse at all. The Sonnets, which had appeared relatively recently in the 1609 quarto, are not remotely referred to. The Folio tributes use a dozen classical literary and mythological names, but Venus, Adonis, Lucrece, and Tarquin are not among them.

Why this total silence about works already famous? The clue may lie in the Folio's other conspicuous silence: *it makes no mention of Southampton,* to whom all of Shakespeare's major nondramatic poetry had been addressed. *Venus* and *Lucrece* had been dedicated to him in warm terms. Again and again the Sonnets proclaim that all the poet's work is devoted to Southampton and that he wishes his name to be "buried." The Folio fulfills this wish exactly. It is dedicated not to Southampton, but to William and Philip Herbert, earls of Pembroke and Montgomery. The dedication praises them for having "prosecuted both them [the plays] and their author, living, with so much favour" that they are the book's natural "patrons." But there is no evidence that either brother ever patronized the plays or their author. The patron of the King's Men was the king himself. The only ostensible patron the poet Shakespeare ever had was Southampton. Most readers in 1623 would not recall that Montgomery had married Oxford's daughter Susan Vere in 1604—or that Pembroke had once been a candidate for the hand of another of his daughters, Bridget. One aim of the Folio, I submit, was to portray Shakespeare as a mere untitled common player, "fellow" of Heminge and Condell and "servant" to Pembroke and Montgomery, thereby implicitly dissociating him from Southampton and the poems written in his honor—thus burying any memory of the homosexual amour between Oxford and Southampton, who was still very much alive and to be reckoned with. After the 1601 Essex rebellion, Southampton appeared doomed; he had in fact been sentenced to death. Yet his life was spared, and his fortunes made an amazing recovery. When James I acceded to the throne in 1603, Southampton was not only released from prison but restored to his title and possessions. His marriage to Elizabeth Vernon proved very happy for both of them. By 1623, he was a fully respectable—and powerful—nobleman of fifty who would not have welcomed any reminder of his wild youth, least of all his love affair with an eccentric and notorious older man. The compilers of the Folio steered carefully around him. Nobody could know that he would die suddenly in 1624, on a military expedition in the Netherlands.

Even Mr. Shakspere had to be made as unlike an earl as possible. His modest title of "gentleman" is not mentioned in the Folio. The careful reader might gather that he has a "monument" in a town called Stratford, and Jonson calls him "sweet swan of Avon." Otherwise he is a disembodied figure. Nothing memorable about the man himself is recorded; he is discussed in superlatives rather than details. He is merely "so worthy a friend and fellow," whose "memory" may be kept "alive" by this "humble offer of his plays to your most noble patronage." The unstated implication is that Shakespeare's poetry would *not* keep that memory alive.

The Folio eulogies stress Shakespeare's disembodied quality. They say repeatedly that his fame will not depend on anything but his plays. Jonson's poem calls him "a monument without a tomb." Leonard Digges' poem predicts that Shakespeare's name will "outlive Thy tomb" when "time dissolves thy Stratford monument." A sonnet by Milton in the Second Folio, published in 1632, expands the theme:

> What needs my Shakespeare for his honour'd bones
> The labour of an age in piled stones,
> Or that his hallow'd relics should be hid
> Under a star y-pointing pyramid?
> Dear son of memory, great heir of fame,
> What need'st thou such weak witness of thy name?
> Thou in our wonder and astonishment
> Hast built thyself a livelong monument . . .

The 1623 Folio deliberately focused entirely on the plays and so reinvented Shakespeare. It created, subtly and tacitly, but decisively, a distance between him and his Southampton poems, which constituted all his published nondramatic poetry. If Oxford's scandalous connection to Southampton was to be effaced, neither he nor the poems he inspired could be named or alluded to in the Folio. They could only be totally ignored. A whole persona had to be constructed for Shakespeare: a great playwright, of course, but also a mere actor and "fellow" of actors, under the patronage of "the most noble and incomparable pair of brethren," the Herbert brothers.

Mr. Shakspere was now officially Shakespeare—a modest bust of him, with an inscription likening him to Nestor, Socrates, and Virgil, was commissioned and placed in the parish church in Stratford. In a few years, Oxford was all but forgotten.

If the purpose of the Folio was to obscure not only Oxford but the Southampton poems, it was a total success. *Venus, Lucrece,* and the Sonnets fell into total neglect until the late eighteenth century, when Edmond Malone became the first editor to give them the attention they deserve; some editions of the works of Shakespeare, including Samuel Johnson's, omitted them altogether. And though over the past century the Sonnets have been appreciated as never before, the two long poems have not recovered anything approaching their original stature among the works of Shakespeare. Almost nobody today would rank them as masterpieces, which is understandable, or as milestones in the poet's development, which is another matter.

Nobody seriously tried to piece Mr. Shakspere's life together until late in the eighteenth century, when Malone and others took up the task. Since then, not only biographers but nearly all the scholars and critics have based their work on the assumption that he was, as the Folio assured its readers, William Shakespeare. But if Oxford's early efforts are also Shakespeare's, we must trace the trajectory of the poet's development from a new starting point, understanding *Venus* and *Lucrece* as pivotal works, not minor departures. For when Oxford decided to publish *Venus and Adonis,* a poem whose central purpose was to glorify his homosexual lover Southampton, he faced a serious problem. It was not enough to publish it anonymously; he needed a blind to divert suspicion about his relations with the younger earl. He chose the name William Shakespeare, a slightly more elegant adaptation of the rather homely William Shakspere. Was Mr. Shakspere one of the actors in his employ? This seems likely. Mr. Shakspere clearly had some role in the Lord Chamberlain's Men, of which he is named a few years later as a shareholder. That he was directly attached to Oxford also seems probable, since he disappears from the London records for several years after Oxford's death in June 1604. William Shakespeare is listed among the actors in the king's coronation procession in March of that year, but he is missing from another record in August. It would seem that he returned to Stratford when Oxford died.

For nearly three centuries, beginning with Nicholas Rowe, thousands of scholars, many of them subsidized by government treasuries, have searched for connections between Mr. Shakspere and his imputed works. This massive search, consuming countless professorial man-hours, has turned up nothing of significance—and has failed to banish doubts about Mr. Shakspere's authorship. Meanwhile, a handful of amateurs, many of them innocent of rigorous method and hardly knowing where to look for materials, have managed, in a relatively short period, to amass an impressive case for Oxford's authorship. For all their defects, quirks, and disadvantages, the amateurs keep gaining adherents. One might object that the many apparent links between Shakespeare's works and Oxford's life, milieu, poems, letters, and biblical annotations may be coincidental. In that case, we are forced to ask not only why there are so many of them, but why Mr. Shakspere's records, over hundreds of years, have yielded none. When all is said, the case for Mr. Shakspere's authorship still stands just where it stood in 1623, when the Folio, under the authority of the Herbert brothers, made it official.

It is the Stratfordian view, not the Oxfordian, that lacks all literary pertinence. It has proven utterly sterile—as sterile as the Baconian view—for our understanding of Shakespeare's works. This is most apparent in the Sonnets, whose basic question of factuality has profoundly confused mainstream scholars. The Oxfordian view, trimmed of its crankish excesses, opens a door to a completely new understanding of the great plays and poems, promising rewards, now hardly imaginable, for those readers and scholars who can bear to let go of the old view. It will surely bring about radical renewal in biography, literary history, criticism, and the Shakespeare canon itself. As Oxford's poems and letters are recovered, our conception of Shakespeare's development will be greatly enriched. We will acquire new ways of determining whether the author of *King Lear* and *Hamlet* also wrote such disputed plays as *Sir Thomas More* and *Edward III*. It may become possible to see how Oxford's acquaintances—including Golding, Lyly, Spenser, Nashe, Southampton, Burghley, and Elizabeth I herself—fit into the most amazing literary career of all time.

However it happens, Oxford's acceptance as Shakespeare will change Shakespeare studies beyond recognition. Nearly half a century ago, Harold Clarke Goddard wrote hauntingly: "I believe we are nearer the beginning than the end of our understanding of Shakespeare's genius." Those may prove the most prophetic words yet written about our ever-living poet.

APPENDIXES

M r . S h a k s p e r e ' s W i l l

*M*r. Shakspere's will, dated 1616, is the only document in which he speaks in the first person. It may have been composed by his lawyer, Francis Collins; and this doubt of his authorship calls his very literacy into question.

But even if Mr. Shakspere did write it, the will lacks any personal detail or spark of style that might mark it as Shakespearean. It is difficult to imagine the great poet writing a document of more than 1300 words without leaving a single recognizable touch of his literary personality, distinctive expression, or sheer verbal energy. The document bespeaks a respectable citizen of some wealth and local social connections, with old friends in the London theater. He gives no indication of literary talent or interest. He bequeaths no books, manuscripts, musical instruments, or other tokens of what we would recognize as an artistic bent. He shows no acquaintance with Shakespeare's supposed patrons, the earls of Southampton, Pembroke, and Montgomery, or with any men of letters, though the poet Michael Drayton lived in a nearby town.

After all, there is no good reason why the style of the will should be anything other than entirely humdrum, and it in no way suggests an ability, or desire, to turn a phrase. Mr. Shakspere, contemplating death, no doubt had many things on his mind. Perhaps pretending to be the poet and playwright William Shakespeare was not one of them.

> In the name of God, Amen! I William Shackspeare, of Stratford upon Avon in the county of Warr., gent., in perfect health and memory, God be praised, do make and ordain this my last will and testament in manner and form following; that is to say, first, I commend my soul into the hands of God my Creator, hoping and assuredly believing, through the only merits of Jesus Christ my Savior to be made partaker of life everlasting, and my body to the earth whereof it is made. Item, I give and bequeath unto my daughter Judith one hundred and fifty pounds of lawful English money, to be paid unto her in the manner and form following; that is to say, one hundred pounds in discharge of her marriage portion within one year after my decease, with consideration after the rate of two shillings in the pound for so long time as the same shall be unpaid unto her after my decease, and the fifty pounds residue thereof upon her surrendering of, or giving of such sufficient security as the overseers of this my will shall like of, to surrender or grant all her estate and right that shall descend or come unto her after my decease, or that she now hath, of, in, or to, one copyhold tenement, with the appurtenances, lying and being in Stratford upon Avon aforesaid in the said county of Warr., being parcel or holden of the manor of Rowington, unto my daughter Susanna Hall and her heirs forever. Item, I give and bequeath unto my said daughter Judith one hundred and fifty pounds more, if she or any issue of her body be living at the end of three years next ensuing the day of the date of this my will, during which time my executors are to pay her consideration from my decease according to the rate aforesaid; and if she die within the said term without issue of her body, then my will is, and I do give and bequeath one hundred pounds thereof to my niece Elizabeth Hall, and the fifty pounds to be set forth to my executors during the life of my sister Joan Hart, and the use and profit thereof coming shall be paid to my said sister Joan, and after her decease the said 50 pounds shall remain amongst the children of my said sister, equally to be divided amongst them; but if my said daughter Judith be living at the end of the said three years, or any issue of her body, then my will is, and so I devise and bequeath the said hundred and fifty pounds to be set out by my executors and overseers for the best benefit of her and her issue, and the stock to be paid unto her so long as she shall be married and covert baron; but my will is, that she shall have the consideration yearly paid unto her during her life, and, after her decease, the said stock and consideration to be paid to her children, if she have any, and if not, to her executors or assigns, she living the said term after my decease. Provided that if such husband as she shall at the end of

the said three years be married unto, or at any after, do sufficiently assure unto her and the issue of her body lands answerable to the portion by this my will given unto her, and to be adjudged so by my executors and overseers, then my will is, that the said 150 pounds shall be paid to such husband as shall make such assurance, to his own use.

Item, I give and bequeath unto my said sister Joan 20 pounds and all my wearing apparel, to be paid and delivered within one year after my decease; and I do will and devise unto her the house with the appurtenances in Stratford, wherein she dwelleth, for her natural life, under the yearly rent of 12 pence. Item, I give and bequeath unto her three sons, William Hart, ——— Hart, and Michael Hart, five pounds apiece, to be paid within one year after my decease. Item, I give and bequeath unto the said Elizabeth Hall, all my plate, except my broad silver and gilt bowl, that I now have at the date of this my will.

Item, I give and bequeath unto the poor of Stratford aforesaid ten pounds; to Mr. Thomas Combe my sword; to Thomas Russell, Esquire, five pounds; and to Francis Collins, of the borough of Warr. in the county of Warr., gentleman, thirteen pounds, six shillings, and eightpence, to be paid within one year after my decease. Item, I give and bequeath to Hamlet Sadler 26 s. 8 d. to buy him a ring; to William Reynolds, gent., 26 s. 8 d. to buy him a ring; to my godson William Walker 20 s. in gold; to Anthony Nash, gent., 26 s. 8 d.; and to Mr. John Nashe 26 s. 8 d.; and to my fellows John Hemings, Richard Burbage, and Henry Condell, 26 s. 8 d. apiece to buy them rings. Item, I give, will, bequeath, and devise, unto my daughter Susanna Hall, for better enabling of her to perform this my will, and towards the performance thereof, all that capital messuage or tenement with the appurtenances, situate, lying, and being in Henley Street, within the borough of Stratford aforesaid; and all my barns, stables, orchards, gardens, lands, tenements, and hereditaments whatsoever, situate, lying, and being, or to be had, received, perceived, or taken, within the towns, hamlets, villages, fields, and grounds, of Stratford upon Avon, Oldstratford, Bushopton, and Welcombe, or in any of them in the said county of Warr. And also all that messuage or tenement with the appurtenances, wherein one John Robinson dwelleth, situate, lying, and being, in the Blackfriars in London, near the Wardrobe; and all my other lands, tenements, and hereditaments whatsoever, to have and to hold all and singular the said premises, with their appurtenances, unto the said Susanna Hall, for and during the term of her natural life, and after her decease, to the first son of her body lawfully issuing, and to the heirs males of the body of the said first son lawfully issuing; and for the default of such issue, to the second son of her body, lawfully issuing, and to the heirs males of the body of the said second son lawfully issuing; and for default of such heirs, to the third son of the body of the said Susanna lawfully issuing, and of the heirs males of the body of the said third son lawfully issuing; and for default of such issue, the same so to be and remain to the fourth, fifth, sixth, and seventh sons of her body lawfully issuing, one after another, and to the heirs males of the bodies of the said fourth, fifth, sixth, and seventh sons lawfully issuing, in such manner as it is before limited to be and remain to the first, second, and third sons of her body, and to their heirs males; and for default of such issue, to my daughter Judith, and the heirs males of her body lawfully issuing; and for default of such issue, to the right heirs of me the said William Shackspeare forever.

Item, I give unto my wife my second best bed with the furniture. Item, I give and bequeath to my said daughter Judith my broad silver gilt bowl. All the rest of my goods, chattel, leases, plate, jewels and household stuff whatsoever, after my debts and legacies paid, and my funeral expenses discharged, I give, devise, and bequeath to my son in law, John Hall, gent., and my daughter Susanna, his wife, whom I ordain and make executors of this my last will and testament. And I do entreat and appoint the said Thomas Russell Esquire and Francis Collins, gent., to be overseers hereof, and do revoke all former wills, and publish this to be my last will and testament. In witness whereof I have hereunto put my hand, the day and year first above written.

By me William Shakspeare

Appendix 2 ～

Oxford's Poems

*B*ecause no plays bearing Oxford's name are extant, his known poems provide the best basis for comparing his writing with Shakespeare's.

The poems are variously judged; some critics rank them as brilliant and accomplished, but C.S. Lewis comments: "Edward de Vere, Earl of Oxford, shows, here and there, a faint talent, but is for the most part undistinguished and verbose." These are, after all, youthful poems. One of them was published in 1573, when Oxford was twenty-three; in another, Oxford refers to himself as a "young man." Nobody knows exactly when any of the others were written; Professor Steven May puts the latest possible date for any of them at 1593, and they were probably written long before that. Some suspect that most were written before 1573. Few would call them works of genius. How, then, can they be Shakespeare's? Perhaps because they are early poems. They certainly display strong similarities to the artificially rhetorical manner of much of Shakespeare's earlier work and his nondramatic poetry. We must bear in mind that whoever wrote *The Tempest* was at one time capable of writing *Titus Andronicus,* a play so inferior to Shakespeare's mature work that its authorship was formerly in doubt.

The crucial question is whether the parallels between Oxford's twenty or so known poems and Shakespeare's work are more numerous than can reasonably be assigned to coincidence and poetic convention. These poems bear hundreds of resemblances to Shakespeare's phrasing, far too many to be dismissed as insignificant. The kinship is evident in these poems' themes, turns of phrase, word associations, images, rhetorical figures, various other mannerisms, and, above all, general diction.

Not all of the parallels are of the same order. Some are trivial or conventional; others are highly distinctive and idiosyncratic. But, while we may disagree over particular cases, the sheer number of examples is overwhelming. The following poems ascribed to Oxford are followed by noteworthy parallels from the Shakespearean canon.

labouring man 'let the magistrates be labouring men' *2 Henry VI* 4.2.18. **tills the fertile soil** 'fertile England's soil' *2 Henry VI* 1.1.238. 'soil's fertility' *Richard II* 3.4.39. **reaps the harvest fruit** 'after the man That the main harvest reaps' *As You Like It* 3.5.103. 'And reap the harvest which that rascal sow'd' *2 Henry VI* 3.1.381. 'We are to reap the harvest of his son.' *3 Henry VI* 2.2.116. 'To reap the harvest of perpetual peace' *3 Henry VI* 5.2.15. 'My poor lips, which should that harvest reap' *Sonnets* 128.7. **harvest . . . toil** 'Scarce show a harvest of their heavy toil' *Love's Labour's* 4.3.323. **He pulls the flowers, he plucks but weeds** 'They bid thee crop a weed, thou pluck'st a flower.' *Venus* 946. 'which I have sworn to weed and pluck away' *Richard II* 2.3.167. 'He weeds the corn, and still lets grow the weeding.' *Love's Labour's* 1.1.96. **high degree** 'Thou wast installed in that high degree.' *1 Henry VI* 4.1.17. 'And thou art but of low degree.' *Othello* 2.3.94. 'Take but degree away, untune that string, And hark what discord follows' *Troilus* 1.3.109. {**The mason poor that builds the lordly halls . . .**} **The idle drone that labours not at all, Sucks up the sweet of honey from the bee** 'For so work the honey-bees . . . The singing masons building roofs of gold . . .} the lazy yawning drone' *Henry V* 1.2. {187, 198, 204. 'Not to eat honey like a drone from others' labors' *Pericles* 2.ch.18 'Where the bee sucks' *Tempest* 5.1.88. 'Drones suck not eagles' blood, but rob beehives.' *2 Henry VI* 4.1.109. 'Death, that hath suck'd the honey of thy breath' *Romeo* 5.3.92. 'That suck'd the honey of his music vows' *Hamlet* 3.1.156. 'And suck'd the honey which thy chaste bee kept.' *Lucrece* 840. **Who worketh most to their share least doth fall** 'the fewer men, the greater share of honour' *Henry V* 4.3.22. **most/least** (see below) **The swiftest hare unto the mastive slow** 'like a brace of greyhounds, Having the fearful flying hare in sight' *3 Henry VI* 2.5.130. **The greyhound thereby doth miss his game** 'like greyhounds in the slips . . . The game's afoot!' *Henry*

The labouring man that tills the fertile soil,
And reaps the harvest fruit, hath not indeed
The gain, but pain; and if for all his toil
He gets the straw, the lord will have the seed.
The manchet file falls not unto his share;
On coarsest cheat his hungry stomach feeds.
The landlord doth possess the finest fare;
He pulls the flowers, he plucks but weeds.
The mason poor that builds the lordly halls,
Dwells not in them; they are for high degree;
His cottage is compact in paper walls,
And not with brick or stone, as others be.
The idle drone that labours not at all,
Sucks up the sweet of honey from the bee;
Who worketh most to their share least doth fall,
With due desert reward will never be.
The swiftest hare unto the mastive slow
Oft-times doth fall, to him as for a prey;
The greyhound thereby doth miss his game we know
For which he made such speedy haste away.
So he that takes the pain to pen the book,
Reaps not the gifts of goodly golden muse;
But those gain that, who on the work shall look,
And from the sour the sweet by skill doth choose;
For he that beats the bush the bird not gets,
But who sits still and holdeth fast the nets.

V 3.1.31. 'thy greyhounds are as swift' *Shrew* ind.2.47. **speedy haste** 'Good lords, make all the speedy haste you may' *Richard III* 3.1.60. **the sour the sweet** 'Speak sweetly, man, although thy looks be sour' *Richard II* 3.2.193. 'How sour sweet music is When time is broke' *Richard II* 5.5.42. 'that thy sour leisure gave sweet leave' *Sonnets* 39.10. 'Sweetest nut hath sourest rind.' *As You Like It* 3.2.109. 'Touch you the sourest points with sweetest terms.' *Antony* 2.2.24. 'For sweetest things turn sourest by their deeds.' *Sonnets* 94.13. 'To that sweet thief which sourly robs from me.' *Sonnets* 35.14. 'The sweets we wish for turn to loathed sours.' *Lucrece* 867. **For he that beats the bush the bird not gets, But who sits still and holdeth fast the nets.** 'Poor bird, thou'dst never fear the net nor lime.' *Macbeth* 4.2.34. 'Look how a bird lies tangled in a net' *Venus* 67. 'Birds never lim'd no secret bushes fear.' *Lucrece* 88. Sh often has 'lim'd bushes.' **takes the pain . . . sits still** Shakespeare uses both expressions many times.

Ev'n as the wax doth melt, or dew consume away/Before the sun, so I, behold, through careful thoughts decay 'as soon decay'd and done As is the morning's silver melting dew Against the golden splendor of the sun' *Lucrece* {23}. 'her wax must melt' *3 Henry VI* 3.2.51. 'solid flesh would melt, Thaw, and resolve itself into a dew.' *Hamlet* 1.2.129. 'let virtue be as wax And melt in her own fire' *Hamlet* 3.4.85. 'when sun doth melt their snow' *Lucrece* 1218. 'that melted at the sweet tale of the sun's' *1 Henry IV* 2.4.121. 'melted away with rotten dews' *Coriolanus* 2.3.32. 'cold snow melts with the sun's hot beams' *2 Henry VI* 3.1.223. 'As mountain snow melts with the midday sun' *Venus* 750. 'Scarce had the sun dried up the dewy morn' *Passionate Pilgrim* 6.1. 'That you in pity may dissolve to dew' *Richard II* 5.1.9. 'To dew the sovereign flower and drown the weeds' *Macbeth* V.2.30. **consume away** 'Therefore let Benedick, like cover'd fire, Consume away in sighs, waste inwardly.' *Much Ado* 3.1.78. 'consume away in rust' *King John* 4.1.65. **that hath myself in hate** 'My name, dear saint, is hateful to myself.' *Romeo* 2.2.55. 'He scowls and hates himself for his offense.' *Lucrece* 738. 'Whose deed hath made herself herself detest.' *Lucrece* 1566. **And he that beats the bush the wished bird not gets, But such, I see, as sitteth still and holds the fowling nets** (see above) **The drone more honey sucks, that laboureth not at all** (see above) **to whose most pain least pleasure doth befall** 'no pains, sir, I take pleasure in singing, sir' *Twelfth Night* 2.4.68. 'Having no other pleasure of his gain But torment that it cannot cure his pain' *Lucrece* 860. **So I the pleasant grape have pulled from the vine** 'For one sweet grape who will the vine destroy?' *Lucrece* 215. **I wove the web of woe** 'Now she unweaves the web that she hath wrought' *Venus* 991. **weed . . . grow** 'To weed my vice and let his grow' *Measure* 3.2.70.

Ev'n as the wax doth melt, or dew consume away
Before the sun, so I, behold, through careful thoughts decay;
For my best luck leads me to such sinister state,
That I do waste with others' love, that hath myself in hate.
And he that beats the bush the wished bird not gets,
But such, I see, as sitteth still and holds the fowling nets.

The drone more honey sucks, that laboureth not at all,
Than doth the bee, to whose most pain least pleasure doth befall:
The gard'ner sows the seeds, whereof the flowers do grow,
And others yet do gather them, that took less pain I trow.
So I the pleasant grape have pulled from the vine,
And yet I languish in great thirst, while others drink the wine.
Thus like a woeful wight I wove the web of woe,
The more I would weed out my cares, the more they seem'd to grow:
The which betokeneth, forsaken is of me,
That with the careful culver climbs the worn and wither'd tree,
To entertain my thoughts, and there my hap to moan,
That never am less idle, lo! than when I am alone.

crown of bays 'an olive branch and laurel crown' *3 Henry VI* 4.6.34. 'crowns, sceptres, laurels' *Troilus* 1.3.107. **The more I follow'd one, the more she fled away** 'The more I hate, the more he follows me.' *Midsummer* 1.1.197. 'I follow'd fast, but faster he did fly' *Midsummer* 3.3.4. **As Daphne did full long agone, Apollo's wishful prey** 'Apollo flies, and Daphne holds the chase' *Midsummer* 2.1.231. 'Tell me, Apollo, for thy Daphne's love' *Troilus* 1.1.98. **The more my plaints I do resound, the less she pities me; The more I sought, the less I found** 'And so by hoping more they have but less' *Lucrece* 137. 'Not that I loved Caesar less, but that I loved Rome more.' *Caesar* 3.2.22. 'A little more than kin, and less than kind.' *Hamlet* 1.2.65. 'More than I seem, and less than I was born to' *3 Henry VI* 3.1.56. 'That moves in him more rage and lesser pity' *Lucrece* 468. 'The lesser thing should not the greater hide.' *Lucrece* 663. 'The repetition cannot make it less, For more it is than I can well express.' *Lucrece* 1285. 'An eye more bright than theirs, less false in rolling' *Sonnets* 20.5. **Melpomene** Muse of tragedy. **doleful tunes** 'a very doleful tune' *Winter's Tale* 4.4.262. **Drown me with trickling tears** 'we drown our gains in tears' *All's Well* 4.3.68. 'which burns Worse than tears drown' *Winter's Tale* 2.1.112. 'My heart is drown'd with grief, Whose flood begins to flow within mine eyes.' *2 Henry VI* 3.1.198. 'Lest with my sighs or tears I blast or drown' *3 Henry VI* 4.4.23. 'tears shall drown the wind' *Macbeth* 1.7.25. 'drown the stage with tears' *Hamlet* 2.2.562. 'Then can I drown an eye unus'd to flow' *Sonnets* 30.5. 'But floods of tears will drown my oratory' *Titus* 5.3.90. 'who drown'd their enmity in my true tears' *Titus* 5.3.107. 'To drown me in thy sister's flood of tears' *Errors* 3.2.46. **these hands to rend my hairs** 'Is it not as this mouth should tear this hand For lifting food to 't?' *Lear* 3.4.15. 'These hands shall tear her' *Much Ado* 4.1.191. 'Whose breath indeed these hands have newly stopp'd' *Othello* 5.2.202. 'Let him have time to tear his curled hair' *Lucrece* 981. **On whom the scorching flames of love doth feed** 'whom flaming war doth scorch' *Kinsmen* 1.1.91. 'feed'st thy light's flame' *Sonnets* 1.6. 'To feed for aye her lamp and flames of love' *Troilus* 3.2.160. **you muses nine** 'Be thou the tenth muse' *Sonnets* 38.9. **An anchor's life to lead** 'An anchor's cheer in prison be my scope!' *Hamlet* 3.2.219. **scratch . . . grave . . . worms** Cf. the dying Mercutio: 'A scratch, a scratch . . . Ask for me tomorrow, and you shall find me a grave man. . . . They have made worms' meat of me.' *Romeo* 3.1.93 ff. 'Let's talk of graves, of worms, and epitaphs' *Richard II* 3.2.145. **Where earthly worms on me shall feed, Is all the joy I crave** 'I wish you all joy of the worm.' *Antony* 5.2.260. 'And food for —' 'For worms, brave Percy.' *1 Henry IV* 5.4.86.

A crown of bays shall that man wear,
   That triumphs over me;
   For black and tawny will I wear,
Which mourning colours be.

The more I follow'd one,
     the more she fled away,
As Daphne did full long agone,
     Apollo's wishful prey.
The more my plaints I do resound,
     the less she pities me;
The more I sought the less I found,
     that mine she meant to be.

Melpomene alas, with doleful tunes help than;
And sing *Bis,* woe worth on me forsaken man.

Then Daphne's bays shall that man wear,
     that triumphs over me;
For black and tawny will I wear,
     which mourning colours be.
Drown me with trickling tears,
     you wailful wights of woe;
Come help these hands to rend my hairs,
     my rueful haps to show.
On whom the scorching flames
     of love doth feed you see;
Ah a lalalantida, my dear dame,
     hath thus tormented me.

Wherefore you muses nine,
     with doleful tunes help than,
And sing *Bis,* woe worth on me forsaken man.
Then Daphne's bays shall that man wear,
     that triumphs over me;
For black and tawny will I wear,
     which mourning colours be.

An anchor's life to lead,
     with nails to scratch my grave,
Where earthly worms on me shall feed,
     is all the joys I crave;

past all recovery 'For grief that they are past recovery' *2 Henry VI* 1.1.116. **My life, through ling'ring long** 'life, which false hope lingers in extremity' *Richard II* 2.2.72. **My death delay'd to keep from life the harm of hapless days.** 'In the delaying death.' *Measure* 4.2.164. 'His days may finish ere that hapless time.' *1 Henry VI* 3.1.200. **deep distress** 'deeply distress'd' *Venus* 814. **distress are drown'd** Ophelia, drowning, is 'incapable of her own distress' *Hamlet* 4.7.178. **loss of my good name** 'good name' occurs eight times in Sh; see Iago esp. **of my griefs the ground** 'the true ground of all these piteous woes' *Romeo* 5.3.180. 'the grounds and motives of her woe' *Lover's Complaint* 63. **Such piercing plaints as answer might, or would my woeful case** 'Hearing how our plaints and prayers do pierce' *Richard II* 5.3.127. **with tears upon my face** 'Cooling his hot face in the chastest tears' *Lucrece* 682. 'Poor soul, thy face is much abus'd with tears.' *Romeo* 4.1.29. **Of all that may in heaven or hell, in earth or air be found** 'Whether in sea or fire, in earth or air, Th'extravagant and erring spirit hies To his confine.' *Hamlet* 1.1.153. 'i'th'air, or th'earth?' *Tempest* 1.2.388. **To wail with me this loss of mine** 'Wailing our losses, whiles the foe doth rage' *3 Henry VI* 2.3.26. 'Wise men ne'er sit and wail their loss' *3 Henry VI* 5.4.1. 'That she hath thee is of my wailing chief, A loss in love that touches me more dearly.' *Sonnets* 42.3. **Help fish, help fowl** 'Of more pre-eminence than fish and fowls.' *Errors* 2.1.23. 'Ay, when fowls have no feathers, and fish have no fin.' *Errors* 3.1.79. **salt sea soil** 'salt-sea shark' *Macbeth* 4.1.24. 'salt sea' *Henry V* 1.2.209. 'this salt flood' *Romeo* 3.5.134. 'Neptune's salt wash' *Hamlet* 3.2.156. **Help echo that in air doth flee, shrill voices to resound** 'And fetch shrill echoes from the hollow earth' *Shrew* ind.2.46. 'As is the maiden's organ, shrill and sound.' *Twelfth Night* 1.4.33. 'What shrill-voiced suppliant makes this eager cry?' *Richard II* 5.3.75.

And hide myself from shame,
>   sith that mine eyes do see,
Ah a lalalantida, my dear dame,
>   hath thus tormented me.
And all that present be,
>   with doleful tunes help than,
And sing *Bis* woe worth, on me forsaken man.

Fram'd in the front of forlorn hope past all recovery,
I stayless stand, t' abide the shock of shame and infamy.
My life, through ling'ring long, is lodg'd in lair of loathsome ways;
My death delay'd to keep from life the harm of hapless days.
My sprites, my heart, my wit and force, in deep distress are drown'd;
The only loss of my good name is of these griefs the ground.

And since my mind, my wit, my head, my voice and tongue are weak,
To utter, move, devise, conceive, sound forth, declare and speak,
Such piercing plaints as answer might, or would my woeful case,
Help crave I must, and crave I will, with tears upon my face,
Of all that may in heaven or hell, in earth or air be found,
To wail with me this loss of mine, as of these griefs the ground.

Help gods, help saints, help sprites and powers that in the heaven do dwell,
Help ye that are aye wont to wail, ye howling hounds of hell;
Help man, help beasts, help birds and worms, that on the earth do toil;
Help fish, help fowl, that flock and feed upon the salt sea soil,
Help echo that in air doth flee, shrill voices to resound,
To wail this loss of my good name, as of these griefs the ground

I am not as I seem to be 'I am not what I am.' *Othello* 1.1.65. **Nor when I smile I am not glad** 'I am not merry; but I do beguile The thing I am by seeming otherwise.' *Othello* 2.1.125. **most in mirth, most pensive sad** 'I show more mirth than I am mistress of' *As You Like It* 1.2.3. 'With mirth in funeral, and with dirge in marriage' *Hamlet* 1.2.12. 'So mingled as if mirth did make him sad' *Kinsmen* 5.3.52. 'But sorrow that is couch'd in seeming gladness Is like that mirth fate turns to sudden sadness' *Troilus* 1.1.40. 'sad tales doth tell To pencill'd pensiveness' *Lucrece* 1496. **As Hannibal that saw in sight/His country soil with Carthage town, By Roman force defaced down** 'And see the cities and the towns defac'd' *1 Henry VI* 3.3.45. Sh has four mentions of Hannibal and seven of Carthage. **Pompey** Two Roman plays and five others refer to Pompey. **A flood of tears he seemed to shed** 'to drown me in thy sister's flood of tears' *Errors* 3.2.46. 'Return thee therefore with a flood of tears' *1 Henry VI* 3.3.56. 'the tears that she hath shed for thee Like envious floods o'errun her lovely face.' *Shrew* ind.2.66. 'But floods of tears will drown my oratory' *Titus* 5.3.90. **I, Hannibal that smile for grief; And let you Caesar's tears suffice; The one that laughs at his mischief; The other all for joy that cries. I smile to see me scorned so, You weep for joy to see me woe** 'Then they for sudden joy did weep, And I for sorrow sung, That such a king should play bo-peep, And go the fools among.' *Lear* 1.4.175. 'weeping joys' *2 Henry VI* 1.1.34. 'how much better is it to weep at joy than to joy at weeping!' *Much Ado* 1.1.28. **a heart by Love slain dead** 'Number there in love was slain' *Phoenix* 28. 'Presume not on thy heart when mine is slain.' *Sonnets* 22.13. **O cruel hap and hard estate/That forceth me to love my foe** 'My only love sprung from my only hate!' *Romeo* 1.5.138. 'Prodigious birth of love it is to me, That I must love a loathed enemy!' *Romeo* 1.5.140. **Accursed be so foul a fate** 'I doubt some foul play . . . O cursed spite!' *Hamlet* 1.5.188. **So long to fight with secret sore/And find no secret salve therefore** (see below) **But I in vain do breathe my wind** 'You breathe in vain' *Timon* 3.5.59. 'no wind of blame shall breathe' *Hamlet* 4.7.66. **mirth . . . sad . . . flood of tears . . . annoy . . . grief . . . tears suffice** Compare *Lucrece* 1109–13 and 1676–80:

> For mirth doth search the bottom of annoy;
> Sad souls are slain in merry company;
> Grief best is pleas'd with grief's society.
> > True sorrow then in feelingly suffic'd
> > When with like semblance it is sympathiz'd.

> 'Dear lord, thy sorrow to my sorrow lendeth
> Another power; no flood by raining slaketh.
> My woe too sensible thy passion maketh,
> > More feeling-painful. Let it then suffice
> > To drown one woe, one pair of weeping eyes.'

I am not as I seem to be,
Nor when I smile I am not glad;
A thrall, although you count me free,
I most in mirth, most pensive sad.
I smile to shade my bitter spite
As Hannibal that saw in sight
His country soil with Carthage town,
By Roman force defaced down.

And Caesar that presented was,
With noble Pompey's princely head;
As 'twere some judge to rule the case,
A flood of tears he seemed to shed;
Although indeed it sprung of joy;
Yet others thought it was annoy.
Thus contraries be us'd I find,
Of wise to cloak the covert mind.

I, Hannibal that smile for grief;
And let you Caesar's tears suffice;
The one that laughs at his mischief;
The other all for joy that cries.
I smile to see me scorned so,
You weep for joy to see me woe,
And I, a heart by Love slain dead,
Presents in place of Pompey's head.

O cruel hap and hard estate
That forceth me to love my foe;
Accursed be so foul a fate,
My choice for to prefix it so.
So long to fight with secret sore
And find no secret salve therefore;
Some purge their pain by plaint I find,
But I in vain do breathe my wind.

Reason's reins my strong affection stay 'for now I give my sensual race the rein' *Measure* 2.4.160. 'What rein can hold licentious wickedness' *Henry V* 3.3.22. 'curb his heat, or rein his rash desire' *Lucrece* 706. 'he cannot Be rein'd again to temperance' *Coriolanus* 3.3.28. **quiet breast** 'Truth hath a quiet breast.' *Richard II* 1.3.96. 'Into the quiet closure of my breast' *Venus* 782. **secret thoughts** 'Nor shall he smile at thee in secret thought.' *Lucrece* 1065. 'the history of all her secret thoughts' *Richard III* 3.5.28. **lurks in my breast** 'Or tyrant folly lurk in gentle breasts' *Lucrece* 851. **my grief through Wisdom's power oppress'd** 'To counterfeit oppression of such grief.' *Richard II* 1.4.14. **But who can leave to look on Venus' face, Or yieldeth not to Juno's high estate? What wit so wise as gives not Pallas place?** 'great and high estate' *Pericles* 4.4.16. 'his high estate' *Lucrece* 92. etc. 'The shrine of Venus, or straight-pight Minerva' *Cymbeline* 5.5.164. **What worldly wight can hope for heavenly hire** 'These earthly godfathers of heaven's lights' *Love's Labour's* 1.1.88. 'heaven's praise with such an earthly tongue' *Love's Labour's* 4.2.118. 'My vow was earthly, thou a heavenly love.' *Love's Labour's* 4.3.64. 'a heavenly effect in an earthly actor.' *All's Well* 2.3.23. 'Between this heavenly and this earthly sun' *Venus* 198. 'Such heavenly touches ne'er touch'd earthly faces.' *Sonnets* 17.8. **roll the restless stone** 'That stands upon the rolling restless stone' *Henry V* 3.6.29. **Yet Phoebe fair disdained the heavens above, To joy on earth her poor Endymion's love.** 'And the moon sleeps with Endymion.' *Merchant* 5.1.109. **happy star** 'a happy star Led us to Rome' *Titus* 4.2.32. **A slavish smith, of rude and rascal race, Found means in time to gain a Goddess' grace.** 'as like as Vulcan and his wife' *Troilus* 1.3.168. **streams of tears** 'my eye shall be the stream' *Merchant* 3.2.46. 'weeping as fast as they stream forth thy blood' *Caesar* 3.1.201. 'mine eyes . . . shall gush pure streams' *Lucrece* 1076. 'And round about her tear-distained eye Blue circles stream'd' *Lucrece* 1587. **pine and die** 'To love, to wealth, to pomp, I pine and die.' *Love's Labour's* 1.1.31.

If care or skill could conquer vain desire,
Or Reason's reins my strong affection stay:
There should my sighs to quiet breast retire,
And shun such signs as secret thoughts betray;
Uncomely Love which now lurks in my breast
Should cease, my grief through Wisdom's power oppress'd.

But who can leave to look on Venus' face,
Or yieldeth not to Juno's high estate?
What wit so wise as gives not Pallas place?
These virtues rare each God did yield a mate;
Save her alone, who yet on earth doth reign,
Whose beauty's string no God can well distrain.

What worldly wight can hope for heavenly hire,
When only sighs must make his secret moan?
A silent suit doth seld to grace aspire,
My hapless hap doth roll the restless stone.
Yet Phoebe fair disdain'd the heavens above,
To joy on earth her poor Endymion's love.

Rare is reward where none can justly crave,
For chance is choice where reason makes no claim;
Yet luck sometimes despairing souls doth save,
A happy star made Gyges joy attain.
A slavish smith, of rude and rascal race,
Found means in time to gain a Goddess' grace.

Then lofty Love thy sacred sails advance,
My sighing seas shall flow with streams of tears,
Amidst disdains drive forth thy doleful chance,
A valiant mind no deadly danger fears;
Who loves aloft and sets his heart on high
Deserves no pain, though he do pine and die.

What wonders love hath wrought 'Love wrought these miracles.' *Shrew* 5.1.124. **Paris, Priam's son** 'As Priam was for all his valiant sons.' *3 Henry VI* 2.5.120. 'a son of Priam' *Troilus* 3.3.26. 'the youngest son of Priam' *Troilus* 4.5.96. 'sons, Half of the number that King Priam had' *Titus* 1.1.80. 'Had doting Priam check'd his son's desire.' *Lucrece* 1490. 'all Priam's sons' *Troilus* 2.2.126. 'One of Priam's daughters' *Troilus* 3.3.194. 'great Priam's seed' *Troilus* 4.5.121. 'A bastard son of Priam's.' *Troilus* 5.7.15. 'You valiant offspring of great Priamus.' *Troilus* 2.2.207. **the god of sleep** 'the god of sleep' *1 Henry IV* 3.1.217. Note that neither Shakespeare nor Oxford uses the god's name, Hypnos or Somnus. **cometh but by fits** 'a woman's fitness comes by fits.' *Cymbeline* 4.1.6

The lively lark stretched forth her wing, The messenger of Morning bright 'Lo here the gentle lark, weary of rest, From his moist cabinet mounts up on high, And wakes the morning.' *Venus* 853. 'the morning lark' *Midsummer* 4.1.94 and *Shrew* ind.2.44. 'the lark, the herald of the morn' *Romeo* 3.5.6. 'And then my state (Like to the lark at break of day arising From sullen earth) sings hymns at heaven's gate.' *Sonnets* 29.10. 'Hark! Hark! The lark at heaven's gate sings, And Phoebus 'gins arise.' *Cymbeline* 2.3.22. **cheerful voice** 'Lords, with one cheerful voice welcome my love.' *2 Henry VI* 1.1.36. **The Day's approach** 'the approach of day' *Henry V* 4.1.88. **When that Aurora blushing red** 'And yonder shines Aurora's harbinger, At whose approach, ghosts, wandering here and there, Troop home to churchyards.' *Midsummer* 3.2.380-2. 'When lo the blushing morrow Lends light to all' *Lucrece* 1082. **Thetis' bed** 'Aurora's bed' *Romeo* 1.1.136. 'Hymen's purest bed' *Timon* 4.3.383. 'Cytherea, how bravely thou becom'st thy bed!' *Cymbeline* 2.2.15. 'Cupid grant all tongue-tied maidens here bed' *Troilus* 3.2.211. 'Juno's crown, O blessed bond of board and bed!' *As You Like It* 5.4.142. 'Whom Jove hath mark'd The honour of your bed' *Kinsmen* 1.1.30. **The courteous knight** 'You are right courteous knights.' *Pericles* 2.3.27. **What things did please and what did pain** 'But since you make your pleasure of your pains' *Twelfth Night* 3.3.2.

The trickling tears that fall along my cheeks 'trickling tears' *1 Henry IV* 2.4.391. 'With cadent tears fret channels in her cheeks.' *Lear* 1.4.285. 'Tears' & 'cheeks' oft together in Sh. **The secret sighs that show my inward grief** 'my grief lies all within' *Richard II* 4.1.295. 'A plague of sighing and grief!' *1 Henry IV* 2.4.332. 'Consume away in sighs, waste inwardly' *Much Ado* 3.1.78. **present pains** ''Tis good for men to love their present pains.' *Henry V* 4.1.18. **Bid me renew my cares without relief** 'And by her presence still renew his sorrows' *Titus* 5.3.82. **thy mortal foe** 'But I return his sworn and mortal foe.' *3 Henry VI* 3.3.257. 'I here

My meaning is to work what wonders love hath wrought,
Wherewith I must, why men of wit have love so dearly bought.
For love is worse than hate, and eke more harm hath done;
Record I take of those that rede of Paris, Priam's son.

It seemed the god of sleep had maz'd so much his wits,
When he refused wit for love, which cometh but by fits.
But why accuse I him, whom th'earth hath cover'd long?
There be of his posterity alive, I do him wrong.
Whom I might well condemn, to be a cruel judge
Unto myself, who hath the crime in others that I grudge.

The lively lark stretch'd forth her wing,
The messenger of Morning bright;
And with her cheerful voice did sing,
The Day's approach, discharging Night;
When that Aurora blushing red,
Descried the guilt [gilt?] of Thetis' bed.

I went abroad to take the air, and in the meads I met a knight,
Clad in carnation colour fair; I did salute this gentle wight:
Of him I did his name inquire,
He sigh'd and said it was Desire.

Desire I did desire to stay; awhile with him I crav'd to talk,
The courteous knight said me no nay, but hand in hand with me did walk;
Then of Desire I ask'd again,
What things did please and what did pain?
He smil'd and thus he answer'd than: 'Desire can have no greater pain,
Than for to see another man, that he desireth to obtain;
Nor greater joy can be than this:
Than to enjoy that others miss.'

The trickling tears that falls along my cheeks,
The secret sighs that shows my inward grief,
The present pains perforce that Love aye seeks,
Bids me renew my cares without relief;
In woeful song, in dole display,
My pensive heart for to bewray.

proclaim myself thy mortal foe.' *3 Henry VI* 5.1.94. **The stricken deer hath help to heal his wound** 'Why, let the stricken deer go weep' *Hamlet* 3.2.287. 'My pity hath been balm to heal their wounds' *3 Henry VI* 14.8.41. **The haggard hawk with toil is made full tame** *Shrew;* see below. **The strongest tower, the cannon lays on ground** 'a tower of strength' *Richard III* 5.3.12. 'topples down Steeples and moss-grown towers' *1 Henry IV* 3.1.32. 'Who in a moment even with the earth Shall lay your stately and air-braving towers' *1 Henry VI* 3.1.12. 'When sometime lofty towers I see down rased' *Sonnets* 64.3. **thrall to Love by Cupid's sleights** 'Love makes young men thrall and old men dote.' *Venus* 837. **weigh my cause with equal weights** 'you weigh equally' *Measure* 2.2.126. 'I have in equal balance justly weigh'd' *2 Henry IV* 4.1.67. 'Commit my cause in balance to be weigh'd' *Titus* 1.1.55. 'equalities are so weighed' *Lear* 1.1.6. 'In equal scale weighing delight and dole' *Hamlet* 1.2.13. 'acquainted with a weighty cause' *Shrew* 4.4.26. **She is my joy, she is my care and woe** 'Your tributary drops belong to woe, Which you, mistaking, offer up to joy.' *Romeo* 3.2.103. **She is my pain, she is my ease therefore** 'Give physic to the sick, ease to the pain'd' *Lucrece* 901. **She is my death, she is my life also** 'Showing life's triumph in the map of death' *Lucrece* 402. 'But that life liv'd in death, and death in life' *Lucrece* 406. 'life imprison'd in a body dead' *Lucrece* 1456. 'Yet in this life Lie hid moe thousand deaths.' *Measure* 3.1.39. 'And seeking death, find life' *Measure* 3.1.44. 'That life is better life, past fearing death.' *Measure* 5.1.397. **She is my salve, she is my wounded sore** 'The humble salve which wounded bosoms fits' *Sonnets* 120.12. 'To see the salve doth make the wound ache more.' *Lucrece* 1116. 'such a salve can speak That heals the wound' *Sonnets* 34.8. 'A salve for any sore that may betide' *3 Henry VI* 4.6.88. 'My pity hath been balm to heal their wounds.' *3 Henry VI* 4.8.41. 'your majesty may salve The long-grown wounds of my intemperance' *1 Henry IV* 3.2.155. **save and end my life** 'Some happy mean to end a hapless life.' *Lucrece* 1045. **And shall I live on earth to be her thrall?** 'but I, my mistress' thrall' *Sonnets* 154.12. **And let her feel the power of all your might, And let her have her most desire with speed, And let her pine away both day and night** 'Since my young lady's going into France, sir, the fool hath much pined away.' *Lear* 1.4.73. 'Go to Flint Castle, there I'll pine away.' *Richard II* 3.2.209. **And let her moan, and none lament her need; And let all those that shall her see, Despise her state and pity me.** 'This you should pity rather than despise.' *Midsummer* 3.2.235. Compare *Lucrece* 981:

> 'Let him have time to tear his curled hair,
> Let him have time against himself to rave,
> Let him have time of time's help to despair,
> Let him have time to live a loathed slave,
> Let him have time a beggar's orts to crave,
>   And time to see one that by alms doth live
>   Disdain to him disdained scraps to give.'

Bewray thy grief, thou woeful heart with speed;
Resign thy voice to her that caused thee woe;
With irksome cries, bewail thy late done deed,
For she thou lov'st is sure thy mortal foe.
And help for thee there is none sure,
But still in pain thou must endure.

The stricken deer hath help to heal his wound,
The haggard hawk with toil is made full tame;
The strongest tower, the cannon lays on ground,
The wisest wit that ever had the fame,
Was thrall to Love by Cupid's sleights;
Then weigh my cause with equal weights.

She is my joy, she is my care and woe;
She is my pain, she is my ease therefore;
She is my death, she is my life also,
She is my salve, she is my wounded sore:
In fine, she hath the hand and knife
That may both save and end my life.

And shall I live on th'earth to be her thrall?
And shall I sue and serve her all in vain?
And kiss the steps that she lets fall,
And shall I pray the gods to keep the pain
From her that is so cruel still?
No, no, on her work all your will.

And let her feel the power of all your might,
And let her have her most desire with speed,
And let her pine away both day and night,
And let her moan, and none lament her need;
And let all those that shall her see,
Despise her state and pity me.

Fain would I sing, but fury makes me fret 'Fain would I woo her, yet I dare not speak' *1 Henry VI* 5.3.65. **fury makes me fret, And Rage** 'And with the wind in greater fury fret' *Lucrece* 648. 'the furious winter's rages' *Cymbeline* 4.2.259. 'Rancorous spite, more furious raging broils' *1 Henry VI* 4.1.185. **Rage hath sworn to seek revenge of wrong** 'seek not t'allay My rages and revenges' *Coriolanus* 5.3.85. 'And you both have vow'd revenge On him' *3 Henry VI* 1.1.55. 'I will revenge his wrong to Lady Bona' *3 Henry VI* 3.3.197. **fury . . . My mazed mind** 'wise, amaz'd, temp'rate, and furious' *Macbeth* 2.3.108. **in malice so is set** 'Nothing extenuate, Nor set down aught in malice' *Othello* 5.2.343. **As Death shall daunt my deadly dolours long** 'As ending anthem of my endless dolour' *Two Gentlemen* 3.1.242. 'But none where all distress and dolour dwell'd' *Lucrece* 1446. 'To think their dolour others have endured' *Lucrece* 1582. **Patience perforce is such a pinching pain** 'Patience perforce with willful choler meeting' *Romeo* 1.5.89. **As die I will or suffer wrong again** 'patience, tame to sufferance' *Sonnets* 58.7. 'a present remedy, at least a patient sufferance' *Much Ado* 1.3.9. 'what wrongs we suffer' *2 Henry IV* 4.1.68. 'the wrongs I suffer' *Errors* 3.1.16. 'Shall tender duty make me suffer wrong?' *Richard II* 2.1.164. 'such suffering souls That welcome wrongs' *Caesar* 2.1.140. **to suffer such abuse** 'he shall not suffer indignity' *Tempest* 3.2.37. **Nor will I frame myself to such as use** 'And frame my face to all occasions' *3 Henry VI* 3.2.185. 'That she preparedly may frame herself To the way she's forc'd to' *Antony* 5.1.55. 'Frame yourself to orderly soliciting' *Cymbeline* 2.3.46. **such despite** 'thrown such despite and heavy terms upon her' *Othello* 4.2.116. 'she fram'd thee in high heaven's despite' *Venus* 731. **No quiet sleep shall once possess mine eye** 'Sin of self-love possesseth all mine eye' *Sonnets* 62.1. 'What a strange drowsiness possesses them!' *Tempest* 2.1.199. **some device** 'Every day thou daff'st me with some device' *Othello* 4.2.175. 'plot some device of further misery' *Titus* 3.1.134. 'by some device or other' *Errors* 1.2.95. 'entrap thee by some treacherous device' *As You Like It* 1.1.151. 'I think by some odd gimmors or device' *1 Henry 6* 1.2.41. **pay Despite his due** 'More is thy due than more than all can pay.' *Macbeth* 1.4.21. 'Pay him the due of honey-tongued Boyet.' *Love's Labour's* 5.2.334. 'duer paid to the hearer than the Turk's tribute' *2 Henry IV* 3.2.307. 'be spent, And as his due writ in my testament' *Lucrece* 1183. **raze the ground** 'raze the sanctuary' *Measure* 2.2.170. 'raz'd oblivion' *Sonnets* 122.7. etc. **in rage of ruthful mind refus'd** 'in rage With their refusal' *Coriolanus* 2.3.259. **ruthful mind** 'ruthful deeds' *3 Henry VI* 2.5.95. 'ruthful work' *Troilus* 5.3.48.

Fain would I sing, but fury makes me fret,
And Rage hath sworn to seek revenge of wrong;
My mazed mind in malice so is set,
As death shall daunt my deadly dolours long;
Patience perforce is such a pinching pain,
As die I will or suffer wrong again.

I am no sot to suffer such abuse
As doth bereave my heart of his delight;
Nor will I frame myself to such as use
With calm consent to suffer such despite;
No quiet sleep shall once possess mine eye
Till Wit have wrought his will on Injury.

My heart shall fail, and hand shall lose his force,
But some device shall pay Despite his due;
And Fury shall consume my careful corse,
Or raze the ground whereon my sorrow grew.
Lo, thus in rage of ruthful mind refus'd,
I rest reveng'd of whom I am abus'd.

sweet boy 'sweet boy' *Venus* 155, 583, 613. 'sweet boy' *Sonnets* 108.5. **Fresh youth** 'whose youth and freshness Wrinkles Apollo's' *Troilus* 2.2.78. **Sad sighs** 'Sad sighs, deep groans' *Two Gentlemen* 3.1.232. **What had'st thou then to drink? Unfeigned lovers' tears.** 'drink my tears' *King John* 4.1.62. 'Ye see I drink the water of my eye.' *3 Henry VI* 5.4.75. 'Thy napkin cannot drink a tear of mine.' *Titus* 3.1.140. 'as lovers they do feign' *As You Like It* 3.3.22. 'Dismiss your vows, your feigned tears' *Venus* 425. **What Cradle wert thou rocked in?** 'And rock his brains In cradle of the rude . . .' *1 Henry IV* 3.1.19. 'If drink rock not his cradle' *Othello* 4.4.28. **What lulled thee to thy sleep?** 'the virgin voice That babies lull asleep' *Coriolanus* 3.2.115. **Sweet thoughts** 'But these sweet thoughts do even refresh my labours' *Tempest* 3.1.14. 'That I in your sweet thoughts would be forgot' *Sonnets* 71.7. **What feedeth most thy sight? To gaze on beauty still.** 'with gazing fed' *Merchant* 3.2.68. 'I have fed mine eyes on thee.' *Troilus* 4.5.231. 'Her eye must be fed.' *Othello* 2.1.225. 'But when his glutton eye so full hath fed' *Venus* 399. 'He fed them with his sight' *Venus* 1104. 'That makes me see, and cannot feed mine eye?' *All's Well* 1.1.221. 'I feed Most hungerly on your sight' *Timon* 1.1.252. 'Fold in the object that did feed her sight.' *Venus* 822. 'starves the ears she feeds' *Pericles* 5.1.112. **Will ever age or death/Bring thee into decay?** 'Death, desolation, ruin, and decay' *Richard III* 4.4.409. 'folly, age, and cold decay' *Sonnets* 11.6.

Wing'd with desire, I seek to mount on high 'Whose haughty spirit, winged with desire' *3 Henry VI* 1.1.267. 'Borne by the trustless wings of false desire' *Lucrece* 2. 'the gentle lark, weary of rest, From his moist cabinet mounts up on high' *Venus* 854. 'That mounts no higher than a bird can soar' *2 Henry VI* 2.1.14. **Sith comfort ebbs, and cares do daily flow** 'And sorrow ebbs, being blown with wind of words.' *Lucrece* 1330. 'Thus ebbs and flows the current of her sorrow.' *Lucrece* 1569. 'ebb and flow with tears' *Romeo* 3.5.133. 'The sea will ebb and flow' *Love's Labour's* 4.3.212. 'ebb and flow like the sea' *1 Henry IV* 1.2.31. 'great ones, That ebb and flow by th' moon' *Lear* 5.3.19. **But sad despair would have me to retire, When smiling hope sets forward my desire** 'our hope but sad de-

When wert thou born, Desire?
      In Pomp and prime of May.
By whom, sweet boy, wert thou begot?
      By good Conceit, men say.
Tell me who was thy Nurse?
      Fresh youth, in sugar'd Joy.
What was thy meat and daily food?
      Sad sighs with great Annoy.
What had'st thou then to drink?
      Unfeigned lovers' tears.
What Cradle wert thou rocked in?
      In Hope devoid of Fears.
What lulled thee to thy sleep?
      Sweet speech that lik'd me best.
And where is now thy dwelling place?
      In gentle hearts I rest.
Doth Company displease?
      It doth in many a one.
Where would Desire then choose to be?
      He likes to muse alone.
What feedeth most your sight?
      To gaze on Favour still.
Whom find'st thou most thy foe?
      Disdain of my good will.
Will ever Age or Death
      Bring thee unto decay?
No, no, Desire both lives and dies
      Ten thousand times a day.

Winged with desire, I seek to mount on high;
Clogged with mishap yet am I kept full low;
Who seeks to live and finds the way to die,
Sith comfort ebbs, and cares do daily flow.
  But sad despair would have me to retire,
    When smiling hope sets forward my desire.

I still do toil and never am at rest,
Enjoying least when I do covet most;
With weary thoughts are my green years oppress'd,
To danger drawn from my desired coast.

spair' *3 Henry VI* 2.3.9. 'Where hope is coldest and despair most fits' *All's Well* 2.1.144. 'past hope, and in despair' *Cymbeline* 1.1.137. 'Despair and hope makes thee ridiculous.' *Venus* 988. **Enjoying least when I do covet most . . . With least abode where best I feel content . . . Then least alone when most I seem to lurk** 'With what I most enjoy contented least' *Sonnets* 29.8. 'When most impeach'd stands least in thy control' *Sonnets* 125.14. 'In least speak most' *Midsummer* 5.1.105. 'Seeming to be most which we indeed least are' *Shrew* 5.2.175. **Now craz'd with Care** 'The grief hath craz'd my wits' *Lear* 3.4.170. **feigned joy** 'And all that poets feign of bliss and joy' *3 Henry VI* 1.2.31. **twixt fear and comfort toss'd** 'Is madly toss'd between desire and dread' *Lucrece* 171. **I speak of peace, and live in endless strife** 'as thou liv'st in peace, die free from strife' *Richard II* 5.6.27. 'And for the peace of you I hold such strife' *Sonnets* 75.3. **Bragging of heaven yet feeling pains of hell** 'If not to heaven, then hand in hand to hell.' *Richard III* 5.3.313. 'To shun the heaven that leads men to this hell.' *Sonnets* 129.14. 'Though this a heavenly angel, hell is here.' *Cymbeline* 2.2.50. 'If not in heaven, you'll surely sup in hell.' *2 Henry VI* 5.1.216. **sweet friend** the vocative 'sweet'

Now craz'd with Care, then haled up with Hope,
With world at will yet wanting wished scope.

I like in heart, yet dare not say I love,
And looks alone do lend me chief relief.
I dwelt sometimes at rest yet must remove,
With feigned joy I hide my secret grief.
    I would possess, yet needs must flee the place
    Where I do seek to win my chiefest grace.
Lo thus I live twixt fear and comfort toss'd,
With least abode where best I feel content;
I seld resort where I should settle most,
My sliding times too soon with her are spent.
    I hover high and soar where Hope doth tower,
    Yet froward Fate defers my happy hour.

I live abroad but still in secret grief,
Then least alone when most I seem to lurk;
I speak of peace, and live in endless strife,
And when I play then are my thoughts at work;
    In person far than am in mind full near,
    Making light show where I esteem most dear.

A malcontent yet seem I pleased still,
Bragging of heaven yet feeling pains of hell.
But Time shall frame a time unto my will,
Whenas in sport this earnest will I tell;
    Till then (sweet friend) abide these storms with me,
    Which shall in joys of either fortunes be.

Whereas the Heart at Tennis plays and men to gaming fall 'stuff'd tennis-balls' *Much Ado.* 'tennis-court-keeper' *2 Henry IV* 2.2.18. 'tennis-balls, my liege' *Henry V* 1.2.258. 'There was 'a gaming; . . . There falling out at tennis' *Hamlet* 2.1.56. 'The faith they have in tennis and tall stockings' *Henry VIII* 1.3.30. 'brought to play at tennis.' *Kinsmen* 5.2.56. **Sir Argus' hundred eyes, where-with to watch and pry** 'Watch me like Argus.' *Merchant* 5.1.230. 'purblind Argus, all eyes and no sight' *Troilus* 1.2.29. **Racket . . . Ball** 'When we have match'd our rackets to these balls' *Henry V* 1.2.261. 'But that the tennis-court-keeper knows better than I, for it is a low ebb of linen with thee when thou keepest not racket there.' *2 Henry IV* 2.2.18. **Court . . . chase** 'That all the courts of France will be disturb'd With chases.' *Henry V* 1.2.266.

What cunning can express 'Neither rhyme nor reason can express how much.' *As You Like It* 3.2.398. '"My tongue cannot express my grief"' *Venus* 1069. 'For more it is than I can well express' *Lucrece* 1286. **A thousand Cupids** 'arm'd with thousand Cupids.' *Kinsmen* 2.2.31. **That kindleth soft sweet fire** 'his love-kindling fire' *Sonnets* 153.3. **The lily in the field, That glories in his white, Fair Cynthia's silver light** 'Cynthia for shame obscures her silver shine' *Venus* 728. ''Tis but the pale reflex of Cynthia's brow' *Romeo* 3.5.20. 'Cynthia with her borrowed light' *Kinsmen* 4.1.153. **Compares not with her white, So bright my Nymph doth shine, With this there is a red, Exceeds the Damask-rose; Which in her cheeks is spread, Whence every favour grows.** 'feed on her damask cheek' *Twelfth Night* 2.4.112. 'Upon the blushing rose usurps her cheek' *Venus* 591. 'Her lily hand her rosy cheek lies under' *Lucrece* 386. 'The air hath starved the roses in her cheeks.' *Two Gentlemen* 4.4.154. 'Meantime your cheeks do counterfeit our roses' *1 Henry VI* 2.4.62. 'The roses in thy lips and cheeks shall fade' *Romeo* 4.1.99. 'With cherry lips and cheeks of damask roses' *Kinsmen* 4.1.74. 'rosy lips and cheeks' *Sonnets* 116.9. 'But no such roses see I in her cheeks.' *Sonnets* 130.6. 'as those cheek-roses Proclaim you are no less!' *Measure* 1.4.16. **In sky there is no star, But she surmounts it far.** 'The brightness of her cheek would shame those stars' *Romeo* 2.2.19. **When Phoebus from the bed/Of Thetis doth arise** 'And Phoebus 'gins arise' *Cymbeline* 2.3.21. Sh makes 5 refs to Thetis. **The morning blushing red** 'a blush Modest as morning' *Troilus*

Love Compared to a Tennis Play

Whereas the Heart at Tennis plays and men to gaming fall,
Love is the Court, Hope is the House, and Favour serves the Ball.
The Ball itself is True Desert, the Line which Measure shows
Is Reason, whereon Judgment looks how players win or lose.
The Getty is deceitful Guile, the Stopper, Jealousy,
Which hath Sir Argus' hundred eyes, wherewith to watch and pry.
The Fault wherewith fifteen is lost is want of wit and Sense,
And he that brings the Racket in is double diligence.
And lo, the Racket is Freewill, which makes the Ball rebound,
And Noble Beauty is the chase, of every game the ground.
But Rashness strikes the Ball awry, and where is Oversight?
'A Bandy ho!' the people cry, and so the Ball takes flight.
        Now in the end Goodlyking proves
            Content the game and gain.
        Thus in a Tennis knit I Love,
            A Pleasure mix'd with Pain.

What cunning can express
The favour of her face?
To whom in this distress,
I do appeal for grace.
    A thousand Cupids fly
    About her gentle eye.

From whence each throws a dart,
That kindleth soft sweet fire:
Within my sighing heart,
Possessed by Desire.
    No sweeter life I try,
    Than in her love to die.

The lily in the field,
That glories in his white,
For pureness now must yield,
And render up his right;
    Heaven pictur'd in her face
    Doth promise joy and grace.

1.3.229. **In fair carnations wise; He shows in my Nymph's face, As Queen of every grace. This pleasant lily white, This taint of roseate red; This Cynthia's silver light, This sweet fair Dea spread; These sunbeams in mine eye, These beauties make me die.** Compare this poem with the second stanza of *Venus*:

'Thrice fairer than myself,' thus she began,
'The field's chief flower, sweet above compare,
Stain to all nymphs, more lovely than a man,
More white and red than doves or roses are;
    Nature that made thee with herself at strife
    Saith that the world hath ending with thy life.'

The first stanza introduces the hero as 'rose-cheek'd Adonis.'

Fair Cynthia's silver light,
That beats on running streams,
Compares not with her white,
Whose hairs are all sunbeams;
    Her virtues so do shine,
    As day unto mine eyne.

With this there is a Red,
Exceeds the Damask-Rose;
Which in her cheeks is spread,
Whence every favour grows.
    In sky there is no star,
    That she surmounts not far.

When Phoebus from the bed
Of Thetis doth arise,
The morning blushing red,
In fair carnation wise;
    He shows it in her face,
    As Queen of every grace.

This pleasant lily white,
This taint of roseate red;
This Cynthia's silver light,
This sweet fair Dea spread;
    These sunbeams in mine eye,
    These beauties make me die.

Who taught thee first to sigh, alas, my heart? 'Who taught thee how to make me love thee more . . . ?' *Sonnets* 150.9. **Who taught thy tongue the woeful words of plaint?** 'And if I were thy nurse, thy tongue to teach . . .' *Richard II* 5.3.113. 'To teach my tongue to be so long' *Passionate Pilgrim* 18.52 'How angerly I taught my brow to frown' *Two Gentlemen* 1.2.62. 'And teach your ears to list me with more heed' *Errors* 4.1.101. 'Teach not thy lip such scorn' *Richard III* 1.2.171. 'Those eyes that taught all other eyes to see' *Venus* 952. 'O, she doth teach the torches to burn bright!' *Romeo* 1.5.44. 'Teaching the sheets a whiter hue than white' *Venus* 398. 'Teaching decrepit age to tread the measures' *Venus* 1148. 'Teaching stern murder how to butcher thee' *Richard II* 1.2.32. **woeful words** 'As if they heard the woeful words they told' *Venus* 1126. **tears of bitter smart** 'bitter tears' *Titus* 3.1.6 and 3.1.129. **Who gave thee grief and made thy joys so faint? Who first did paint with colours pale thy face?** 'Affection faints not like a pale-fac'd coward.' *Venus* 569. 'As burning fevers, agues pale and faint' *Venus* 739. **break thy sleeps** 'break not your sleeps for that.' *Hamlet* 4.7.30. 'broke their sleep' *2 Henry IV* 4.5.68; *Coriolanus* 4.4.19. **quiet rest** 'And so God give you quiet rest tonight.' *Richard III* 5.3.43. **strive in virtue . . . In constant truth** 'I did strive to prove The constancy and virtue of your love.' *Sonnets* 117.13. ''gainst the stream of virtue they may strive' *Timon* 4.1.27. **In constant truth to bide so firm and sure** 'Oaths of thy love, thy truth, thy constancy' *Sonnets* 152.10. 'so firm, so constant' *Tempest* 1.2.207. **With patient mind each passion to endure** 'have patience and endure' *Much Ado* 4.1.254. 'endure the toothache patiently' *Much Ado* 5.1.36. 'God of his mercy give You patience to endure' *Henry V* 2.2.180. 'I must have patience to endure the load' *Richard III* 3.7.230. 'I must have patience to endure all this.' *Titus* 2.3.88. 'I have the patience to endure it now.' *Caesar* 4.3.192.

king . . . command content 'Was ever king that joy'd an earthly throne, And could command no more content than I?' *2 Henry VI* 4.9.2. 'a king crown'd with content' *3 Henry VI* 3.1.66. **content . . . obscure . . . A kingdom or a cottage or a grave** 'The king shall be contented; . . . I'll give . . . My gorgeous palace for a hermitage, . . . And my large kingdom for a little grave, A little little grave, an obscure grave.' *Richard II* 3.3.145. 'the obscure grave' *Merchant* 2.7.51. **no thoughts should me torment** 'the torture of the mind' *Macbeth* 3.2.21. 'the thought whereof Doth like a poisonous mineral gnaw my inwards' *Othello* 2.1.296. 'But ah, thought kills me' *Sonnets* 44.9. Compare *Richard II, Henry IV, Henry V,* and *Henry VI* on the woes of kings.

Who taught thee first to sigh, alas, my heart?
  Who taught thy tongue the woeful words of plaint?
Who filled your eyes with tears of bitter smart?
  Who gave thee grief and made thy joys so faint?
Who first did paint with colours pale thy face?
  Who first did break thy sleeps of quiet rest?
Above the rest in court who gave thee grace?
  Who made thee strive in virtue to be best?
In constant truth to bide so firm and sure,
  To scorn the world regarding but thy friend?
With patient mind each passion to endure,
  In one desire to settle to thy end?
Love then thy choice wherein such faith doth bind,
  As nought but death may ever change thy mind.

Were I a king I might command content;
  Were I obscure unknown would be my cares,
And were I dead no thoughts should me torment,
  Nor words, nor wrongs, nor love, nor hate, nor fears;
A doubtful choice of these things which to crave,
A kingdom or a cottage or a grave.

Sitting alone upon my thought in melancholy mood, In sight of sea, and at my back an ancient hoary wood 'Sitting on a bank' *Tempest* 3.2.390. 'Sitting by a brook' *Passionate Pilgrim* 4.1. 'Venus, with Adonis sitting by her' *Passionate Pilgrim* 11.1. **melancholy mood** 'moody and dull melancholy' *Errors* 5.1.79. **Clad all in colour of a nun, and covered with a veil** 'Where beauty's veil doth cover every blot' *Sonnets* 95.11. 'But like a cloistress she will veiled walk.' *Twelfth Night* 1.1.27. **discern her face** 'I could discern no part of his face' *2 Henry IV* 2.2.80. **see a damask rose hid under crystal glass** 'as sweet as damask roses' *Winter's Tale* 4.4.220. 'I have seen roses damask'd, red and white' *Sonnets* 130.5. 'Who glaz'd with crystal gate the glowing roses' *Lover's Complaint* 286. **her soft hand** 'her soft hand's print' *Venus* 353. 'thy soft hands' *Venus* 633. **And sigh'd so sore as might have mov'd some pity in the rocks** 'He is a stone, a very pebble stone, and has no more pity in him than a dog.' *Two Gentlemen* 2.3.11. 'No beast so fierce but knows some touch of pity.' *Richard III* 1.2.71. 'Rush all to pieces on thy rocky bosom.' *Richard III* 4.4.235. 'Beat at thy rocky and wrack-threat'ning heart.' *Lucrece* 590. 'What rocky heart to water will not wear?' *Lover's Complaint* 291. 'My brother's heart, and warm it to some pity, Though it were made of stone' *Kinsmen* 1.1.129. 'hard'ned hearts, harder than stones' *Lucrece* 978. 'O if no harder than a stone thou art, Melt at my tears, and be compassionate; Soft pity enters at an iron gate.' *Lucrece* 593. 'I would to God my heart were flint, like Edward's, Or Edward's soft and pitiful like mine.' *Richard III* 1.3.140. 'May move your hearts to pity if you mark him' *Richard III* 1.3.348. 'I am not made of stones, But penetrable to your kind entreats.' *Richard III* 3.7.224. 'Pity, you ancient stones, those tender babes' *Richard III* 4.1.98. 'a stony adversary' *Merchant* 4.1.4. 'whetted on thy stony heart' *2 Henry IV* 4.5.107. 'the stony-hearted villains' *1 Henry IV* 2.2.26. 'preaching to stones would make them capable . . . piteous action' *Hamlet* 3.4.125–30? 'you blocks, you stones, you worse than senseless things' *Caesar* 1.1.35. 'See whe'er their basest metal be not mov'd.' *Caesar* 1.1.61. 'You are not wood, you are not stones, but men' *Caesar* 3.2.142. 'move The stones of Rome to rise and mutiny' *Caesar* 3.2.230. 'O, you are men of stones!' *Lear* 5.3.258. 'No, my heart is turned to stone.' *Othello* 4.1.183. 'O perjur'd woman, thou dost stone my heart' *Othello* 5.2.63. 'And with a sigh so piteous and profound' *Hamlet* 2.1.91. '. . . And passion in the gods.' *Hamlet* 2.2.515? 'barbarism itself would have pitied him.' *Richard II* 5.2.36. 'Who moving others are themselves as stone.' *Sonnets* 94.3. '"O pity," gan she cry, "flint-hearted boy"' *Venus* 95. (Compare Oxford's 1572 letter: 'on whose tragedies we have a number of French Aeneases in this city, that tell of their own overthrows with tears falling from their eyes, a piteous thing to hear but a cruel and far more grievous thing we must deem it them to see.' 'To see sad sights more moves than hear them told.' *Lucrece* 1324.) **From sighs and shedding amber tears into**

Sitting alone upon my thought in melancholy mood,
In sight of sea, and at my back an ancient hoary wood,
I saw a fair young lady come, her secret fears to wail,
Clad all in colour of a nun, and covered with a veil;
Yet (for the day was calm and clear) I might discern her face,
As one might see a damask rose hid under crystal glass.

Three times, with her soft hand, full hard on her left side she knocks,
And sigh'd so sore as might have mov'd some pity in the rocks;
From sighs and shedding amber tears into sweet song she brake,
When thus the echo answered her to every word she spake:

Oh heavens! who was the first that bred in me this fe*ver?* Vere.
Who was the first that gave the wound whose fear I wear for e*ver?* Vere.
What tyrant, Cupid, to my harm usurps thy golden qui*ver?* Vere.
What wight first caught this heart and can from bondage it deli*ver?* Vere.

Yet who doth most adore this wight, oh hollow caves tell true? You.
What nymph deserves his liking best, yet doth in sorrow rue? You.
What makes him not reward good will with some reward or ruth? Youth.
What makes him show besides his birth, such pride and such untruth?
   Youth.

May I his favour match with love, if he my love will try? Ay.
May I requite his birth with faith? Then faithful will I die? Ay.
      And I, that knew this lady well,
         Said, Lord how great a miracle,
     To her how Echo told the truth,
         As true as Phoebus' oracle.

sweet song she brake 'eyes purging thick amber' *Hamlet* 2.2.198. Sh. has 'shedding tears' twenty-four times; tears and sighs eleven times; 'sigh' with 'weep, 'groan,' 'grief,' etc., many more times. When thus the echo answered her 'Echo replies . . .' *Venus* 695. 'And still the choir of echoes answer so.' *Venus* 840. **to every word she spake** 'And every word doth almost tell my name' *Sonnets* 76.7. **bred in me this fever** 'the raging fire of fever bred' *Errors* 5.1.75. **Who was the first that gave the wound whose fear I wear for ever?** Sh both uses and parodies 'wound' as metaphorical extravagance: 'When griping griefs? the heart doth wound, And doleful dumps the mind oppress' *Romeo* 4.5.126. **What tyrant, Cupid, to my harm usurps thy golden quiver?** 'Cupid have not spent all his quiver in Venice.' *Much Ado* 1.1.272. Sh often uses 'usurp' figuratively. **from bondage it deliver?** 'Cassius from bondage will deliver Cassius.' *Caesar* 1.3.90. **oh hollow caves tell true** 'Else would I tear the cave where Echo lies' *Romeo* 2.2.161. 'And fetch shrill echoes from the hollow earth' *Shrew* ind.2.46. **match with love . . . requite his birth with faith** 'To make a more requital to your love!' *King John* 2.1.34. 'I will requite you with as good a thing' *Tempest* 5.1.169. 'And Benedick, love on, I will requite thee.' *Much Ado* 3.1.111. 'And I do with an eye of love requite her.' *Much Ado* 5.4.24. 'love me to madness, I shall never requite him.' *Merchant* 1.2.65. 'Thou shalt find I will most kindly requite' *As You Like It* 1.1.138. 'I will requite your loves.' *Hamlet* 1.2.250. Not to mention 'unrequited love.' **As true as Phoebus' oracle** 'And in Apollo's name, his oracle' *Winter's Tale* 3.2.118. 'There is no truth at all i'th oracle!' *Winter's Tale* 3.2.140. 'Apollo said, Is't not the tenor of his oracle' *Winter's Tale* 5.1.38. (Phoebus=Apollo).

My mind to me a kingdom is, such perfect joy therein I find 'the perfectest herald of joy' *Much Ado* 2.1.306. **all other bliss that world affords** 'What other pleasure can the world afford?' *3 Henry VI* 3.2.147. 'The spacious world cannot again afford.' *Richard III* 1.2.245. 'The world affords no law to make thee rich.' *Romeo* 5.1.73. 'the sweet degrees that this brief world affords' *Timon* 4.3.253. **grows by kind** 'Your cuckoo sings by kind.' *All's Well* 1.3.63. 'Fitted by kind for rape and villainy' *Titus* 2.1.116. **Though much I want which most men have, yet still my mind forbids to crave.** Compare: 'My library Was dukedom large enough.' *Tempest* 1.2.109. 'O God, I could be bounded in a nutshell, and count myself a king of infinite space, were it not that I have bad dreams.' *Hamlet* 2.2.254. **No princely pomp, no wealthy store** 'To love, to wealth and pomp, I pine and die.' *Love's Labour's* 1.1.31. 'O, him she stores, to show what wealth she had.' *Sonnets* 67.13. **no force to win the victory** 'you have won a happy victory to Rome' *Coriolanus* 5.3.186. **No wily wit** 'upon my

In Praise of a Contented Mind

My mind to me a kingdom is, such perfect joy therein I find,
That it excels all other bliss that world affords or grows by kind;
Though much I want which most men have, yet still my mind forbids to
crave.

No princely pomp, no wealthy store, no force to win the victory,
No wily wit to salve a sore, no shape to feed each gazing eye,
To none of these I yield as thrall; for why? My mind doth serve for all.

I see how plenty suffers oft, how hasty Climbers soon do fall;
I see that those that are aloft, mishap doth threaten most of all;
They get with toil, they keep with fear, such cares my mind could never
bear.

wit, to defend my wiles' *Troilus* 1.2.261. **to salve a sore** 'a salve for any sore that may betide' *3 Henry VI* 4.6.88. **no shape to feed each gazing eye** 'So is mine eye enthralled to thy shape.' *Midsummer* 3.1.139. 'No shape but his can please your dainty eye.' *1 Henry VI* 5.3.38. 'mine eyes have drawn thy shape' *Sonnets* 24.10. (see 'feed'/'eye' above) 'Gaze'/'eyes': together twelve times in Sh. **eye . . . thrall** 'enthralled to thy shape,' above. 'Whose sudden sight hath thrall'd my wounded eye' *Shrew* 1.1.220. **I seek no more than may suffice** 'and have no more of life than may suffice' *Pericles* 2.1.74. **Lo thus I triumph like a king, content with that my mind doth bring.** 'Poor and content is rich and rich enough; But riches fineless is as poor as winter to him that ever fears he shall be poor.' *Othello* 3.3.172. 'For 'tis the mind that make the body rich.' *Shrew* 4.3.172. **Some have too much yet still do crave, I little have and seek no more; They are but poor though much they have and I am rich with little store. They poor, I rich** 'If thou art rich, thou'rt poor' *Measure* 3.1.25. 'Wise things seem foolish and rich things but poor' *Love's Labour's* 5.2.378. 'Fairest Cordelia, that art most rich being poor' *Lear* 1.1.250. 'Rich gifts wax poor' *Hamlet* 3.1.100. 'poorly rich' *Lucrece* 97. 'My riches are these poor habiliments' *Two Gentlemen* 4.1.13. Compare this stanza from *Lucrece* 134–40:

> Those that much covet are with gain so fond
> That what they have not, that which they possess,
> They scatter and unloose it from their bond,
> And so, by hoping more, they have but less;
> Or, gaining more, this profit of excess
>   Is but to surfeit, and such griefs sustain
>   That they prove bankrupt in this poor-rich gain.

I laugh not at another's loss, I grudge not at another's gain 'laugh'd at my losses, mock'd at my gains' *Merchant* 3.1.55. 'I earn that I eat, get that I wear, owe no man hate, envy no man's happiness, glad of other men's good, content with my harm.' *As You Like It* 3.2.74. **No worldly waves my mind can toss** 'By waves from coast to coast is toss'd' *Pericles* 2.ch.34. 'Your mind is tossing on the ocean' *Merchant* 1.1.8. **toss . . . dread** 'madly toss'd between desire and dread' *Lucrece* 171. **I loathe not life** 'the weariest and most loathed worldly life' *Measure* 3.1.128. 'Why then, though loath, yet must I be content.' *3 Henry VI* 4.6.48. **cloaked craft** 'To cloak offenses with a cunning brow' *Lucrece* 749. **My wealth is health and perfect ease** 'Leaving his wealth and ease' *As You Like It* 2.5.52. 'With honor, wealth, and ease in waning age' *Lucrece* 142. **breed offense** 'sith love breeds such offense' *Othello* 3.3.380.

Content I live, this is my stay, I seek no more than may suffice;
I press to bear no haughty sway, look what I lack my mind supplies.
Lo thus I triumph like a king, Content with that my mind doth bring.

Some have too much yet still do crave, I little have and seek no more;
They are but poor though much they have and I am rich with little store.
They poor, I rich, they beg, I give, They lack, I leave, they pine, I live.

I laugh not at another's loss, I grudge not at another's gain,
No worldly waves my mind can toss, my state at one doth still remain;
I fear no foe nor fawning friend, I loathe not life nor dread my end.

Some weigh their pleasure by their lust, their wisdom by their rage of
will,
Their treasure is their only trust, and cloaked craft their store of skill;
But all the pleasure that I find, is to maintain a quiet mind.

My wealth is health and perfect ease, my conscience clear my chief
defense;
I neither seek by bribes to please, nor by desert to breed offense.
Thus do I live, thus will I die, would all did so well as I.

By service long to purchase their good will 'Which I will purchase with my duteous service' *Richard III* 2.1.64. 'purchase us a good opinion' *Caesar* 2.1.145. **how frail those creatures are** 'Frailty, thy name is woman.' *Hamlet* 1.2.146. **To mark the choice they make, and how they change** 'She must change for youth: when she is sated with his body, she will find the error of her choice. She must have change, she must.' *Othello* 1.3.355. **haggards** 'If I do prove her haggard' *Othello* 3.3.260. 'Another way I have to man my haggard.' *Shrew* 4.1.193. **train them to our lure** 'For then she never looks upon her lure.' *Shrew* 4.1.192. **subtle oath** Compare *Sonnets* 138.1–4:

> When my love swears that she is made of truth,
> I do believe her, though I know she lies,
> That she might think me some untutor'd youth,
> Unlearned in the world's false subtleties.

In Peascod time 'these nine and twenty years, come peascod-time' *2 Henry IV* 2.4.383. **when hound to horn gives ear** 'with horn and hound' *Titus* 1.1.494. 'hounds and horns' *Titus* 2.3.27. 'She hearkens for his hounds and for his horn' *Venus* 868. 'Anon Adonis comes with horn and hounds' *Passionate Pilgrim* 9.6. **with pipes of Corn sit keeping beasts in field** 'And in the shape of Corin sat all day, playing on pipes of corn' *Midsummer* 2.1.67. {'When shepherds pipe on oaten straws' *Love's Labour's* 5.2.903.} **parch'd my face with Phoebus** 'parch in Afric sun' *Troilus* 1.3.369. 'Lo! whilst I waited on my tender lambs, And to sun's parching heat display'd my cheeks' *1 Henry VI* 1.2.77. 'Phoebus' burning kisses' *Coriolanus* 2.1.218. 'that am with Phoebus' amorous pinches black' *Antony* 1.5.28. 'Sweats in the eye of Phoebus' *Henry V* 4.1.273. **And there I found the strangest dream, that ever young man had** 'I have had a dream, past the wit of man to say what dream it was.' *Midsummer* 4.1.205. 'Strange dream, that gives a dead man leave to think' *Romeo* 5.1.7. 'the rarest dream that e'er dull'd sleep' *Pericles* 5.1.161. **Christmas game** 'a Christmas gambold' *Shrew* ind.2.138. **I lack the skill to draw** 'I have no skill in sense To make distinction' *All's Well* 3.4.39. 'Sir, I have not much skill in grass.' *All's Well* 4.5.21. 'Had I sufficient skill to utter them' *1 Henry VI* 5.5.13. 'with the little skill I have' *Titus* 2.1.43. 'I have not the skill.' *Hamlet* 3.2.362. 'Julius Caesar Smil'd at their lack of skill' *Cymbeline*

If women could be fair and yet not fond,
Or that their love were firm, not fickle still,
I would not marvel that they make men bond,
By service long to purchase their good will;
    But when I see how frail those creatures are,
    I muse that men forget themselves so far.

To mark the choice they make, and how they change,
How oft from Phoebus do they flee to Pan,
Unsettled still like haggards wild they range,
These gentle birds that fly from man to man;
    Who would not scorn and shake them from the fist
    And let them fly, fair fools, which way they list

Yet for disport we fawn and flatter both,
To pass the time when nothing else can please,
And train them to our lure with subtle oath,
Till, weary of their wiles, ourselves we ease;
    And then we say when we their fancy try,
    To play with fools, O what a fool was I.

In Peascod time when hound to horn gives ear while Buck is kill'd,
    And little boys with pipes of Corn sit keeping beasts in field,
I went to gather Strawberries tho' when woods and groves were fair,
    And parch'd my face with Phoebus lo, by walking in the air.
I lay me down all by a stream and banks all over head,
    And there I found the strangest dream, that ever young man had.

Methought I saw each Christmas game, both revels all and some,
    And each thing else that man could name or might by fancy come,
The substance of the thing I saw, in Silence pass it shall,
    Because I lack the skill to draw, the order of them all;
But Venus shall not scape my pen, whose maidens in disdain,
    Sit feeding on the hearts of men, whom Cupid's bow hath slain.

And that blind Boy sat all in blood, bebathed to the Ears,
    And like a conqueror he stood, and scorned lovers' tears.
'I have more hearts,' quod he, 'at call, than Caesar could command.
    And like the deer I make them fall, that overcross the land.'

I do increase their wand'ring wits, till that I dim their sight.
    'Tis I that do bereave them of their Joy and chief delight.'

2.4.22. 'if I have any skill' *Kinsmen* 5.2.53. 'Which far exceeds his barren skill to show' *Lucrece* 81. 'With too much labour drowns for want of skill.' *Lucrece* 1099. **But Venus shall not scape my pen** 'thou shalt not escape calumny' *Hamlet* 3.1.136. 'and who shall scape whipping?' *Hamlet* 2.2.530. 'the villain shall not scape' *Lear* 2.1.80. 'in sooth you scape not so' *Shrew* 2.1.240. 'we shall not scape a brawl' *Romeo* 3.1.3. **Cupid's bow hath slain** 'Cupid's bow-string' *Much Ado* 3.2.10. 'I swear to thee, by Cupid's strongest bow' *Midsummer* 1.1.169. 'slain in Cupid's wars' *Pericles* 1.1.38. 'by Cupid's bow she doth protest' *Venus* 581. **And that blind Boy sat all in blood, bebathed to the Ears** 'bath'd in maiden blood' *Titus* 2.3.232. 'And let us bathe our hands in Caesar's blood' *Caesar* 3.1.106. 'Or bathe my dying honour in the blood' *Antony* 4.2.6. 'The mailed Mars shall on his altar sit Up to the ears in blood' *1 Henry IV* 4.1.117. **scorned lovers' tears** 'Scorn and derision never come in tears.' *Midsummer* 3.2.123. 'My manly eyes did scorn an humble tear.' *Richard III* 1.2.164. 'Hunting he lov'd, but love he laugh'd to scorn.' *Venus* 4. So mild that patience seem'd to scorn his woes.' *Venus* 1505. **like a conqueror he stood** 'which he stood seiz'd of to the conqueror' *Hamlet* 1.1.89. **conqueror . . . Caesar** 'a kind of conquest Caesar made here' *Cymbeline* 3.1.22. 'What conquest brings [Caesar] home?' *Caesar* 1.1.32. **Caesar:** 'Have I in conquest stretch'd mine arm so far' *Caesar* 2.2.66. 'O mighty Caesar . . . Are all thy conquests, glories, triumphs, spoils' *Caesar* 3.1.149. 'our Caesar tells, "I am conqueror of myself"' *Antony* 4.14.62. **than Caesar could command** 'Hath given the dare to Caesar and commands The empire of the sea' *Antony* 1.2.184. 'As i'th' command of Caesar' *Antony* 3.13.25. 'fit to stand by Caesar And give direction' *Othello* 2.3.122. **like the deer I make them fall** 'Here wast thou bayed, brave hart; Here didst thou fall . . . How like a deer strucken by many princes Doth thou here lie!' *Caesar* 3.1.205. **dim their sight** 'Gazing on that which seems to dim thy sight' *2 Henry VI* 1.2.6. **bereave them of their Joy and chief delight** 'joy delights in joy' *Sonnets* 8.2. 'bereave him of his wits with wonder' *1 Henry VI* 5.3.195. 'restoring his bereaved sense' *Lear* 4.4.9. **this bragging Boy . . . wanton toys** 'To toy, to wanton, dally, smile, and jest' *Venus* 106. 'toys Of feather'd Cupid' *Othello* 1.3.268. 'wanton tricks' *Lucrece* 320. Sh. associates 'wanton' with 'Cupid' and 'boys' six times. **my panting breast** 'To ease his breast with panting' *Coriolanus* 2.2.122. **royal seat** 'The rightful heir of England's royal seat' *2 Henry VI* 5.1.178. 'in the seat royal of this famous isle' *Richard III* 3.1.164. 'this poor seat of England' *Henry V* 1.2.269. 'in Richard's seat to sit' *Richard II* 4.1.218. 'this the regal seat' *3 Henry VI* 1.1.26. 'Have shaken Edward from the regal seat' *3 Henry VI* 4.6.2. 'the supreme seat' *Richard III* 3.7.118. 'the seat of majesty' *Richard III* 3.7.169. **cured were my wound** 'and cureless are my wounds.' *3 Henry VI* 2.6.23. 'For with a wound I must be cur'd.' *Antony* 4.14.78. 'A smile recures the

Thus did I see this bragging Boy advance himself even then,
    Deriding at the wanton toys, of foolish loving men.
Which when I saw for anger then my panting breast did beat,
    To see how he sat taunting them, upon his royal seat.
O then I wish'd I had been free, and cured were my wound.
    Methought I could display his arms, and coward deeds expound.

But I perforce must stay my muse, full sore against my heart
    For that I am a Subject wight, and lanced with his dart.
But if that I achieve the fort, which I have took in charge,
    My Hand and Head with quivering quill, shall blaze his name at large.

wounding of a frown.' *Venus* 465. 'the deer That hath receiv'd some unrecuring wound.' *Titus* 3.1.90. **coward deeds expound** 'to expound His beastly mind' *Cymbeline* 1.6.152. **my muse** 'But my muse labours, And thus she is deliver'd.' *Othello* 2.1.127. 'How can my muse want subject to invent' *Sonnets* 38.1. 'my slight muse' *Sonnets* 38.13. 'So oft have I invok'd thee for my muse' *Sonnets* 78.1. 'And my sick muse doth give another place' *Sonnets* 79.4. 'I grant thou wert not married to my muse' *Sonnets* 82.1. 'My tongue-tied muse in manners holds her still' *Sonnets* 85.1. 'Alack, what poverty my muse brings forth' *Sonnets* 103.1. **achieve the fort** 'the half-achiev'd Harfleur' *Henry V* 3.3.8. **with quivering quill, shall blaze his name** 'One that exceeds the quirks of blazoning pens' *Othello* 2.1.63.

O x f o r d ' s   L e t t e r s

O xford's letters furnish a very different, but equally rich, sampling of his manner of expression. We owe the survival of most of Oxford's letters to the fact that his father-in-law was Lord Burghley, who put his correspondence in the official files. Only one of these letters can be described as literary, and I will return to it in Appendix 4; the rest are casual communications on various subjects, often reflecting the tense and sometimes explosive relations between the two men. Even so, the letters bear many of the verbal mannerisms and idiosyncrasies of Shakespeare. They are the sort of evidence scholars once hoped would turn up in Stratford.

These letters do not show Oxford at inspired moments; most were hastily written and unrevised. They are a chance selection of his correspondence, most of which has been lost; but they furnish a sampling of his way of expressing himself in his everyday dealings, especially with a difficult and overbearing father-in-law.

Many pet words seem to have been borrowed from Shakespeare's plays. One letter, for example, uses the phrase "yet so extenuated"; in *1 Henry IV*, we find "Yet such extenuation let me beg," and "so extenuate" occurs in *Measure for Measure* and *Much Ado About Nothing*. Oxford writes: "This I am assured your Lordship hath good cause to remember"; Shakespeare, in *2 Henry*

IV, writes: "I am assured, if I be measured rightly,/Your majesty hath no just cause to hate me." Oxford writes: "But these things I call only to mind for your Lordship's better remembrance"; Shakespeare, in *Timon of Athens*, writes: "Let it not cumber your better remembrance." Oxford writes of being "eased of many griefs"; Shakespeare, again in *Timon,* uses the phrase "to ease them of their griefs."

Many of the echoes are more than verbal; they often involve themes and images common to Oxford and Shakespeare. Oxford cites the Latin maxim *Finis coronat opus* ("The end crowns the work"). In *2 Henry VI*, we find the maxim in French: *"La fin couronne les oeuvres"*). It appears in English in *Troilus* ("The end crowns all") and in *All's Well:* "All's well that ends well. Still the fine's the crown./What'er the course, the end is the renown."

Oxford writes: "But now time and truth have unmasked all difficulties"; Shakespeare, in *The Rape of Lucrece,* writes: "Time's glory is to calm contending kings,/To unmask falsehood and bring truth to light." Oxford uses the phrase "bring all my hope in her Majesty's words to smoke"; *Lucrece* gives us "this helpless smoke of words," and *King John* yields "calm words folded up in smoke."

In his indispensable study, *"Shakespeare" Revealed in Oxford's Letters,* from which most of these examples are taken, William Plumer Fowler keenly observes a number of links in syntax and rhetoric between Oxford and Shakespeare, such as a marked fondness for the gerund (often accompanied by the definite article and sometimes an adjective as well). When Oxford turns such phrases as "to signify your liking" or "to supply in writing the want of speaking" or "for my liking of Italy," we hear a familiar Shakespearean mannerism. A single paragraph in Oxford's preface to Bedingfield yields four gerunds: *the setting forth, the publishing of your book, profited in the translating, reap knowledge by the reading.* A paragraph in another letter also contains four: *the wise proceeding and orderly dealing, the better achieving, the great liking.* A paragraph in still another letter bears no less than six: *evil dealings, the changing of the name, [the] putting in another, the cozening of so many tenants, the forfeiting of my lease, for forbearing my suit.*

And Oxford several times associates the same pairs of words that Shakespeare does, as when he says he hopes Robert Cecil "will make the end answerable to the rest of your most friendly proceeding"; similarly, Shakespeare says, "If his own life answer the straitness of his proceeding" *(Measure for Measure),* "a feigned friend to our proceedings" *(3 Henry VI),* "equal friendship and proceeding" *(Henry VIII).* Oxford's "promised expedition" finds a mirror twin in Shakespeare's "his expedition promises/Present approach" *(Timon);*

likewise, Oxford's "conceit, which is dangerous" and Shakespeare's "dangerous conceits" *(Othello);* and again, Oxford's "an end according to my expectation" is reflected in Shakespeare's "Our expectation hath this day an end" *(Henry V)*.

Oxford's phrase "in an eternal remembrance to yourself" has a Shakespearean ring, even if we do not immediately think of "Together with remembrance of ourselves" *(Hamlet)*. Oxford writes that "although it be some discouragement to me, yet I cannot alter the opinion I have conceived of your constancy"; Ford, in *The Merry Wives of Windsor,* muses: "Though Page be a secure fool, and stands so firmly on his wife's frailty, yet I cannot put off my opinion so easily."

When Oxford writes "in all kindness and kindred," we may be reminded of Hamlet's "a little more than kin, and less than kind." Oxford's phrase "decked with pearls and precious stones" has its twin in Shakespeare's "decked with diamonds and Indian stones" *(3 Henry VI)*. His "by these lewd fellows" as closely matches Shakespeare's "by this lewd fellow" *(Measure for Measure)*. His "experience doth manifest" resembles Shakespeare's "manifest experience" *(All's Well)*. Of course, one may put too much weight on small and common expressions, and each of these by itself proves little. But the accumulation of them at least is what we should expect if Oxford was Shakespeare. No two writers are likely to overlap this much in their choice of words, even those words that show no special distinction. That Oxford and Shakespeare are both addicted to such adverbs as "earnestly" and "heartily" is one more small sign that they may be the same writer. So is their use (once each) of the rare verb "repugn."

Consider Oxford's letter to Burghley from Siena, dated January 3, 1576. It begins:

> My Lord, I am sorry to hear how hard my fortune is in England, as I perceive by your Lordship's letters, but knowing how vain a thing it is to linger a necessary mischief, (to know the worst of myself, & to let your Lordship understand wherein I would use your honorable friendship) in short I have thus determined, that whereas I understand, the greatness of my debt, & greediness of my creditors, grows so dishonorable to me, and troublesome unto your Lordship, that that land of mine which in Cornwall I have appointed to be sold according to that first order for mine expenses in this travel be gone through withal.

Some of these phrases, though they occur in Shakespeare, are commonplace: "I am sorry to hear," "to let your Lordship understand," "the greatness of my debt." Others are more arresting. "To linger a necessary mischief" reminds us of "To linger out a purposed overthrow" (Sonnet 90) and "And linger not our sure destructions on!" *(Troilus)*. "To stop my creditors' exclamations" recalls "we shall stop her exclamation" *(King John)* and "thus will I drown your exclamations" *(Richard III)*.

On another occasion, Oxford writes angrily to Burghley: "I serve her Majesty, and I am that I am." He is warning Burghley to respect his dignity. Both clauses have their significant counterparts in Shakespeare, where the same simple phrases carry the speaker's sense of his own worth. In *King Lear,* Kent, about to be put in the stocks, protests indignantly: "I serve his majesty"—meaning by the phrase, as Oxford does, that he is not answerable to the man he is addressing at the moment, but only to the monarch. Sonnet 121 also has the proud phrase "I am that I am": "No, I am that I am, and they that level/At my abuses, reckon up their own."

"I have no help but of mine own, and mine is made to serve me and myself, not mine," Oxford writes in another letter to Burghley—echoed in "I must serve my turn out of mine own" *(Timon)*. The closing of the letter— "Thus I leave you to the protection of almighty God"—is likewise echoed (also in *Timon*) by "So I leave you/To the protection of the prosperous gods." Not only is the wording similar; the sentiment and the rhythm are identical. When, writing of his properties, Oxford says, "The woods were preserved, the game cherished, the forest maintained in their full state," he summons a similar triad of verbs in *Richard III:* "preserved, cherished, and kept."

Oxford tells Burghley he would be loath "to trouble your Lordship with so much if I were not kept back here with this tedious suit"; Shakespeare has the phrases "to trouble you with no more suit" (in *The Merchant of Venice*) and "kept a tedious fast" (in *Richard II*). Oxford's letters abound in expressions which, though unremarkable in themselves, Shakespeare habitually uses: *yet notwithstanding, if it please you, find means, bear with me, take another course, ill bestowed, as I perceive, think it strange, stand indebted, put in mind, think fit, most especial, as concerning, most singular, friendly help, I dare presume, laid open, with all kindness, amend the fault, take occasion, give opportunity, as I take it, bear with patience, through ignorance, dearly welcome, in this cause*—as well as slightly more unusual words such as *propound, intercept, endued, privity, molestation, commodious,* and *decipher.*

The verb "decipher," as used in these contexts, deserves special attention. Both Oxford and Shakespeare apply it metaphorically to persons. Oxford writes of his enemies Howard, Southwell, and Arundel that "I do not but so to decipher them to the world," that is, to expose them for what they are: traitors. Shakespeare has "Which is the natural man,/And which the spirit;

who deciphers them?" (*The Comedy of Errors*) and "The white will decipher her well enough" (*Merry Wives*).

As Fowler observes, Oxford displays Shakespeare's penchant for antithesis and paradox: even in these relatively few letters, Oxford plays much like Shakespeare on the opposition of great and small, hope and despair, words and deeds, forgetting and remembering, doing and not doing, shadow and substance, something and nothing, beginning and ending. His phrase "to supply in writing the want of speaking" is characteristic. So is "but of a hard beginning we may hope a good and easy ending," suggesting as it does "Find sweet beginning but unsavory end" (*Venus and Adonis*). Oxford's "if by mine industry I could make something out of this nothing" has several Shakespearean cousins, as in *Richard II:* "For nothing hath begot my something grief,/Or something hath the nothing that I grieve." And in *Lucrece:* "Make something nothing by augmenting it." In the same passage, Oxford writes of his "only desiring you to remember that you may know I do not forget," recalling lines from *The Two Gentlemen of Verona:* "I will forget that Julia is alive,/Remembering that my love to her is dead" and from Sonnet 122: "To keep an adjunct to remember thee/Were to import forgetfulness in me."

Elsewhere Oxford employs what may be Shakespeare's favorite antithesis when he writes: "But the world is so cunning as of a shadow they can make a substance, and of a likelihood a truth." Fowler finds fourteen passages in Shakespeare that play on "shadow' and "substance," including these:

Whilst that this shadow doth such substance give (Sonnet 37)

What is your substance, whereof you are made,
That millions of strange shadows on you tend? (Sonnet 53)

He takes false shadows for true substances. *(Titus Andronicus)*

Each substance of a grief hath twenty shadows. *(Richard II)*

By the Apostle Paul, shadows tonight
Have struck more terror to the soul of Richard
Than can the substance of ten thousand soldiers. *(Richard III)*

In *Measure for Measure*, Shakespeare writes: "For truth is truth to the end of reckoning." Oxford in one letter writes something arrestingly similar: "for truth is truth though never so old, and time cannot make that false which was once true." The theme and phrasing occur several times in Shakespeare: "Truth is truth" (*Love's Labour's Lost*); "A truth's a truth" (*All's Well*); "But truth is truth" (*King John*); "Is not the truth the truth?" (*1 Henry IV*). All these may be oblique plays on the punning motto of the de Veres, *Vero nihil verius*

("Nothing is truer than truth"), as Oxford's letter plays on it; he loved to pun on his name, in English and Latin. It looks as if he did so under the guise of Shakespeare.

Shakespeare uses legal metaphors so freely that several books (assuming that he was Mr. Shakspere) have argued that he must have spent his "lost" years as a legal clerk. Of course, there is no evidence that he was; if he had been, his signature would be found on old wills, depositions, and other documents. But Oxford did have legal training, and his letters often discuss his legal affairs. A letter of 1590 mentions a "lease" that is "supposed void," recalling Sonnet 107: "Can yet the lease of my true love control,/Supposed as forfeit to a confined doom."

The letter refers to "casualties and defects," technical words that Shakespeare uses too. It also uses the terms *eligit, fieri facias,* and *levare facias.* Oxford's other letters employ dozens of legal terms: *acquitted, annuity, arbitrement, arrearages, attainder, champerty, copyholder, detriment, escheat, feoffs, furtherance, jointure, license, monopoly, nominate, patent, petition, precedent, preemption, prescription, proportion, prosecute, redress, solicitation, sureties, tales, testimony,* and many others.

Shakespeare uses more than six hundred legal terms; in the Sonnets alone he employs these: *accessory, account, adverse, advocate, allege, appeal, arrest, audit, bail, bankrupt, bond, cancel, cause, charge, charter, compound, contract, count, counterfeit, debtor, decease, defect, defendant, determinate, due, empanel, exchequer, executor, forfeit, grant, heir, impediment, impeach, informer, inheritor, interest, issue, judgment, lawful, league, lease, misprision, moiety, mortgage, pardon, part, party, patent, plea, possession, privilege, quest, quietus, receipt, recompense, release, render, rent, revenues, seal, session, slander, statute, suborn, subscribe, succession, suit, sum, summon, surety, tenant, title, treason, use, usurer, verdict, will, witness.*

Most of these words, or their close relations, occur in Oxford's letters, especially his 1595 letters on tin mining, which deal with legal details: *account, adversary, allege, appeal, audit, bond, cause, charge, compounded, contract, count, counterfeit, debt, defects, defend, determination, due, exchequer, execute, forfeit, grant, heirs, impeach, informations, inheritance, interest, issue, judgment, lawful, lease, moiety, mortgage, pardon, parties, patent, plead, possession, receipt, recompense, render, rent, revenues, seal, slanderously, statute, successor, suit, sum, sureties, tenants, title, treasons, usage, witness.*

The lexicon of law flows easily from Shakespeare, and its idiom often appears in ingenious figurative combinations (see Sonnets 13, 30, 35, 46, 49, 58, 87, 117, 125, 126, 134, and 146). By contrast, there is only one theatrical metaphor in the Sonnets (23). This tends to suggest a man whose formative years owed more to the law than to the stage. If Mr. Shakspere were our man, we should expect the ratio to be reversed, on the presumption that he knew more about the stage than the law. One biographer, Hesketh Pearson, observes plaintively that legal terms "occur again and again in [Shakespeare's] work, very often to the detriment of his poetry and to the impairment of character."

The same letter of 1590 speaks of "the supply of my present wants," a formula Shakespeare employs several times. Antonio in *The Merchant of Venice* tells Shylock he wishes to "supply the ripe wants of my friend," and Shylock in turn says he would "supply your present wants"; *Richard II* uses the phrase "send them after to supply our wants."

Writing to Robert Cecil in 1603, Oxford sadly refers to Elizabeth's death as "the common shipwreck," an image Shakespeare is fond of. In *Timon* we find "the common wrack" (of Athens), in *Titus Andronicus* "his shipwrack and his commonwealth's," in *Macbeth* "his country's wrack," and in *2 Henry VI* "The commonwealth hath daily run to wrack." Oxford's "among the alterations of time and chance" chimes closely with several passages in Shakespeare, such as this from *2 Henry IV*:

> How chances mock
> And changes fill the cup of alteration
> With divers liquors!

Extending the shipwreck metaphor, Oxford says the queen's death has left him "either without sail whereby to take advantage of any prosperous gale, or without anchor to ride till the storm be overpast." In Shakespeare we find many such nautical images, such as "a prosperous south-wind friendly" *(The Winter's Tale)*, a "happy gale" *(The Taming of the Shrew)*, "auspicious gales" *(The Tempest)*, "anchored in the bay where all men ride" *(Sonnet 137)*, and "till the dregs of the storm be past" *(The Tempest)*.

It is notable that Oxford does express himself spontaneously in metaphor, often military or maritime, even in his casual letters and business dealings. He will speak of himself as "having passed the pikes of so many adversaries." Compare "bristly pikes that ever threat his foes" in *Venus and Adonis*. Oxford writes of his family and Burghley's as being "knit in alliance." Shakespeare uses the same metaphor more than a dozen times. In *Antony and Cleopatra*, Antony and Octavius Caesar are said to be "forever knit together" by Antony's marriage to Octavia; John of England proposes to Philip of France that the two kings "knit our powers" (the same phrase recurs in *2 Henry IV*), and elsewhere he says, "This royal hand and mine are newly knit"; Iago tells Roderigo that "I confess me knit to thy deserving"; and Sonnet 26 begins: "Lord of my love, to whom in vassalage/Thy merit hath my duty strongly knit."

One of Oxford's letters uses the phrase "when the serpent lay hid in the herb." The image occurs several times in Shakespeare. *Romeo* has "O serpent's heart, hid with a flow'ring face!" *Macbeth* contains the famous exhortation, "Look like the innocent flower,/But be the serpent under't." *Richard II* gives us: "And when they from thy bosom pluck a flower,/Guard it, I pray thee, with a lurking adder."

When Oxford writes of "fruits of golden promises," we may think of Shakespeare even if we do not recall "golden promises" from *Titus Andronicus.* But when he writes that he has cause "to bury my hopes in the deep abyss and bottom of despair," few will deny the Shakespearean cadence—there are many specific echoes, from *Richard III*'s "In the deep bosom of the ocean buried" to *The Tempest*'s "In the dark backward and abysm of time." One might also include: "Is not my sorrow deep, having no bottom?" *(Titus Andronicus);* "And deeper than oblivion do we bury/Th'incensing relics of it" *(All's Well);* "Finds bottom in the uncomprehensive deeps" *(Troilus);* "Or dive into the bottom of the deep" *(1 Henry IV);* "In so profound abysm I throw all care" (Sonnet 112).

Oxford's "salve so great an inconvenience" is closely akin to Shakespeare's metaphorical use of "salve," as in "salving thy amiss" (Sonnet 35). Two of Oxford's poems, as we have seen, make similar use of the word.

Even in such short samples of Oxford's most casual, everyday writing, we find Shakespeare's pet terms, his free interchanging of parts of speech, his liberty in forging new words, his quick recourse to the figurative, his fondness for the gerund, his easy fluency, his rhythms, his moral attitudes, his intensifiers, and his sheer authority of expression.

The Preface to
Cardanus Comfort

*L*et us return to Oxford's prefatory letter to Thomas Bedingfield's translation of *Cardanus Comfort,* published in 1573,
bearing in mind that this is the book Hardin Craig called "Hamlet's book."
Oxford, addressing Bedingfield, professes to overrule Bedingfield's refined
(and perhaps coy) reluctance to publish his work. This document unmistak-
ably prefigures the Southampton poems of Shakespeare: the Sonnets, *Venus
and Adonis,* and *The Rape of Lucrece.* Written when Oxford was only twenty-
three, the letter anticipates these poems in spirit, theme, image, and other details. Like those poems, it borrows, for figurative use, the languages of law,
commerce, horticulture, and medicine. It speaks of publication as a duty and
of literary works as tombs and monuments to their authors. It has echoes in
the plays, and the points of resemblance to the Southampton poems are especially notable.

> To my loving friend Thomas Bedingfield Esquire, one of Her Majesty's gen-
> tlemen pensioners.
>
> After I had perused your letters, good Master Bedingfield, finding in them
> your request far differing from the desert of your labour, I could not choose
> but greatly doubt whether it were better for me to yield you your desire, or

execute mine own intention towards the publishing of your book. For I do confess the affections that I have always borne towards you could move me not a little. But when I had thoroughly considered in my mind of sundry and divers arguments, whether it were best to obey mine affections or the merits of your studies, at the length I determined it better to deny your unlawful request than to grant or condescend to the concealment of so worthy a work. Whereby as you have been profited in the translating, so many may reap knowledge by the reading of the same, that shall comfort the afflicted, confirm the doubtful, encourage the coward, and lift up the base-minded man, to achieve to any true sum or grade of virtue, whereto ought only the noble thoughts of men to be inclined.

And because next to the sacred letters of divinity, nothing doth persuade the same more than philosophy, of which your book is plentifully stored, I thought myself to commit an unpardonable error, to have murdered the same in the waste bottoms of my chests; and better I thought it were to displease one, than to displease many: further considering so little a trifle cannot procure so great a breach of our amity, as may not with a little persuasion of reason be repaired again. And herein I am forced like a good and politic captain oftentimes to spoil and burn the corn of his own country, lest his enemies thereof do take advantage. For rather than so many of your countrymen should be deluded through my sinister means of your industry in studies (whereof you are bound in conscience to yield them an account) I am content to make spoil and havoc of your request, and that, that might have wrought greatly in me in this former respect, utterly to be of no effect or operation: and when you examine yourself what doth avail a mass of gold to be continually imprisoned in your bags, and never to be employed to your use? I do not doubt even so you think of your studies and delightful Muses. What do they avail, if you do not participate them to others? Wherefore we have this Latin proverb: *Scire tuum nihil est, nisi te scire hoc sciat alter.* What doth avail the tree unless it yield fruit unto another? What doth avail the vine unless another delighteth in the grape? What doth avail the rose unless another took pleasure in the smell? Why should this tree be accounted better than that tree, but for the goodness of his fruit? Why should this vine be better than that vine, unless it brought forth a better grape than the other? Why should this rose be better esteemed than that rose, unless in pleasantness of smell it far surpassed the other rose?

And so it is in all other things as well as in man. Why should this man be more esteemed than that man, but for his virtue, through which every man desireth to be accounted of? Then you amongst men I do not doubt, but will aspire to follow that virtuous path, to illuster yourself with the ornaments of virtue. And in mine opinion as it beautifieth a fair woman to be decked with pearls and precious stones, so much more it ornifieth a gentleman to be furnished in mind with glittering virtues.

Wherefore considering the small harm I do to you, the great good I do to others, I prefer mine own intention to discover your volume before your request to secret the same; wherein I may seem to you to play the part of the cunning and expert mediciner or physician, who, although his patient in the extremity of his burning fever is desirous of cold liquor or drink to qualify his sore thirst, or rather kill his languishing body, yet for the danger he doth evidently know by his science to ensue, denieth him the same. So you being sick of too much doubt in your own proceedings, through which infirmity you are desirous to bury and insevill your works in the grave of oblivion, yet I, knowing the discommodities that shall redound to yourself thereby (and which is more, unto your countrymen) as one that is willing to salve so great an inconvenience, am nothing dainty to deny your request.

Again, we see if our friends be dead, we cannot show or declare our affection more than by erecting them of tombs; whereby when they be dead indeed, yet make we them live as it were again through their monument; but with me, behold, it happeneth far better, for in your lifetime I shall erect you such a monument, that as I say [in] your lifetime you shall see how noble a shadow of your virtuous life shall hereafter remain when you are dead and gone. And in your lifetime, again I say, I shall give you that monument and remembrance of your life, whereby I may declare my good will, though with your ill will as yet that I do bear you in your life.

Thus earnestly desiring you in this one request of mine (as I would yield to you in a great many) not to repugn the setting forth of your own proper studies, I bid you farewell. From my new country muses at Wivenghole, wishing you as you have begun, to proceed in these virtuous actions. For when all things shall else forsake us, virtue yet will ever abide with us, and when our bodies fall into the bowels of the earth, yet that shall mount with our minds into the highest heavens.

By your loving and assured friend,

—*E. Oxenford.*

Oxford sweetly accuses Bedingfield of hiding his virtues, just as the early Sonnets lovingly accuse the "beauteous and lovely youth," presumably Southampton, of hoarding his beauty from the world. In Shakespeare, we often find the theme that the possessor of a virtue has a duty to share it, as when Cominius chides Coriolanus for his reluctance to allow his heroism to be praised:

> You shall not be
> The *grave* of your *deserving;* Rome must know
> The value of her own. 'Twere a *concealment*
> Worse than a theft, no less than a traducement,
> To hide your doings (1.9.19–23)

Oxford refers to the *desert* of Bedingfield's labor, decides that its *concealment* would be wrong, and charges the translator with wanting to bury it in the *grave* of oblivion. Oxford's *so worthy a work* is also echoed in Menenius Agrippa's praise of Coriolanus' *worthy work.*

Compare also the Duke's speech to Angelo in the first scene of *Measure for Measure:*

> Thyself and thy belongings
> Are not thine own so proper, as to waste
> Thyself upon thy virtues, they on thee.
> Heaven doth with us as we with torches do,
> Not light them for themselves; for if our virtues
> Did not go forth of us, 'twere all alike
> As if we had them not. (1.1.29–35)

Nearly every word Oxford uses in the Bedingfield letter, including the odd *repugn,* is also used somewhere by Shakespeare. Considering the vastness of Shakespeare's vocabulary, this may seem unsurprising. But Oxford displays a wide-ranging—and specifically Shakespearean—vocabulary of his own even in this short letter.

Indeed, there are about ninety distinctive words that also appear in the Sonnets; for example, *perused, desert, labour, doubt, yield, publishing, confess, affections, considered, arguments, merits, determined,* and *unlawful.* A single one of these correspondences would mean next to nothing, but their combination is very suggestive, as when *sum* and *account* both appear in the letter, a paragraph apart; the phrase *sum my count* appears in Sonnet 2. The word *account* is found in four other Sonnets, and 136 speaks of *thy stores' account;* the word *stored* occurs in the same passage of the letter. Oxford's *encourage the coward* is matched by *courage to the coward* in *Venus* (line 1158).

Setting aside common and unavoidable words, we should look in this letter for words used in a Shakespearean manner. Nothing distinguishes a writer more sharply than his use of figurative language, and Oxford, with rhetorical brio, uses more than two dozen images, metaphors, and figures of speech in the short Bedingfield letter. More remarkably, *all of them also appear in Shakespeare's Southampton poems.*

Oxford asks Bedingfield: "[W]hat doth avail a mass of *gold* to be continually imprisoned in your bags, and never to be employed to your *use?*" The theme of use, as opposed to waste, looms large in the early Sonnets and in *Venus,* where we are told (line 768) that *"gold* that's put to *use* more *gold* begets." The youth of the *Sonnets* must think of his "beauty's *use*" (2); his "beauty" must not die *"unused"* (4); legitimate *"use"* must not be confused with "forbidden *usury*" (6).

Oxford's *rose, smell, ornaments, virtue, fair,* and *beautifieth* conjure Shakespeare too; these words, their cognates, and their synonyms occur dozens of times in the poems written for Southampton. Sonnet 54 demands comparison:

> Oh, how much more doth *beauty beauteous* seem
> By that *fair ornament* which truth doth give:
> The *rose* looks *fair,* but *fairer* we it deem
> For that sweet *odor* which doth in it live.
> But, for their *virtue* only is their show, . . .

And Oxford's *"decked* with pearls and precious *stones"* has its near relation in *"decked* with diamonds and Indian *stones"* in *3 Henry VI.* Oxford's "What doth avail the *vine* unless another delighteth in the *grape?"* looks forward to a strikingly similar rhetorical question in *Lucrece* (line 215): "For one sweet *grape* who will the *vine* destroy?"

Oxford says he would have *murdered* Bedingfield's manuscript if he had failed to publish it, Sonnets 9 and 10 call the youth *murd'rous* for failing to beget a copy of himself. Venus (line 54) *"murders* with a kiss" what Adonis is about to say; Adonis' eyes, she later says (at 502), have *"murdered* this poor heart of mine"; her own eyes are "as *murd'red* with the view" of his corpse (at 1031). Lucrece, in her bitter apostrophe to Opportunity (at 885), accuses it: "Thou smother'st honesty, thou *murd'rest* troth"; in killing herself to expiate Tarquin's rape, she says (at 1189): "For in my death I *murder* shameful scorn."

Oxford uses another favored image of Shakespeare's when he speaks of gold as *"imprisoned* in your bags." The *Sonnets* yield us "a liquid *prisoner* pent in walls of glass" (5); "his *imprison'd* pride" (52); *"th'imprisoned* absence of your liberty (58); and *"prison* my heart in thy steel bosom's ward" (133). *Venus* gives us "a lily *prison'd* in a jail of snow" (line 362); *"prison'd* in her eye like pearls of glass" (980); and "the wind *imprison'd* in the ground" (1046). *Lucrece* has darkness stowing day "in her vaulty *prison*" (119); Lucrece's desperate hope that "true respect will *prison* false desire" (642); "life *imprison'd* in a body dead" (1456); Lucrece's honor "ta'en *prisoner* by the foe" (1608); and her ravished body as the "polluted *prison*" of her soul (1726).

Oxford, likening himself to a *physician* whose *patient* craves what would harm him, speaks of a *burning fever* and an *infirmity* in the same paragraph; in *Venus* we find *infirmities* (735) and *burning fevers* (739) four lines apart. Sonnet 147 uses the same thought and the same images:

> My love is as a *fever,* longing still
> For that which longer nurseth the disease,
> Feeding on that which doth preserve the ill,
> The uncertain sickly appetite to please.
> My reason, the *physician* to my love, . . .

And *Lucrece* says (line 904): "The *patient* dies while the *physician* sleeps."

Sharing Shakespeare's fondness for medicinal figures, Oxford also uses the word *salve* metaphorically ("to salve so great an inconvenience"). In the Southampton poems, Shakespeare uses the word the same way, as both noun and verb: "such a salve" (Sonnet 34), "salving thy amiss" (35), "the humble *salve*" (120), "Earth's sovereign salve" (*Venus,* line 28), "To see the salve doth make the wound ache more" (*Lucrece,* line 1116).

Oxford ironically accuses Bedingfield of being "desirous to *bury* and in-sevill your works in the *grave* of *oblivion*." This phrase is Shakespearean, in sentiment, diction, and rhetoric. Sonnet 1 uses the same imagery as Oxford's letter and makes the same protest, that his subject is doing himself wrong:

> Thou that art now the world's fresh *ornament,*
> And only herald to the gaudy spring,
> Within thine own bud *buriest* thy content,
> And, tender churl, mak'st *waste* in niggarding.
> Pity the world, or else this glutton be,
> To eat the world's due, by the *grave* and thee.

And compare Sonnet 31: "Thou art the *grave* where *buried* love doth live."

Shakespeare is partial to images of graves and burial. He feels the pathos of oblivion and an "obscure grave" (the phrase is used in both *Richard II* and *The Merchant of Venice*) and speaks often, as Oxford does in this letter, of the need for *tombs, monuments, remembrances,* and the like against "devouring time," mortality, and forgetfulness. A monument may even be literary: "Your *monument* shall be my gentle verse," Sonnet 81 assures the youth, even though the poet himself is doomed to "a common *grave*" when his young friend shall be "*entombed* in men's eyes." And Oxford similarly tells Bedingfield that in publishing his book, he is erecting him a "*monument* and *remembrance* of your life." (Compare also Henry V's "*tombless*, with no *remembrance* over them.")

Venus, scolding Adonis in the same terms in which the *Sonnets* scold the youth for not marrying, asks (757–62):

> What is thy body but a swallowing *grave,*
> Seeming to *bury* that posterity
> Which by the rights of time thou needs must have,
> If thou destroy them not in dark *obscurity?*
> If so, the world will hold thee in disdain,
> Sith in thy pride so fair a hope is *slain.*

Note here the kinship of "obscurity" to *oblivion* and of the figurative use of "slain" to the similar use of *murder.* In *Lucrece* (946–7), we read that "Time's glory" is, among other things, "To fill with wormholes stately *monuments,*/To feed *oblivion* with decay of things." And compare two phrases from *All's Well That Ends Well: "oblivion* is the *tomb"* (II, 3, 139) and "deeper than *oblivion* do we *bury"* (V, 3, 24). Oxford reminds Bedingfield that by "erecting . . . tombs" (a phrase Shakespeare uses twice, in *1 Henry VI* and *Much Ado*) for our friends, "whereby when they be dead indeed, yet we make them live as it were again through their monument"; but Bedingfield's case is better, because Oxford, by publishing his book, is making him "such a monument that . . . [in] your lifetime you shall see how noble a *shadow* of your virtuous life shall hereafter remain when you are dead and gone." Compare the terms in which *Venus* urges Adonis (and Shakespeare implicitly urges Southampton) to beget a son (lines 171–4):

> By law of nature thou art bound to breed,
> That thine may *live when thou thyself art dead;*
>   And so *in spite of death* thou dost *survive,*
>   In that thy *likeness* still is left *alive.*

Sonnet 17 offers the hope that the young man will "live twice": in a son and in the poet's rhyme. Many other sonnets sound the theme embodied by "To bury and insevill your works in the grave of oblivion." "So long lives this, and this gives life to thee" (18); "My love shall in my verse ever live young" (19); "That in black ink my love may still shine bright" (65); and see also in Sonnets 3, 17, 77, 101, and 4; and in *Venus* 244, *Tempest* 5.1.312, *Titus* 5.3.192, *Richard II* 1.4.15 and 3.2.145, *Richard III* 1.1, *Romeo and Juliet* 2.3.9 and 5.3.83, *Tempest* 4.1.55, *Winter's Tale* 2.1.155, *Two Noble Kinsmen* 5.3.45 and *Timon* 5.1.222. Perhaps most striking, however, are the parallel uses of "monument": "Your monument shall be my gentle verse" (81); "And thou in this shalt find thy monument" (107); "Not marble nor the gilded monuments/Of princes shall outlive this powerful rhyme" (55.1–2); *Hamlet* 5.1.297; *Macbeth* 3.4.71; and in the lovely Sonnet 81:

> Your name from hence immortal life shall have,
> Though I, once gone, to all the world must die;
> The earth can yield me but a common grave,
> When you entombed in men's eyes shall lie.
> Your monument shall be my gentle verse . . .

> You still shall live—such virtue hath my pen—
> Where breath most breathes, even in the mouths of men
> (81.5–9, 13-14)

Oxford's letter is Shakespearean in a wider respect too. in its overwhelming warmth and generosity, verging on excess, yet controlled by a pleasant irony. He loves to praise, but he avoids the risk of fulsomeness by disguising praise as admiring accusation. "For shame!" he says: "You want to hoard your own excellence, deny your virtue to the world!" This is exactly the rhetorical strategy of Sonnets 1 through 17, using much the same language and many of the same images, where Shakespeare lovingly tells his young friend that he is his own worst enemy; for example, "Thyself thy foe, to thy sweet self too cruel. (1), but see also especially Sonnets 4, 9, and 10. Venus, in the same vein, accuses Adonis of self-murder (lines 763–6):

> So in thyself thyself art made away;
> A mischief worse than civil home-bred strife,
> Or theirs whose desperate hands themselves do slay,
> Or butcher sire that reaves his son of life.

Of course, the poetry of the Sonnets and *Venus and Adonis* is far richer than the prose of the Bedingfield letter, which is, after all, a young man's work. Nevertheless, there is ample reason to believe that young man was Shakespeare in embryo.

T h e F u n e r a l E l e g y

S hakespeare scholarship recently enjoyed a rare burst of public-
ity when Vassar College professor Donald Foster presented a
case for Shakespeare's authorship of a long-neglected poem, titled *A Funeral
Elegy*. Its full title, as given on the title page, is *A Funeral Elegy in Memory of the
Late Virtuous Master William Peter of Whipton near Excester* (an old spelling of
Exeter); the author is identified only as "W.S."

The 578-line poem was published as a pamphlet in 1612 by Thomas
Thorpe, who had also published *Shake-speares Sonnets* in 1609. It purports to
be about a young gentleman named William Peter, who, as Foster has ascer-
tained, had been murdered in Exeter in January 1612. The initials W.S. would
have invited the reading public to assume that the author was William Shakespeare; several plays published under these initials in those days clearly adver-
tised his authorship, though nearly all of them were spurious. (Several
authentic plays, on the other hand, were published without identifying him
as the playwright.) But Thorpe was an unusually honest publisher who never,
as far as we know, tried to defraud the public.

The Elegy, as Foster is the first to have noticed, sounds remarkably like
Shakespeare. It begins:

Since Time, and his predestinated end,
Abridg'd the circuit of his hopeful days,
Whiles both his youth and virtue did intend
The good endeavors of deserving praise,
What memorable monument can last
Whereon to build his never-blemish'd name
But his own worth, wherein his life was grac'd,
Sith as it ever he maintain'd the same?
Oblivion in the darkest day to come,
When sin shall tread on merit in the dust,
Cannot rase out the lamentable tomb
Of his short-liv'd deserts; but still they must,
Even in the hearts and memories of men,
Claim fit respect, that they, in every limb
Rememb'ring what he was, with comfort then
May pattern out one truly good by him.

Using stylistic tests and aided by a computer, Foster concludes that Shakespeare was indeed the author of *A Funeral Elegy*. Foster appears to have no interest in the more general authorship controversy; he takes for granted that Shakespeare is Mr. Shakspere of Stratford, so he sees no difficulty in imputing to him a poem written in 1612. But if he is right about the poem's date and origin, his conclusions have inescapable consequences for the authorship question. It would mean that whoever Shakespeare was, he was still writing in early 1612. This would of course rule out Oxford, who had been dead for eight years, as the author.

The Elegy's style, themes, and language are strikingly similar to those of Shakespeare, particularly in the Sonnets, as Foster argues. Nonetheless, he has committed some oversights in his study of the Elegy, and his errors result from the assumption that Mr. Shakspere was the author of the Shakespearean canon.

First, the Elegy is not about William Peter of Exeter. It was written about someone else, most likely many years before 1612. Foster's research has uncovered a good deal of information about William Peter, but the crucial fact remains that he was killed only three years after his marriage at the age of twenty-nine. Moreover, the publisher Thomas Thorpe registered the Elegy for publication in London only three weeks after Peter's death. The Elegy itself never identifies its subject explicitly or connects him with Exeter. Obviously its first audience was expected to know the man it commemorates, along with other facts it alludes to. But the key facts are only touched on, not spelled out. One of the few facts it does make clear, however, is that the dead man left a widow to whom he had been married for "nine of years," and to whom the poet expresses his sympathy. This cannot refer to William Peter, who had been married for only three years at the time of his death. Here is the critical passage:

As then the loss of one, whose inclination
Strove to win love in general, is sad,
So specially his friends, in soft compassion
Do feel the greatest loss they could have had.
Amongst them all, she who those nine of years
Liv'd fellow to his counsels and his bed
Hath the most share in loss; for I in hers
Feel what distemperature this chance hath bred.
The chaste embracements of conjugal love,
Who in a mutual harmony consent,
Are so impatient of a strange remove
As meager death itself seems to lament,
And weep upon those cheeks which nature fram'd
To be delightful orbs in whom the force
Of lively sweetness plays, so that asham'd
Death often pities his unkind divorce.
Such was the separation here constrain'd
(Well worthy to be term'd a rudeness rather),
For in his life his love was so unfeign'd
As he was both a husband and a father—
The one in firm affection and the other
In careful providence, which ever strove
With joint assistance to grace one another
With every helpful furtherance of love.

A further problem exists. Only three weeks passed between Peter's murder and the registration of the Elegy in London. That would be a short enough time if Peter had been murdered in London, but he was murdered in Exeter, 170 miles away. The news might have reached London within a few days, if it had been urgent to inform anyone there; but we have no reason to think it was. And if, as most scholars believe, Mr. Shakspere had retired to Stratford by 1612, the difficulty of imagining a poem written and prepared for the press in London within three weeks sharply increases. Getting the news of Peter's death to Stratford, the composition of the poem, the conveyance of the poem to London, and the decision to publish it would all have had to be accomplished with improbable haste. Nor is it obvious why the poet and the publisher would have been in a rush to get the poem into print. Peter was a minor gentleman, apparently unknown in London. There would be no public demand for a poem in his honor. The only obvious selling point would be the poet's fame—yet only his initials are given.

The poem itself seems aimed at a private audience of those who knew the dead man. Nothing about it suggests that it was intended primarily for publication, let alone immediate publication. As if all this were not strange enough, the Elegy's publisher was Thomas Thorpe, who only three years earlier, in 1609, had published *Shake-speares Sonnets*—clearly without the poet's cooperation. If, as the scholars generally agree, Mr. Shakspere had been furious at seeing his most intimate poems in print without his permission, he would have regarded Thorpe as his enemy. He would hardly have rushed to favor him with another poem in 1612. This, at any rate, is what the orthodox view requires us to suppose.

Foster acknowledges other difficulties. There is no evidence that William Peter ever met Mr. Shakspere; Foster can only surmise that they became friends in the town of Oxford, which lay on the road between London and Stratford, while Peter was a student at the university during the early 1600s. Peter cannot be placed in London or Stratford at any time.

To make matters darker, the poet refers to himself and the dead man as being in their "youth." How can this fit Mr. Shakspere, who was forty-seven in January of 1612? Foster suggests that the poet is speaking of his own age figuratively. But this seems a rather desperate explanation. There is no obvious reason why the poet should take such an eccentric liberty. It could only confuse the Elegy's intended audience, when everything else in the poem implies that the poet and the dead man, who was clearly young at the time of his death, are contemporaries and close friends. Thus, if we accept the standard view, we are left with a poet who figuratively describes himself as "old" in the Sonnets in 1593, and then figuratively describes himself as in his "youth" in 1612. In the Elegy he complains of an injured reputation, of "my country's thankless misconstruction cast Upon my name and credit"; yet he hopes in time to restore his good name. But in the Sonnets he has given up. He is a ruined man and he accepts his lot with bitter resignation. Is there any way out of this confusion? Only if we abandon the orthodox assumption about authorship. Once we free ourselves of the burden of squeezing these poems into Mr. Shakspere's life, the problem becomes much simpler: the Elegy appears to have been written *before* the Sonnets—many years before. The poet wrote the Elegy when he was relatively young, just as he says, and the Sonnets when he was relatively old—just as he says.

This position is confirmed by the styles of the poems. The Elegy shows poetic talent; the poet has mastered rhyme and meter. But the poem lacks the subtlety, emotional resonance, and poetic suavity of the Sonnets. The frequency of its run-on lines leads Foster to conclude that the Elegy is contemporary with Shakespeare's late plays, but this is not tenable. The verse of the Elegy is extremely regular iambic pentameter; the verse of the late plays is dramatically jagged, unique in its syntax. We can see this at once by comparing the rather sententious Elegy with any long speech from *Antony and Cleopatra, The Winter's Tale,* or *The Tempest.*

Ye elves of hills, brooks, standing lakes, and groves,
And ye that on the sands with printless foot
Do chase the ebbing Neptune, and do fly him
When he comes back; you demipuppets that
By moonshine do the green sour ringlets make,
Whereof the ewe not bites; and you whose pastime
Is to make midnight mushrumps, that rejoice
To hear the solemn curfew; by whose aid,
Weak masters though ye be, I have bedimm'd
The noontide sun, call'd forth the mutinous winds,
And 'twixt the green sea and the azur'd vault
Set roaring war; to the dread rattling thunder
Have I given fire, and rifted Jove's stout oak
With his own bolt; the strong-bas'd promontory
Have I made shake, and by the spurs pluck'd up
The pine and cedar; graves at my command
Have wak'd their sleepers, op'd, and let 'em forth
By my so potent art. But this rough magic
I here abjure; and when I have requir'd
Some heavenly music (which even now I do)
To work mine end upon their senses that
This airy charm is for, I'll break my staff,
Bury it certain fathoms in the earth,
And deeper than did ever plummet sound,
I'll drown my book.

Assuming a decade passed between the Elegy and the Sonnets, the Elegy would have been written by the early 1580s, when Mr. Shakspere was still a teenager in Stratford. It is hardly plausible that he, at that age, had formed a bosom friendship with a married gentleman several years his senior, and had cause to complain that his reputation was already besmirched throughout "my country. " Thus, the poet of the Elegy cannot possibly be Mr. Shakspere. The Elegy can be added to the works of Shakespeare only if we deny Mr. Shakspere's authorship of the rest of the canon. If Oxford wrote the Elegy, the difficulties vanish. He would have written it in the late 1570s, when he could still speak of being in his "days of youth." He was prominent enough, and proud enough, to complain of "my country's thankless misconstruction" and some "shame," though what these terms refer to we can only guess. It would have been especially presumptuous for a man of lesser rank to bring his own troubles into an elegy, but less presumptuous for a man of some stature and public notoriety, who perhaps had powerful enemies, to do so. Indeed, the references to the poet's injured reputation undercut the idea that the Elegy was intended for immediate publication. They probably mean that he was writing for a private audience that already knew about his troubles.

So, if Oxford was the author, we can imagine this scenario: Thorpe acquired *A Funeral Elegy* along with the Sonnets and *A Lover's Complaint* sometime after Oxford's death in 1604. He published the Sonnets and the *Complaint* in one volume in 1609. The 1609 volume caused him some trouble, so he had to sit on the Elegy for a time. But when he heard of the violent death of another man named Peter in 1612, he recognized a plausible pretext on which to publish the Elegy. He did so at once—this time, in order to avoid more trouble, using only "Shakespeare's" initials. (Nobody in London, of course, would know of the discrepancies between William Peter of Exeter and the subject of the poem; Thorpe himself probably did not know of them.) If we assume that the Elegy was *already written and in Thorpe's possession* when William Peter was killed, we avoid the problem of explaining how a poem about an event in Exeter could have appeared in print in London so swiftly.

Most of the scholars who reject the Elegy do so on the grounds that the poem is far below Shakespeare's standard. This objection would have merit if the Elegy were, as Foster assumes, a late work. But its sententious rhetoric and rather ponderous moralism are unlike Shakespeare's highly elliptical late style; if the poet had written a defective poem in his later years, it would have been defective in a manner very different from the Elegy. The faults of the Elegy, such as they are, are in Shakespeare's early manner—that is, before he became "Shakespeare."

Notes

Name-and-page references (e.g. "Matus, 1") are to books (or essays) of authors listed in Works Cited. When an author has more than one work listed, the title is also given (e.g. "Wells, *Shakespeare: A Life in Drama,* 22").

Page

1   Bloom, 84
2   Matus, 1.
3   Durning-Lawrence, 84–102.
3   Allen, 74, 98, 120–21, 131
5   Schoenbaum, *Shakespeare's Lives,* 629
7   Evans and Evans, 24.
7   Wright and LaMar, xxvi–xxvii.
8   Schoenbaum, *Shakespeare: The Globe and the World,* 183.
8   Bentley, 16–18.
8   Fraser, 137.
8   Wells, *Shakespeare: A Life in Drama.*
9   Bloom, 52
9   Greer, 5.
9   Whitman: quoted by Ogburn, 151, 255.
10   Milano, viii.
11   Bloom, 84
33   Warren Austin's study is discussed by Schoenbaum *(William Shakespeare: A Compact Documentary Life),* 156–57, and Ogburn, 62–64.
33   Moore: private conversations with author.

Page

48   Rowse, 58.

50   Taylor, 121–23.

56   James: cited by Ogburn, 151–52, 819.

59–60   Schoenbaum, *William Shakespeare: A Compact Documentary Life,* 75.

61–62   Rowse, 37–58.

62   "historical investigation," etc: Rowse, vii.

62   "no aristocrat": Rowse, 162.

62   Marlowe as Rival Poet: Rowse, 175–98.

62   Dark Lady: Rowse, 197.

63   O'Connor, 9, 36, 294.

67   Lambin: quoted in Campbell and Quinn, 392.

67   Grillo, 32.

68–69   Grillo, 97–98.

69–70   Grillo, 135–37.

80–81   Schoenbaum, *William Shakespeare: A Compact Documentary Life,* 180.

81   Quennell, 120.

81   Wells, 39.

81   Winny, 24.

81   Booth, 549.

81   Halliday, 210.

82–83   Bush, 9–10.

83   Barber, 300.

83   Wright and LaMar, xxii.

83   Pearson, 33.

83   Auden, xvii.

83–84   Frye, 26–27.

84   Ramsey, 19.

84   Edwards, 13.

84   Lewis, 503.

84–85   Bradley, 331.

85   Eliot, 56.

85   Kerrigan, 11.

91   Brooke, 81.

92–93   Rollins: quoted in Ingram and Redpath, 3.

93   Ingram and Redpath, 3.

93   Rollins, viii–ix.

93–94   Rollins, ix–x.

99   Lewis, 503.

99   Bush, 13.

99   Auden, xxix.

124   Ward, 206.

126   Moore, private conversation with author.

148   Chambers, 446.

152   Bethell, p. 46.

152   Bullough, *passim.*

Page

167   Kermode, liv.

169   Pine, 18.

189–90   Campbell, 133–34, quoted by Ogburn, 528.

189–90   Craig, quoted by Ogburn, 528.

195   Phillips, 144.

205   Halliday, *A Shakespeare Companion,* 519.

205   Schoenbaum, *Shakespeare's Lives,* 468.

206   Wallace: cited by Greenwood, *The Vindicators of Shakespeare,* 172.

206   Halliday, *A Shakespeare Companion,* 59.

206   Burton, 63.

206–7   Wallace: quoted in Schoenbaum, *Shakespeare's Lives,* 468.

207   Alexander, 142.

207   Quennell, 273.

207   Rowse, 338.

207   Schoenbaum, *William Shakespeare: A Compact Documentary Life,* 264.

207   Levi, 267.

207   Payne, 222.

208   Wallace: quoted in Schoenbaum, *Shakespeare's Lives,* 468.

208   Wallace: quoted in Greenwood, *The Vindicators of Shakespeare,* 186.

210   Howell, 5.

210   Sanders: quoted in Howell, 291, n.1.

211   Goodman, liner notes for Wassenaer, *Concerto Armonici,* performed by the Brandenburg Consort, 1993 (Hyperion Records Ltd. CDA 66670).

213   Robinson: see Bartlett, 178.

213   Braithwaite: see Bartlett, 179–80.

213   Drayton: see Bartlett, 142–43.

213   Harbert: see Bartlett, 143.

213   Edwards: see Bartlett, 144–45.

213–14   Southwell: see Bartlett, 145.

214   Covell: see Bartlett, 144.

214   Lane: see Bartlett, 157.

215   Barnfield: see Bartlett, 141–42.

215–16   Harvey: quoted in Halliday, *A Shakespeare Companion,* 209.

216   Parnassus: quoted in *ibid.,* 353–54.

216   Heywood: see Bartlett, 169–70.

216–17   Weever: see Bartlett, 149–50.

217   Freeman: see Bartlett, 176.

218   Chettle: see Bartlett, 141.

223   Goddard, v.

231   May.

277   Pearson, 25.

Works Cited

Adams, Joseph Quincy. *A Life of William Shakespeare.* Boston: Houghton Mifflin, 1913.

Alexander, Peter. *Shakespeare's Life and Art.* New York: New York University Press. (Reprinted 1967.)

————, ed. *Studies in Shakespeare.* London: Oxford University Press, 1964.

Allen, Percy. *Talks with Elizabethans.* London: Rider & Company, 1947.

Auden, W.H. Introduction to *The Sonnets.* New York: New American Library, 1965. (Reprinted in *Forewords and Afterwords,* New York: Random House, 1973.)

Barber, C.L. "An Essay on the Sonnets." *Elizabethan Poetry: Modern Essays in Criticism,* edited by Paul J. Alpers. New York: Oxford University Press, 1967.

Bartlett, Henrietta C. *Mr. William Shakespeare: Original and Early Editions of His Quartos and Folios; His Source Books and Those Containing Contemporary Notices.* New York: Kraus Reprint Company, 1969. (Originally published 1922.)

Bentley, Gerald Eades. *Shakespeare: A Biographical Handbook.* New Haven: Yale University Press, 1961.

Bethell, Tom. "The Case for Oxford." *The Atlantic Monthly,* October 1991, pp. 45–61, 74–78.

Bloom, Harold. *The Western Canon: The Books and School of the Ages.* New York: Harcourt Brace & Company, 1994.

Booth, Stephen, ed. *Shakespeare's Sonnets.* New Haven: Yale University Press, 1977.

Bradley, A.C. *Oxford Lectures on Poetry.* Bloomington: Indiana University Press, 1961.

Brooke, Tucker, ed. *Shakespeare's Sonnets.* New Haven: Yale University Press, 1923.

Bullough, Geoffrey. *Narrative and Dramatic Sources of Shakespeare.* Eight vols. London: Routledge and Kegan Paul, 1957.

Burton, S.H. *Shakespeare's Life and Stage.* Edinburgh: W&R Chambers Ltd., 1989.

Bush, Douglas. Introduction to *The Sonnets,* edited by Douglas Bush and Alfred Harbage. Baltimore: Penguin Books, 1961.

Campbell, Lily B. *Shakespeare's Tragic Heroes.* Cambridge: Cambridge University Press, 1930.

Campbell, Oscar James, and Quinn, Edward G. *The Reader's Encyclopedia of Shakespeare.* New York: Thomas Y. Crowell, 1966.

Chambers, Edmund, and Williams, Charles. *A Short Life of Shakespeare.* Oxford: Oxford University Press, 1933.

Durning-Lawrence, Sir Edwin. *Bacon Is Shakespeare.* New York: John McBride, 1910.

Edwards, Philip. *Shakespeare: A Writer's Progress.* New York, Oxford University Press, 1986.

Eliot, T.S. "Hamlet and His Problems." Often reprinted; here it is taken from *Hamlet: Enter Critic,* edited by Claire Sacks and Edgar Whan. New York: Appleton-Century-Crofts, 1960. (See also Eliot, T.S., *Selected Essays, 1917–1932.* New York: Harcourt, Brace and Company, 1932.)

Evans, Gareth, and Evans, Barbara Lloyd. *Everyman's Companion to Shakespeare.* London: J.M. Dent & Sons, 1978.

Fraser, Russell. *Young Shakespeare.* New York: Columbia University Press, 1988.

Frye, Northrop. "How True a Twain." *The Riddle of Shakespeare's Sonnets,* edited by Edward Hubler. New York: Basic Books, 1962.

Goddard, Harold. *The Meaning of Shakespeare.* Chicago: University of Chicago Press, 1951.

Greenwood, George. *The Vindicators of Shakespeare: A Reply to Critics.* London: Sweeting and Company, n.d.

Greer, Germaine. *Shakespeare.* Oxford: Oxford University Press, 1986.

Grillo, Ernesto. *Shakespeare and Italy.* Glasgow: Robert Maclehose and Company and The University Press, 1949.

Halliday, F.E. *The Life of Shakespeare.* London: Gerald Duckworth & Company, 1964.

———. *A Shakespeare Companion 1564–1964.* New York: Schocken Books, 1964.

Hoster, Jay. *Tiger's Heart.* Columbus, Ohio: Ravine Books, 1993.

Howell, Roger. *Sir Philip Sidney: The Shepherd Knight.* Boston: Little, Brown and Company, 1968.

Ingram, W.G., and Redpath, Theodore, eds. *Shakespeare's Sonnets.* New York: Barnes & Noble, 1965.

Kermode, Frank. Introduction to *The Tempest.* The Arden Shakespeare. London: Methuen, 1954.

Kerrigan, John, ed. *The Sonnets and A Lover's Complaint.* London: Penguin Books, 1986.

Lee, Sidney. *Shakespeare's Life and Work.* London: Macmillan, 1904.

Levi, Peter. *The Life and Times of William Shakespeare.* London: Macmillan, 1988.

Lewis, C.S. *English Literature in the Sixteenth Century.* Oxford: Clarendon Press, 1954.

Matus, Irvin Leigh. *Shakespeare: The Living Record.* New York: St. Martin's Press, 1991.

May, Steven W., ed. "The Poems of Edward de Vere, Seventeenth Earl of Oxford and of Robert Devereux, Second Earl of Essex." *Studies in Philology* 77, 1980.

Milano, Paolo, ed. *The Portable Dante.* New York: The Viking Press, 1947.

Moore, Peter. Private conversations with the author.

Norman, Charles. *So Worthy a Friend: William Shakespeare.* New York: Rinehart & Company, 1947.

O'Connor, Garry. *William Shakespeare: A Life.* London: Sceptre, 1992.

Ogburn, Charlton. *The Mysterious William Shakespeare.* New York: Dodd, Mead & Co., 1984.

Payne, Robert. *By Me, William Shakespeare.* New York: Everest House, 1980.

Pearson, Hesketh. *A Life of Shakespeare.* New York: Walker and Company, 1949.

Phillips, Gerald W. *Lord Burghley in Shakespeare.* London: Thornton Butterworth, 1936.

Pine, L.G. *Heraldry, Ancestry, and Titles.* New York: Gramercy Publishing Company, 1965.

Quennell, Peter. *Shakespeare: A Biography.* Cleveland: The World Publishing Company, 1963.

Ramsey, Paul. *The Fickle Glass.* New York: AMS Press, 1979.

Rollins, Hyder Edward, ed. *Shakespeare's Sonnets.* New York: Appleton-Century-Crofts, 1951.

Rowse, A.L. *William Shakespeare: A Biography.* New York: Harper & Row, 1963.

Schoenbaum, Samuel *Shakespeare: The Globe and the World.* New York: Folger Shakespeare Library and Oxford University Press, 1979.

———. *Shakespeare's Lives.* New York: Oxford University Press, 1970.

———. *William Shakespeare: A Compact Documentary Life.* New York: Oxford University Press, 1977.

Taylor, Gary. *Reinventing Shakespeare.* New York: Weidenfeld & Nicolson, 1989.

Ward, B.M. *The Seventeenth Earl of Oxford, 1550–1604.* London: John Murray, 1928.

Wells, Stanley. *Shakespeare: A Life in Drama.* New York: W.W. Norton & Company, 1995.

———. *Shakespeare: The Writer and His Work.* New York: Charles Scribner's Sons, 1978.

Winny, James. *The Master-Mistress: A Study of Shakespeare's Sonnets.* New York: Barnes & Noble, 1968.

Wright, Louis B., and LaMar, Virginia A. Introduction to *Shakespeare's Sonnets.* Folger Library General Reader's Shakespeare. New York: Washington Square Press, 1967.

Acknowledgments

This book has many debts, but one stands out. Peter Moore gave me invaluable guidance, instruction, correction, and encouragement for nearly a decade. He has shaped my whole understanding of the Elizabethan era. The countless errors he has saved me from are only the least of his services.

Tom Bethell has been a steadfast friend whose conversations on the authorship question and on writing in general have been both helpful and delightful. Other friends, too numerous to list, have listened, argued, offered suggestions; I will mention Robert Royal, Roy Pulsifer, Phil Collier, and the members of the Shakespeare Oxford Society, notably the president, Charles Burford.

Two dear friends, Phil Nicolaides and Bill Rickenbacker, died while this book was being written. Both were brilliant Shakespeare lovers who offered valuable insights.

I am indebted to scholars who completely disagree with my theses. I have yet to ask a favor of Stephen May of Georgetown College that he has failed to grant instantly; Alan Nelson of Berkeley has shared his precious discoveries with equal generosity. Irvin Leigh Matus has argued with vigor but constant good humor. The witty skepticism of my old friends Hugh Kenner of the University of Georgia and Robert Grant of Glasgow University has kept me on my toes and given me the adrenaline to finish this book; I hope they will at least find it amusing.

Adam Bellow is already a legend in publishing; I know why. His strategic advice has much enriched my book. My editor, Stephen Morrow, has gently pruned and reshaped each chapter, and only those who coped with my original manuscript can appreciate my gratitude to him. My agents Glen Hartley and Lynn Chu have performed miracles.

Needless to say, none of these good people are responsible for my conclusions or for any remaining defects in this book. They have merely left me with no excuses.

Index